CUSTOMER RELATIONSHIP MANAGEMENT SYSTEMS HANDBOOK

OTHER AUERBACH PUBLICATIONS

CUSTOMER RELATIONSHIP MANAGEMENT SYSTEMS HANDBOOK

DUANE E. SHARP

AUERBACH PUBLICATIONS

A CRC Press Company
Boca Raton   London   New York   Washington, D.C.

Library of Congress Cataloging-in-Publication Data

Sharp, Duane E.
    Customer relationship management systems handbook / Duane E. Sharp.
      p. cm.
    Includes bibliographical references and index.
    ISBN 0-8493-1143-8 (alk. paper)
     1. Customer relations—Management. 2. Customer relations—Management—Data
processing. I. Title.
    HF5415.5 .S5199 2002
    658.8'12—dc21   2002018592
                                                        CIP

Visit the Auerbach Web site at www.auerbach-publications.com

© 2003 by CRC Press LLC
Auerbach is an imprint of CRC Press LLC

No claim to original U.S. Government works
International Standard Book Number 0-8493-1143-8
Library of Congress Card Number 2002018592
Printed in the United States of America 1 2 3 4 5 6 7 8 9 0
Printed on acid-free paper

Dedication

This Handbook is dedicated to my wife, Myrna, who enabled me to devote my time and energies to the research and writing, to my daughter Heidi, who assisted in gathering and inputting the text, and to my late son Brett, who would have been proud of this work, the culmination of many years of association with information technology.

Contents

1 The Customer Today 1
  Who Is the Customer? 2
  A Shifting Paradigm 3
  A New Look for Marketing 3
    The Customer-Centric Marketing Model 4
    The Challenge 5
    Priorities 6
    Market of Millions to Market of One 7
  Customer Feedback 7
    A Perspective on the Customer 7
  Managing Relationships: The CRM Solution 8
    Relationship Technologies 8
  The Stages of a CRM Strategy 9
    Interacting 10
    Analyzing 10
    Learning 10
    Planning 10

2 The Evolution of Customer Relations to CRM 13
  Planning 14
    A Functioning CRM Solution 14
    Believe in CRM 14
    Moving Away from Mass Marketing 15
  Strategies for Managing Customer Information 16
    Tools to Support CRM 18
    CRM and the New Marketing Paradigm 19
    CRM Provides Answers 20
    Lessons from CRM Successes 22
    Customer Data 22

From Product Focus to Customer Centricity 23
Customer Value 24
The CRM Planning Phase 25
The CRM Plan of Action 26
Selecting the Technology Solutions 27
Changing the Customer Focus 28
CRM Strategy: From Planning to Development 29
A Twelve-Stage CRM Strategy 29
Applying the CRM Strategy 35
Maximizing Individual Customer Experiences 35
CRM Issues, Tactics, and Methodologies 36
CRM Workshops 36
Exact Transaction Analysis 37
Relationship Technologies 38
Knowing the Customer: Another Perspective 39
A Rationale for CRM 40
Two-Way Dialog: Customer Input to CRM 40
The Alert Platform 41
Implementing Alert/Response Applications 42
Integrating with Existing Systems 42
Configuring the Alert/Response Content 43
Referrals 43
Testing and Evaluating CRM Solutions 44
The Difficult and Demanding Customer 45
Loyalty and Long-Term Relationships 46
Three Areas of Evaluation 47
Discovery Testing 47
Dialog Testing 48
Discipline Testing 49
Managing the CRM Program 51
A Program Manager's Perspective 51
CRM Analytics in Data Mining 54
Data Mining 54
CRM: Summing Up the Business Value 55

3   The Technology of CRM 57
An Overview of the Data Warehouse 58
The Healthy Centralized Data Warehouse 58
Data Warehousing Objectives 59
Characteristics of the Data Warehouse 60
Data Warehousing and Customer Relationships 61
Creating a Data Mart Model 62
Corporate Data — The Operational Perspective 63
The Heart of the Data Warehouse 63

Design and Construction of a Data Warehouse 65
    Data in Data Warehouses 66
    Restrictions of Summary Data 66
        Example 1. Retail 66
        Example 2. Consumer Goods Manufacturer 66
Data Marts in the Real World 67
    Data Marts versus Data Warehouses 68
        Advantages and Disadvantages 68
        Comparison of Data Requirements 69
        Supporting Technologies 69
        Business Application 69
    From Data Mart to Data Warehouse 70
    Data Marts, Data Warehouses, and Marketing Campaigns 70
Avoiding the Pitfalls of Data Warehousing 71
    Data Warehousing Processing Environments 72
    Data Granularity and Performance Comparison 73
The Data Warehouse Development Process 73
    Data Warehouse: Business Contents 74
    Bad Data 75
The Operational Data Warehouse 76
    Components of the ODW 77
        JIT Applications 77
        RAD Tools 78
        OLAP Generator 79
        Metadata Repository 79
        Programming API 79
        Business Information Directory 79
    ODW: Problem-Solving Approach 79
    Solutions Using JIT Applications 80
    The ODW in Action 80
    XML Facilities in Search Engines 81
Data Warehousing Computer Platforms 81
    Selection Criteria 81
    Benchmarking 82
    The Mentor Approach to Building a Data Warehouse 83
    Accessing the Data: Query Tool Methodology 84
    Data Warehousing: Processing Methodology 84
Data Warehousing and CRM: Managing the Project 85
    Data Warehousing: The Planning 86
    Project Scope and Resources 86
    Business Discovery: Analyzing Business Issues 87
    Data Warehouse Consultants 87
    Data Warehouse Logical Modeling 88

Data Warehouse Architectural Design 88
Project Implementation 89
Initiating the Data Warehousing Project 90
Select a Scalable Product 90
Measurable Results 91
Departmental or Enterprisewide 91
Data Warehouse Development: One Vendor's Methodology 92
Solution Readiness 92
Physical Data Modeling 93
Data Transformation 94
Client/Server Application Development 94
Data Warehouse Management 95
Elements Of Database Technology 95
Determining Database Requirements 96
The Star Schema 97
The Snowflake Schema 97
The Business Tools: Analytical CRM 97
Integrate Front- and Back-Office Systems 97
Necessary Data 98
Establish Data Standards 98
Automate the Decision-Making Process 99
Data Clustering Offers New Insights 99
Data Warehouse Support and Enhancement 99
Solution Integration 100
Enterprise System Support 101
Logical Design Review 101
Physical Database Design Review 101
Data Warehouse Tuning 101
Data Warehouse Audit 102
Data Warehousing Architectures: Options 102
Special Function Data Warehouses 104
Federated Data Warehouse/Federated Data Mart
(FDW/FDM) 104
Non-Architected Data Marts 105
Implementing the Enterprise Data Warehouse 106
Top-Down EDW 106
EDW Phased Subject Area Development 106
Bottom-Up EDW 107
Analyzing the Organization 108
Challenges for the EDW Project Team 109
Decision Support Systems and Data Warehousing 110
Virtual Data Warehouse 110
Multidimensional Online Analytical Processing (OLAP) 111
Relational OLAP 112

Database Management Systems 112
  Complexity of the Data Model 113
  Number of Concurrent Users 113
  Data Volumes... 113
  Complexity of the Processing Environment.............................. 114
From Data Warehousing to Data Mining 114
  Data Mining Techniques.. 115
  Data Mining: Exploring Corporate Assets 117
  Data Mining versus Other Business Tools................................ 117
  Data Mining Supports CRM Solutions 118
  Data Mining Processes: Selection and Extraction.................... 119
  Data Cleansing and Transformation 119
    Mining, Analysis, and Interpretation.................................. 120
  Creating Models.. 120
  Analyzing Links 121
  Segmenting Databases 121
  Detecting Deviations 121
  Modeling Techniques.. 121
    Creating Predictive Models 121
    Supervised Induction.. 122
    Association Discovery 122
    Sequence Discovery 122
  Data Mining Tools... 122
    Neural Networks.. 122
    Decision Trees 123
    Rule Induction 123
    Data Visualization... 123
  Data Mining Applications 124
  Data Mining: Summing Up.. 125
Data Consistency and Quality.. 125
  Data: A Corporate Asset 125
  Separation of Warehouse Data... 126
  Critical Success Factors 127
Managerial and Organizational Impacts
      of Data Warehousing.. 128
  Adding New Data to the Warehouse 128
  Monitoring the Data Warehouse 129
  Data Warehouse Provides New Tools....................................... 129
  Exploration Warehouses 130
  The Metadata Infrastructure.. 130
  Organizational Growth.. 131
  Proactive Administration 131
  Ensuring Stability.. 131
  User Training 132

Vendors with CRM Technology 133
    Checklist for Vendor Selection 133
Conclusion 133

4 Case Studies in CRM 137
Automotive... 139
    Case Study A1: General Motors (GM)..................................... 139
        CRM Project Objectives.. 139
        Corporate Background.. 139
        The CRM Solution 139
        The Benefits.. 139
        Industry Checklist: Lessons Learned 140
    Case Study A2: Saturn Corporation 140
        CRM Project Objectives.. 140
        Corporate Background.. 140
        The CRM Solution 140
        The Benefits.. 141
        Industry Checklist: Lessons Learned 141
Communications... 141
    Case Study C1: AT&T Wireless Services — Southwest
        Region 141
        CRM Project Objectives.. 141
        Corporate Background.. 141
        The CRM Solution 142
        The Benefits.. 142
        Industry Checklist: Lessons Learned 143
    Case Study C2: Access Integrated Networks 143
        CRM Project Objectives.. 143
        Corporate Background.. 143
        The CRM Solution 143
        The Benefits.. 143
        Industry Checklist: Lessons Learned 144
    Case Study C3: Canada Post 144
        CRM Project Objectives.. 144
        Corporate Background.. 144
        The CRM Solution 144
        The Benefits.. 145
        Industry Checklist: Lessons Learned 145
    Case Study C4: Pele-Phone Communications........................ 145
        CRM Project Objectives.. 145
        Corporate Background.. 145
        The CRM Solution 145
        The Benefits.. 146
        Industry Checklist: Lessons Learned 146

Energy 146
  Case Study E1: Enbridge Consumers Gas........................ 146
    CRM Project Objectives.. 146
    Corporate Background.. 146
    The CRM Solution 147
    The Benefits... 147
    Industry Checklist: Lessons Learned.......................... 148
  Case Study E2: ENMAX Energy 148
    CRM Project Objectives.. 148
    Corporate Background.. 148
    The CRM Solution 148
    The Benefits... 149
    Industry Checklist: Lessons Learned.......................... 149
Entertainment... 149
  Case Study Ent1: BMG Entertainment 149
    CRM Project Objectives.. 149
    Corporate Background.. 150
    The CRM Solution 150
    The Benefits... 151
    Industry Checklist: Lessons Learned.......................... 151
  Case Study Ent2: Harrah's Casinos 151
    CRM Project Objectives.. 151
    Corporate Background.. 151
    The CRM Solution 152
    The Benefits... 152
    Industry Checklist: Lessons Learned.......................... 152
Financial Institutions 152
  Case Study F1: Alberta Treasury Branches (ATB)............ 152
    CRM Project Objectives.. 152
    Corporate Background.. 152
    The CRM Solution 153
    The Benefits... 153
    Industry Checklist: Lessons Learned.......................... 153
  Case Study F2: Guaranty Bank 154
    CRM Project Objectives.. 154
    Corporate Background.. 154
    The CRM Solution 154
    The Benefits... 154
    Industry Checklist: Lessons Learned.......................... 155
  Case Study F3: National Bank of Canada (NBC)............. 155
    CRM Project Objectives.. 155
    Corporate Background.. 155
    The CRM Solution 155

The Benefits.. 156
Industry Checklist: Lessons Learned................................. 156
Case Study F4: The Royal Bank of Canada
    (RBC Financial Services) 156
CRM Project Objectives... 156
Corporate Background... 156
The CRM Solution 157
The Benefits.. 158
Industry Checklist: Lessons Learned................................. 158
Case Study F5: Union Bank of Norway............................. 158
CRM Project Objectives... 158
Corporate Background... 159
The CRM Solution 159
The Benefits.. 159
Industry Checklist: Lessons Learned................................. 160
Fund-Raising 160
Case Study Fund1: United Way of Greater Toronto 160
CRM Project Objectives... 160
Corporate Background... 160
The CRM Solution 161
The Benefits.. 162
Industry Checklist: Lessons Learned................................. 162
Healthcare 162
Case Study H1: Anthem Blue Cross Blue Shield 162
CRM Project Objectives... 162
Corporate Background... 162
The CRM Solution 163
The Benefits.. 164
Industry Checklist: Lessons Learned................................. 164
Case Study H2: Apotex Group 165
CRM Project Objectives... 165
Corporate Background... 165
The CRM Solution 165
The Benefits.. 166
Industry Checklist: Lessons Learned................................. 166
Case Study H3: TLC Laser Eye Centers............................. 166
CRM Project Objectives... 166
Corporate Background... 166
The CRM Solution 166
The Benefits.. 167
Industry Checklist: Lessons Learned................................. 167
Insurance.. 167
Case Study Ins1: Zurich Kemper Life Insurance 167

CRM Project Objectives...167
Corporate Background...167
The Benefits...168
Industry Checklist: Lessons Learned...............................169
Investment 169
Case Study Inv1: Yorkton Securities...................................169
CRM Project Objectives...169
Corporate Background...169
The CRM Solution 169
The Benefits...170
Industry Checklist: Lessons Learned...............................170
Packaging...170
Case Study P1: Tipper Tie..170
CRM Project Objectives...170
Corporate Background...170
The CRM Solution 171
The Benefits...171
Industry Checklist: Lessons Learned...............................171
Recruiting and Training 172
Case Study RT1: Eagle's Flight..172
CRM Project Objectives...172
Corporate Background...172
The CRM Solution 173
The Benefits...173
Industry Checklist: Lessons Learned...............................173
Case Study RT2: Global Interactive and Workopolis..............174
CRM Project Objectives...174
Corporate Background...174
The CRM Solution 174
The Benefits...175
Industry Checklist: Lessons Learned...............................175
Retail..175
Case Study R1: Home Depot 175
CRM Project Objectives...175
Corporate Background...175
The Benefits...176
Industry Checklist: Lessons Learned...............................176
Case Study R2: M&M Meat Shops 176
CRM Project Objectives...176
Corporate Background...176
The Benefits...177
Industry Checklist: Lessons Learned...............................177
Case Study R3: Migros Cooperatives....................................177

CRM Project Objectives 177
Corporate Background 177
The CRM Solution 177
The Benefits 180
Industry Checklist: Lessons Learned 180
Case Study R4: RadioShack Canada 180
CRM Project Objectives 180
Corporate Background 180
The CRM Solution 181
The Benefits 182
Industry Checklist: Lessons Learned 182
Case Study R5: Wal-Mart 182
CRM Project Objectives 182
Corporate Background 182
The CRM Solution 183
The Benefits 183
Industry Checklist: Lessons Learned 183
Technology 184
Case Study Tech1: Canon Canada 184
CRM Project Objectives 184
Corporate Background 184
The CRM Solution 184
The Benefits 185
Industry Checklist: Lessons Learned 185
Case Study Tech2: Hewlett-Packard (HP) 185
CRM Project Objectives 185
Corporate Background 185
CRM Solution #1 186
CRM Solution #2 186
The Benefits 187
Industry Checklist: Lessons Learned 188
Case Study Tech3: Western Digital 188
CRM Project Objectives 188
Corporate Background 188
The CRM Solution 188
The Benefits 189
Industry Checklist: Lessons Learned 190
Transportation and Travel 190
Case Study TT1: AeroXchange 190
CRM Project Objectives 190
Corporate Background 190
The CRM Solution 190
The Benefits 191
Industry Checklist: Lessons Learned 192

Case Study TT2: Burlington Northern Santa Fe Railway
(BNSF) 192
CRM Project Objectives.................................. 192
Corporate Background..................................... 192
The CRM Solution 192
The Benefits... 193
Industry Checklist: Lessons Learned 193
Case Study TT3: Canadian Pacific Railway (CPR).................. 193
CRM Project Objectives.................................. 193
Corporate Background..................................... 193
The CRM Solution 194
The Benefits... 194
Industry Checklist: Lessons Learned 194
Case Study TT4: Delta Airlines 194
CRM Project Objectives.................................. 194
Corporate Background..................................... 195
The CRM Solution 195
The Benefits... 195
Industry Checklist: Lessons Learned 195
Case Study TT5: Travel Unie 196
CRM Project Objectives.................................. 196
Corporate Background..................................... 196
The CRM Solution 196
The Benefits... 196
Industry Checklist: Lessons Learned 197
Wholesale.. 197
Case Study W1: Clearwater Fine Foods 197
CRM Project Objectives.................................. 197
Corporate Background..................................... 197
The CRM Solution 198
The Benefits... 198
Industry Checklist: Lessons Learned 199
Case Study W2: Fujifilm France 199
CRM Project Objectives.................................. 199
Corporate Background..................................... 199
The CRM Solution 199
The Benefits... 200
Industry Checklist: Lessons Learned 201
Analyzing Case Studies for Maximum Benefit........................... 201

5   Privacy in CRM 203
Data Privacy.. 204
Corporate Privacy Policies..................................... 205
Customers Demand Privacy 205

Defining Privacy of Personal Data 206
Government Initiatives 207
Europe and the EU Directive 207
Canada 208
CRM: Opportunities to Address Privacy Concerns 209
Establishing the Privacy Infrastructure 209
Privacy Guidelines — Applying the OECD Principles 211
Advising Customers 212
Privacy and E-Commerce 212
P3P Standard and Definitions 213
P3P Privacy Platform 213
P3P and Customer Databases 214
Industry Support for Privacy Initiatives 215
The Direct Marketing Opt-Out 215
Opt-Out of Disclosure of Personal Data to Third Parties
or Affiliated Organizations 216
Protecting Personal Privacy in CRM 216
Examining the Logical Data Model 217
Addressing Privacy Issues: Benefits 217
Summing Up: Personal Privacy Is a Key Component
of CRM 218

6   Benefits of CRM 219
Benefits of CRM in Four Major Business Sectors 219
Communications 220
Increasing Network Utilization and Profitability 220
Improving Operating Results 221
Analyzing Effects of Competitive Offerings 221
Insurance 221
Manufacturing 222
Transportation 223
The General Value of CRM 224
Determining the ROI for a CRM Solution 224
Justifying Data Warehouse Growth 225
The Ultimate Benefits of CRM 225
Measuring ROI: An Ongoing Process 226
Tangible and Intangible 226

Appendix A   Glossary of CRM and Data Warehouse Terminology .. 229

Appendix B   References and Bibliography 233

Index 235

Introduction

What is clear is that the revolution of rising expectations, which has been one of the chief features of Western society in the past 25 years, is being transformed into a revolution of rising entitlements for the next 25.

— Daniel Bell, The Cultural Contradictions of Capitalism, 1976

The concept of developing better relationships with customers using technology as an enabler has evolved over the past decade to the point where most organizations, in both private and public sectors, realize that the relationship between supplier and customer has changed dramatically.

In the private sector, where competition is frequently a driving force for change, companies strive for ways to reduce the defection of customers to competitive organizations, to increase customer loyalty, and to develop long-term relationships with customers.

At a number of major public and private sector organizations throughout the world, management has turned to sophisticated technologies and new business processes to develop and implement customer relationship management (CRM) systems.

The benefits of CRM are referenced throughout this Handbook and detailed in Chapter 6.

CRM has two faces: (1) the customer face and (2) the supplier face. It embraces several relationship aspects and, therefore, one definition will not suffice. To provide an umbrella under which to develop a CRM solution, the following characteristics of CRM are considered in this Handbook:

- *Modification of customer behavior* over a period of time to enhance the relationship between supplier and customer
- *Relating to customers* on an individual basis
- *Establishing a mutually beneficial environment* where customers provide information in return for services that meet their individual needs

The *Customer Relationship Management Systems Handbook* has been researched, formatted, and written for IS professionals who need a full understanding of the rationale, concepts, technology, insights, and processes involved in the successful development and implementation of a CRM solution in their respective business sectors. A broad and extensive range of corporate information from many sources, including numerous CRM vendors and user organizations with CRM implementations, have been used in its preparation.

Reports, studies, white papers, and surveys on data warehousing, data mining, and CRM, from several consulting organizations were also valuable resources. We are particularly appreciative of the works of authors of other CRM texts, which are cited under References in Appendix B, "References and Bibliography," for their insight and experience, and contributions to this Handbook.

To support the significant benefits CRM has provided to organizations that have developed successful CRM strategies, the research orientation for this Handbook has focused on an analysis of successful CRM implementations from a broad range of major business sectors. These implementations, presented in a case study format, demonstrate successful implementation processes within organizations, the application of appropriate technologies, and the selection of vendor solutions that work.

How to Use This Handbook

The significant change in the customer profile that has occurred over the past decade or more and the growth of customer power are analyzed in Chapter 1, "The Customer Today," to set the stage for a description of the evolution of CRM. This chapter clearly positions the customer as a driving force behind the success of large and small business enterprises in the 21st century — "the century of the customer," as some analysts have defined this era. It is also a historical backdrop for today's marketplace, the customers who inhabit it, and the lead-in to what businesses need to do to attract and retain customers.

Businesses clearly recognize that CRM is a process, not an event, and in Chapter 2, "The Evolution of Customer Relations to CRM," the evolution and formalization of the customer relations model of earlier days, to *customer relationship management,* is described. Detailed descriptions of the process with illustrations and diagrams provide a roadmap for planning, developing, and implementing an enterprisewide CRM strategy.

For CRM, technology is an important enabler, and Chapter 3, "The Technology of CRM," is an in-depth analysis of the technologies that form the basis of a CRM strategy. A selected group of knowledgeable, experienced vendors with CRM products and services is also included, along with Web site contact information.

While every CRM process has not necessarily been successful — there are no ultimate guarantees to success in a marketplace where every corporate culture is different — analyzing successful CRM projects can provide insight and guidelines that can give a more than reasonable chance of success.

Chapter 4, "Case Studies in CRM," a core component of this Handbook, examines and analyzes a series of researched case studies from a broad range of business sectors. The material is presented in a traditional business school case study format to illustrate the methodology applied to develop and implement successful CRM solutions. For each case study, the CRM objectives are defined, corporate background is provided, and the CRM solution is described. The specific benefits of these CRM strategies to each organization are also summarized, and an industry checklist of "lessons learned" is provided.

These case studies demonstrate how CRM benefits organizations in a number of ways, as well as illustrating its almost universal applicability across a broad spectrum of businesses in virtually every business sector.

Where There Are Customers, There Is a Need for CRM

In Chapter 5, the issue of privacy is explored from a global perspective, examining the growth of both government and industry initiatives to manage and control the use of personal information and to protect the privacy of individuals. The internal processes and the technology required to implement privacy structures in CRM systems are also described.

Chapter 6 provides the ultimate *raison d'être* for CRM, a detailed description of the benefits, both overall and in selected business sectors, that can be achieved for both suppliers and customers through the effective application of the principles of customer relationship management.

A Glossary of CRM Terminology is provided to define some of the specific terminology that has emerged as CRM became recognized as a core business process.

An extensive list of references and bibliographic resources on CRM and related topics is also provided, and includes references cited in this Handbook.

Duane Sharp, P.Eng.
Mississauga, Ontario
Canada

Chapter 1

The Customer Today

Once a good product was all you needed. Today, the totality of the experience has equal impact.

In today's marketplace, consumers are a different breed than they were even five years ago. They are much better informed, better educated, and more demanding in the products and services that they require, and they are more familiar with technology. The future belongs to those companies that can capture and share their internal customer knowledge and combine it with new information about their customers.

On the supply side of the market, there is significantly increased competition, with very little product and service differentiation, allowing consumers few clear-cut choices. The end result of these combined factors is that consumers have raised their purchasing power to higher levels than ever before. They are in control.

This scenario in the 21st century consumer market raises many questions among those businesses that need to respond to this new era of consumerism. There are five primary issues that organizations need to address to satisfy demanding consumers:

1. *Retaining* customers and preventing them from defecting to the competition
2. *Determining* which products and services to bundle together to increase customer profitability
3. *Attracting and retaining* profitable customers
4. *Treating* customers as individuals
5. *Implementing technology solutions* that will achieve corporate objectives

These are only a few of the challenges that businesses face today and will face in the future, as customers increase their command of the marketplace.

A business philosophy that focuses on relating to customers will increase revenue, reduce cost, build and retain a loyal customer base, and become a prime motivator in acquiring new customers. The key objective for an organization is to understand every transaction and interaction between the organization and the customer and to communicate effectively with each customer for the life of their association with the organization.

There is a strong economic motive behind this business philosophy. Surveys have shown that it costs about *five times* less to keep customers than to attract new ones. In addition, long-term customers tend to be more profitable.

While many companies are adopting new technologies because they believe that technology is the answer to improving customer service, these companies often end up with mismanaged, misdirected customer relationships. Usually, the reason for this is that they have not taken the time to understand what their customers really want or put in place the human processes in addition to the technology.

Who Is the Customer?

Let's define *customer,* a word which first came into the lexicon about 100 years ago and which many companies are still trying to define. A customer may take many forms; for example, a customer may be one of the following:

- *Consumer* — someone who buys products or services at the retail level
- *Distributor* — someone who buys products at the wholesale level for distribution
- *Business-to-business organization* — a company that buys products and integrates them with their own
- *Internal department* — a department that buys products from other departments

Each of these customers represents a sales opportunity and needs to be treated with an appropriate service level. Even internal customers have options on where to buy their products and services, particularly if they are cost centers responsible for their own operating expenses.

However, different types of customers *do* require different sales and marketing strategies. Organizations that recognize and respond to this will successfully capture the marketplace in their product or service area.

A meaningful relationship with customers is composed of many bits and pieces of information, incidents and events, transactions and interactions, and represents all forms of contact a customer has had with an organization. However, knowing one's customers means more than just collecting this information in a large database. It means being capable of reaching across the data and examining and transforming the behavioral facts into insights about the customer, which can then be converted to action.

A Shifting Paradigm

During the 1990s, external customers began to acquire a certain characteristic they had never had before — one of being sought after by suppliers of products and services. The paradigm of buyer and supplier had shifted, and they were no longer just buyers; they now needed to be treated with respect. Specifically, the buyers expected suppliers to have certain attributes when dealing with customers, attributes these organizations had not necessarily required previously, including the following:

- *Imagination* — using creativity in customer campaigns
- *Individualization of customer needs* — treating each customer as if he or she were the only customer
- *Flexibility* — expecting suppliers to be flexible in product or service offerings

Ultimately, it is the profitable, satisfied, loyal customer who will remain a primary point of focus for those organizations that achieve profitability and growth in the economy of the 21st century. Success in accomplishing these objectives will accrue to organizations that adopt an effective, well-conceived *customer relationship management (CRM)* strategy.

There are numerous examples of how different organizations develop customer awareness and pattern their overall relationships with customers based on the information they gather. In Chapter 4, "Case Studies in CRM," successful CRM projects from a range of business sectors are examined in detail; this examination demonstrates how companies in these sectors have recognized the requirement to become more customer focused in their day-to-day relationships. The lessons learned can be applied to similar businesses in these sectors.

To cite one example in a major business sector, consider a communications company and its customers. As a provider of communications services, the company identifies a customer segment of upper-income customers and prospects, highly profitable, and with some knowledge of technology. It then studies their behavior to understand more fully the types of services they want. Using this information, the company develops a package of bundled products and services under a single name, using a single marketing campaign and a single bill. The result is a customer relationship model that effectively meets the complete communications needs of this market segment, fostering customer loyalty and retention and an ongoing supplier/customer relationship.

A New Look for Marketing

For more than a century, the practice of "marketing" has evolved at a gradual pace, making significant strides only when new ways of reaching the consumer began to mature or when the marketplace itself went through a period of profound economic adjustment.

Its present-day form began with the displacement of the independent store by chains of stores, opening up nationwide channels for the mass distribution of goods. More recently, the Internet has spawned a mini-revolution in marketing methods, opening up global channels to businesses under the umbrella of E-commerce.

Three major economic forces that evolved over the past 20 years have assisted major changes in distribution channels:

1. De-industrialization
2. Segmentation of society along cultural lines
3. Ethnic diversification

These three forces have caused marketers to move away from mass advertising in favor of more segmented messaging, direct-to-consumer channels, and the use of micro-marketing techniques.

In addition, changes in media outlets used by marketers brought new opportunities for organizations to market their products and services. Network television waned as an advertising medium with the expansion of cable services throughout North America. And with PC penetration of households on its way to 80 percent, the Internet has suddenly become a major new force on the advertising scene. Now customers have even more choices about how they contact organizations and how they acquire products or services.

The Customer-Centric Marketing Model

To succeed in this age of global interconnectivity, where distance is irrelevant and a competitor is only a mouse-click away, marketers must learn how to leverage the new tools, synchronize communications activity across multiple channels, and implement a customer-centric infrastructure that meets customer needs. They also have to accept that the traditional rules are no longer valid in a Web-enabled world.

If the old product-centric model of intrusive, ad-based, brand building is not yet irrelevant, it soon will be. Marketing budgets are shifting from the ostrich-like ad agencies, which are still peddling image makeovers, to the new custodians of the customer relationship — large integrated outsourcers whose core business is providing customer-oriented solutions to marketing requirements (see Exhibit 1).

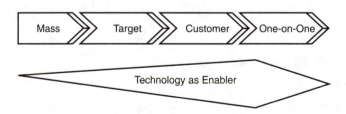

Exhibit 1. The Evolution of Marketing

The Challenge

Corporate marketing departments are significantly behind their organizational counterparts — IT, product development, and accounting — in providing bottom-line business benefits. For example, understanding the effect of marketing investments can have a dramatic impact on a company's performance. The following statistics relating to customer relationships reflect the challenges associated with attracting and retaining customers and how important this objective is to suppliers:

- Most Fortune 50 companies lose 50 percent of their customers in five years.
- It costs seven to ten times more to acquire a new customer than it does to retain an existing customer.
- A 50-percent increase in retention rate can increase profits 25 to 125 percent.
- Up to 50 percent of existing customer relationships are not profitable.
- The average company communicates four times per year with its customers and six times per year with its prospects.

These statistics further underscore the requirement for organizations to adapt, re-engineer, and revamp their customer relationship philosophies — if they had one that could be defined. Marketers from every business sector will have to master the new disciplines of real-time customer dialog, interactive data analysis, and relationship management. They will have to encourage the exchange of information by demonstrating customer benefit in their relationship processes and by ensuring that customer relationship practices are followed in a manner applicable to their business sector. There are seven definable factors involved in this process:

1. Better delivery
2. Better value
3. Better pricing
4. Enhanced product and service customization
5. Greater convenience
6. Loyalty recognition
7. Continuous nurturing of the relationship

Throughout this reformation period, the objective of marketing, more than ever, must be to identify and respond to the individual needs of customers. In today's E-commerce economy, where innovation is likely to offer merely a fleeting advantage, *needs satisfaction* will be the sole way for businesses to survive. Individualization and immediate response will become expected relationship attributes. Get prospects to your site, give them a reason to linger, answer their questions immediately, provide exceptional value, and turn them into recurring customers through consistent positive experiences at every point of interaction. This important factor can be considered the mantra of relationship marketing and the key to successful customer relationships in the E-commerce environment. By forging enduring linkages on the strength and robustness of digital pathways, customers will feel that a true reciprocal relationship has been established, characterized by empowerment, respect, and individualization.

Priorities

While a CRM strategy will encompass numerous customer-oriented elements, there are two major characteristics that must have priority in the development of successful CRM systems. They are:

1. The capability of the CRM system to retain customers
2. The corporate vision to move from markets of millions to markets of one

Every business recognizes that retaining customers is a top priority. Without customers, there is no business, making it imperative that customer satisfaction becomes a *core competency*, if it is not already one (see Exhibit 2).

Consider the retail sector, where frequent changes in customers occur. In fact, retailers suffer customer losses every day. Customers reduce their spending in a store primarily by reducing the store's relative importance in their personal positioning hierarchy. It may begin with an impression created by a common experience in the store: "indifferent service," "not quite the right merchandise," "not exactly the brands I like," and "nobody here knows me."

Over time, every customer builds up a shopping pattern that becomes quite rigid. Customers buy certain items from one store, but go to competitors for other items, even though they are available at the first store. This personal hierarchy supports top-of-mind awareness associated with specific merchandise categories.

Influencing customers, by responding to their precise needs and preferences, broadens a supplier's place in each personal positioning hierarchy. And that is what one-to-one CRM is all about.

Exhibit 2. Three Important Factors in Customer Relationships

Customer retention
Channel purchasing preferences
Propensity models to reduce churn
Changes in life cycle/buying behavior
Lifetime value of customers

Customer acquisition
Integrated detail data form information silos
Build propensity models for new customer acquisitions
Identify customers most likely to purchase
Know when customers touch your business and how to communicate with them

Customer profitability
Identify most profitable customer segments
Discover which new products your most profitable customers are most likely to buy
Determine optimal allocation of marketing dollars

Market of Millions to Market of One

Everyone wants to be an individual and wants to be acknowledged as an individual by having his or her likes and preferences known and acted upon. Businesses in every sector need to build individual relationships with customers based on what the *customer* wants, not on what the *business* wants. For example, in a retail environment, if one customer wants individualized shopping assistance or wants to be called and reminded of special dates, then that is what should be done. Someone else may simply want advance notice of sales, fast alterations, or a particular brand of merchandise. These are only a few of the components that make up the individual fabric of customer relationships.

Personalized customer communications and special preferences acknowledge that a special relationship exists between a company and each individual customer; this connects one person to another in a positive way, providing an aura of civility and pleasantness for every business experience. It is a powerful motivator to repeat this experience again and again.

These relationships are the backbone of a profitable business because they personalize all customer communications. Using every customer contact, it is possible to apply all the components of a customer's history — demographics as well as detailed transaction history — to personalize each element of each campaign.

Customer Feedback

One customer survey by a major consulting firm examined the impact of technology on the delivery of improved customer practices and services. Predictably, the study found that technology alone will not guarantee success in enhancing customer relationships. The key is to select the right technology to meet customer needs — and the right vendor partner to help implement it.

More than 1300 organizations participated in this survey, which found that:

- Organizations that improve customer satisfaction also reap a number of important side benefits.
- Technology alone is not the key to success; organizations that focus on three areas — (1) technology, (2) processes, and (3) customer needs — are the most successful.
- Technology plays a dual role for companies, acting as both a driver and enabler of change in achieving effective CRM.
- Companies with the greatest customer satisfaction ratings were those that integrated the best practices of the three main types of organizations: (1) process focused, (2) customer needs focused, and (3) technology focused.

A Perspective on the Customer

These surveys raise an important and fundamental question for organizations: "Who are my customers?" The answer may point an organization in several directions, because customers take various forms for many organizations; and in today's market, all customer categories enjoy a new range of purchasing power. Most business sectors have four distinct and definable types of customers, as noted previously:

1. *Individuals* who buy products directly from a company
2. *Businesses* that buy from a company
3. *Distribution channels* that buy products for resale to an end user
4. *Internal departments* that buy from other departments

Each of these customers has more power today than ever before, because today's market forces have made organizations more competitive and customers more demanding. Because there is less differentiation in products and services and more product and supplier choices, customers can easily switch suppliers or products, at little cost and effort.

Customers expect customization, and they have the bargaining power to demand it. The popularity of loyalty programs and a variety of incentives — draws, sweepstakes, discounts — that entice customers to stay with a given supplier, attests to the effort companies are making in their marketing campaigns and strategies. Often, these programs become an integral part of a corporate CRM strategy.

Managing Relationships: The CRM Solution

With the customer defined and the nature of the changing marketing experience understood, organizations can now move on to planning, developing, and implementing a CRM solution.

A key objective of CRM is to establish relationships with each individual customer rather than treating customers as a mass market based on a product-centric marketing structure. The new model, referred to as "customer-centric," relates to each customer as if he or she is the only customer. This is a revolutionary approach for organizations that may have thousands or even millions of customers.

As previously noted, today's customers are better educated, better informed, more knowledgeable about technology, and therefore more demanding when it comes to the products and services they buy. Increased competition, with little or no product or service differentiation, further adds to customer purchasing power in the new millennium.

Successfully managing customer relationships means learning about the behavior and needs of customers, anticipating future buying patterns, and finding new opportunities to add value to the relationship.

Relationship Technologies

Relationship technologies are the technology keys to making customer transactions more personal, more individual, and more intimate. Solutions driven by data warehousing systems are designed specifically to expand and enhance relationships with customers — not just to process their data. More than ever, relationship technologies are vital to any company wishing to deal with customers, whether through personal contact or via the Internet or other electronic medium. In Chapter 3, "The Technology of CRM," the core technologies and their application to CRM are described and analyzed, using the experience of successful CRM strategies as foundations on which to build.

CRM has the potential for turning detailed customer information into competitive advantage, enabling businesses to capture and analyze customer interactions, to understand their requirements, and, by responding to them, to build lifetime relationships.

Organizations that achieve high ratings for customer relationships are those that make the relationship something that the customer values from one particular organization over another. To accomplish this, companies need to look at their experiences with customers — not simply the trans-actions and demographics — but every customer interaction: the phone call to a call center, the click on a Web site, and the response to a direct mail campaign.

Building data and information technology architecture around each individual customer — the customer-centric model — enables customers to enjoy a seamless and rewarding experience when doing business with a company.

The Stages of a CRM Strategy

Developing and implementing effective and successful customer relationships through the formal process of a CRM strategy is not an event, but an ongoing process, and it needs to be strategically managed and integrated at all levels within an organization by every employee. Ultimately, CRM is all about increasing customer profitability by identifying detailed customer segmenta-tion, defining marketing communication strategies, and providing the intelli-gent decisions to more effectively drive retention, profitability, and customer satisfaction.

Based on the foregoing analysis of today's customer, there are four distinct stages in establishing and maintaining a successful corporate CRM process:

1. *Interacting* — referring to the series of transactions and interactions that make up a dialog between a customer and an organization (e.g., sales processes)
2. *Analyzing* — applying insightful marketing practices to create relevant interactions that build valued relationships
3. *Learning* — connecting interaction points between a consumer and an organization to obtain knowledge of the customer
4. *Planning* — developing marketing plans and strategies to meet customer requirements

Interacting

A dialog between a customer and an organization consists of a series of transactions and interactions and may take several forms. A transaction may be a telephone or Web-based product order, a cash request from an ATM, a service request, or payment of a monthly bill.

An interaction may also include a call for product information, placement of a product in a shopping cart without purchasing it, a complaint about the quality of a product or service, or a request for the status of a shipment. It might also involve a profile update such as a life-cycle event — change of address, increase in family size, change in marital status, etc.

Each transaction or interaction represents an opportunity to build and develop a relationship with a customer. Even the shortest dialog — a change in telephone number or address — represents a change in a customer's lifestyle. Using this insight to interact with a customer in a follow-up mode (with special marketing offers, for example) is one way of encouraging customer loyalty and retention. These opportunities to relate to customers, if used in a proactive manner, are reflections to the customer of the interest the organization has in this customer's individual needs and the desire to foster an ongoing relationship.

Analyzing

Analyzing customer behavior means applying insight to create relevant inter-actions that build valued relationships. This is the stage where market planning comes in and where marketing campaigns are initiated to build value for customers. Offering a customer something of value emphasizes a desire to retain that customer.

Learning

Learning to apply the knowledge gained from analyzing customer behavior, and applying this knowledge to interaction points between a customer and an organization, defines the third stage in customer relationship management. In this stage, ongoing procedures for maintaining customer contact are established through correspondence, phone calls, or personal meetings — any one-on-one activity that serves to enhance customer relationships by maintaining customer contact.

Planning

A fourth important stage in the CRM process is planning the market strategies that evolve from knowing customers, their purchasing patterns, their product preferences, and their lifestyles. This knowledge is a fundamental requirement to marketing strategies that treat each customer as an individual and can be achieved through constant analysis of the customer's transaction activity.

These four fundamental aspects of maintaining relationships with the knowledgeable customer of today are the basis for a formalization of a customer relationship strategy. On each of these fronts, organizations need to position themselves to gather customer information, store it, and then use the appropriate technology tools to access this information and apply it to manage each and every customer relationship.

One-to-one customer relationships are strengthened by monitoring the individual transaction stream to understand behavior and detect significant changes that lead to the need for a customer dialog. The transaction stream can be used to accurately assess the value of each relationship. Transactions can be viewed from different aspects to provide a consistent, holistic picture by segment, product, or channel. Understanding the customer and the data can enable privacy policies to be implemented, including treating each customer according to his or her individual privacy preferences.

Understanding customers at the most detailed level avoids making false assumptions about their needs and establishes a priority to their needs as individuals — above the vendor's interests. In the networked economy, this is a prerequisite for being in business — to turn transactions into relationships.

An integrated approach to customer relations is an important factor in the CRM solution and reflects the knowledge that every time a customer interacts with the organization, the relationship is enhanced, no matter where the interaction originates, electronically or personally. The tangible benefits of this relationship enhancement are reduced costs, increased revenues, and improved service levels,

In Chapter 2, "The Evolution of Customer Relations to CRM," a comprehensive review is provided concerning the transition that the marketplace is undergoing, from the perspective of both supplier and customer. The evolution of customer relations to the concepts embodied in a complete, enterprisewide customer relationship management solution has resulted in a significant shift in market forces and dynamics, effectively changing forever the customer/supplier landscape.

Chapter 2

The Evolution of Customer Relations to CRM

CRM is a corporatewide approach to understanding customer behavior, influencing it through continuous relevant communication and developing long-term relationships to enhance customer loyalty, acquisition, retention, and profitability. (See also "Glossary" in Appendix A.)

For many corporate senior executives, customer relationship management (CRM) has come into their management perspective and boardroom meetings with mixed reviews — initially appearing to be a great opportunity to increase efficiency, revenues, and profitability, as well as providing a process for getting to know the customer better.

Software companies and consultants have confronted large and small corporations (from old economy and new) with dire predictions, pointing out that if their organizations did not jump on the CRM bandwagon, they would be ground into the dust by competitors that were more aggressive and open to new corporate practices.

CRM is a powerful tool in both the business-to-business and business-to-consumer environments; however, it has been both oversold and underutilized. In many cases, more has been promised for CRM than it could ever possibly deliver; and in other situations, companies have not properly implemented the CRM systems in which they have invested significant time, effort, and money.

There has been a tendency for some vendors and consultants to focus on CRM as a trans-organizational strategy, requiring immediate commitment throughout the organization and rapid re-engineering of processes and philosophies to make the customer the focus of all activities. In reality, as pointed out in this Handbook, the CRM process will be more readily accepted by organizations if the process is a gradual one, building from a series of data marts to an enterprisewide data warehouse and CRM solution. This methodology is highly recommended for those organizations that are just embarking on a CRM solution, as opposed to those companies that have already installed a data warehouse, have already tested the waters with a data mart, and are now prepared to embark on an enterprisewide CRM solution.

When CRM is only seen as a solution that needs to permeate all aspects of an organization's activities to be effective, there is a natural tendency to want to roll it out all at once in what has been called the "big bang" approach. Too often, the big bang turns out to be a big mess!

Organizations confronted with more change than they can handle at one time, may find that the challenges faced by employees are exceeded by the challenges faced by the software. Because of the complex nature of even a modest CRM solution, successful CRM implementation requires above-average consulting. Vendors tend to want to solve all the problems at once, and while consultants can assist in analyzing a business and its processes, there are other issues to be considered, addressed, and solved. The chosen CRM solution needs to be implemented: devise a plan, execute it, and stick to it.

Planning

Companies should not be expending precious financial and human resources on particular communications channels and customer segments out of all proportion to their profitability and practicality. Define a customer service strategy by determining investment priorities, and then select the best supportive technology. Making the proper choice of technology is critical, but it cannot be accomplished without a coherent, executable plan.

Using a gradual approach, a company needs to identify the most important application of CRM and ensure that a stable, viable process is put in place before moving on to the next one. As part of a planned, carefully executed process, specific customer segments and communications channels are identified for the initial execution. Focus on managing these components well before tackling the next segments and channels.

A Functioning CRM Solution

Make sure the business processes are mapped into the underlying technology. Customers are supported by the way you work; the technology you select helps you provide that support. The technology itself should not be in the driver's seat. Companies so often buy CRM technology in the name of customer service and forget about the customer, as implementing the application becomes an internal issue. The focus must be on the customer at all times.

Believe in CRM

For CRM to have long-term practicality and benefits, an organization has to believe in its underlying proposition of improving customer relations. It is more than software and digital switching systems. A customer-focused mindset must take root in the organization, and this takes time. Ideally, it should begin well before the CRM solution is rolled out. Employees require the skill sets to serve customers better; senior executives must show the leadership that encourages a customer-centric culture.

There must be incentives for people to believe in CRM. Customer service has to be more than a slogan; therefore, tangible benefits, whether in data mining that allows sales and marketing to hone their efforts or in measurable successes in repeat customers and overall satisfaction, have to be seen and appreciated. Advances in technology tend to move at breakneck speed; it is often said that an Internet year lasts about four months. But the frantic pace of development does not mean that implementation should also be frantic.

CRM is about cultivating a long-term relationship with the customer by enhancing the value of a company's products or services. Therefore, the process of implementing CRM should be approached as a long-term strategy.

Software-driven CRM systems integrate front-office activities such as sales, customer service, and technical support with back-office resources such as accounting and inventory management. Only a few years ago, the typical CRM operation was seen as a call center with rows full of customer service representatives working telephones in front of computer monitors. An explosion in communications channels, particularly through the Internet, has turned CRM into a multi-channel strategy with the capability to address and integrate telephones, Web presence, e-mail, real-time text chat, and wireless data.

As product offerings became more complex, they became more difficult to implement. CRM's scope has become so ambitious that there are serious doubts as to whether any one vendor can deliver a product that performed as promised. There are now single-vendor products and services available, but the most important factor in CRM success is not what is installed, but *how* the selected implementation process, the external technology resources, and the CRM project team's management capabilities can instill the new customer-centric paradigm into the existing corporate culture.

Some organizations invest millions of dollars and spend thousands of hours deploying corporate applications (e.g., sales force automation (SFA), help desk, enterprise resource planning (ERP), marketing automation, E-commerce, call centers, and Web platforms). These applications implement and support CRM strategies and build customer loyalty through intelligent and trusted communications. Using innovative technologies to achieve this goal while containing costs is a fundamental challenge for every company that embraces CRM.

Moving Away from Mass Marketing

For many organizations that adhere to the old ways of doing business, the move to a CRM strategy begins with the realization that the customer, the market, and the competition have changed and will continue to change. Treating customers as mass markets is no longer a viable business strategy, and success in business in the 21st century requires a new vision — a vision that demands changes in processes, people, and practices, where the customer is involved. These organizations have a greater challenge and need a few years and major changes in corporate culture to evolve to a successful CRM strategy.

For other organizations that have continually examined and revised their methods of relating to customers, as well as adopting appropriate technologies along the way, the evolution to a formalized CRM strategy will be a relatively short step. It may only require a fine-tuning of existing processes, a refinement of current technologies, and additional training of staff to ensure the transition to a complete CRM solution.

Both kinds of organizations need to be aware of the significant changes to the business environment discussed in Chapter 1, "The Customer Today." Businesses merged and grew, customer bases grew, and the customer changed along the way. Armed with their newfound understanding of the levels of service that suppliers should and can provide, they expect much more. And the power they wield in the marketplace can only increase with time.

Companies that have observed these changes and responded, realizing that a new approach to customers was required, will be able to recover some of the customer relations of the days of the corner store. Often, the process involves the formalization of an organization's existing customer relationship policies, requiring several distinct areas of revision of corporate culture, including adopting new methods of managing customer information using new technologies. In Chapter 3, "The Technology of CRM," the enabling technologies required to implement a successful CRM strategy are examined and evaluated with recommendations on planning, developing, implementation, and references to specific vendors and the technologies they have brought to successful CRM implementations.

Strategies for Managing Customer Information

Large organizations routinely collect vast amounts of personal information about their customers through the transactions they conduct. Organizations such as financial institutions, healthcare providers, travel agencies, retailers, automotive manufacturers, and communication companies, among others, collect this data to use in a variety of ways and for several reasons:

- To do targeted marketing based on individual preferences
- To analyze customers for profitability
- To evaluate their own service levels

Cross-functional and pilot teams are keys to success. Employing these teams early in the planning stages of CRM projects saves a tremendous amount of time and effort, by including their insight and expertise and, most importantly, gaining their support.

However, getting positive, measurable business results from these activities does not come from simply gathering information and storing it. Many CRM

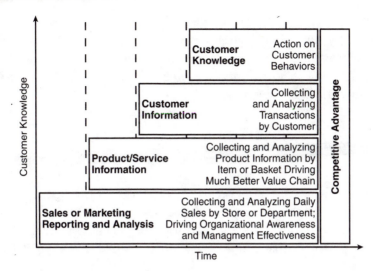

Exhibit 1. Collecting Customer Information

strategies have failed to achieve objectives because of difficulties in developing a strong understanding of who customers are and what they really want, and applying this knowledge to establish customer relationship strategies and processes (see Exhibit 1).

Some companies build multi-terabyte (1000 gigabytes is one terabyte) data warehouses to crunch information about their customers in an effort to determine buying habits or product preferences. Oftentimes, correlation among customer purchasing habits is not properly done; just because data can be correlated does not mean the relationship between one set of data and another is significant from a business viewpoint. Obviously, technology and business processes must be applied in a logical context to ensure that customer data is applied to meet CRM objectives (see Exhibit 2).

CRM brings technology to bear on business processes, enabling organizations to use historical customer transaction data to better manage customer relationships. The concept expressed in the term *customer relationship management* has been adopted by organizations that recognized the benefit of a formal approach to customer relations, one designed to build meaningful,

Exhibit 2. Enhancing Customer Relationships

long-term relationships with customers. CRM is based on a set of technology tools, especially data information-based tools that allow organizations to capture, analyze, and apply the large volumes of detailed customer data needed to achieve a better understanding of their customers and to make more informed business decisions.

Tools to Support CRM

It is important to choose the right technology tools to support a CRM solution. Technologies that directly support CRM, and other technologies that furnish indirect support, such as wireless, voice-over-IP (VoIP), and e-mail-based Internet communications, have evolved to the point of providing many more channels for customer interaction. Business tools that support CRM include:

- Customer contact software
- Marketing campaign programs
- Channel integration
- Product literature

Where legacy systems exist, there may be a requirement to acquire middleware to interface the legacy systems to the CRM solutions. The key challenge for the CRM project team is to select a series of tools that fits the needs of the business and then evaluate these tools to select the best ones. This process is often made difficult because of the state of development of the tools. For many of these tools, the selected product may not be the final version, and this will lead to a product with periodic updates and subsequent software maintenance requirements.

The IT department plays a very prominent role in the development, implementation, and support of a CRM solution because of the various technology tools involved, which need to be selected, analyzed, and acquired. It is important that these tools be seamlessly integrated into the IT environment. This aspect of the CRM strategy requires a formal plan to manage the selection of the tools — from a data warehouse and database software to the business applications and processes.

As noted previously, some companies have adopted formalized CRM strategies early in their corporate histories and are achieving measurable business results through CRM initiatives. Others, however, may have to totally revise their corporate cultures, often to the point of casting aside historical approaches to dealing with customers and in their sales and marketing programs. Organizations that do not have a formal process for managing customers by monitoring and gathering historical transaction data, and then analyzing this data to determine response processes that respond to each customer's needs, will need to put major efforts and budgets into developing CRM strategies.

CRM and the New Marketing Paradigm

While there are several definitions of CRM within the industry, one short, overall definition that best describes the process and its objectives is as follows: the capability of an organization to evolve from a mass marketing model of millions to a market of one. In other words, be able deal with each customer as if he or she were the only customer. This is a new way of thinking for many companies in virtually every business sector noted in Chapter 1 — financial, retail, travel, healthcare, communications, entertainment, automotive, etc. — where customers number in the thousands or millions for many of the organizations in each of these sectors.

Managing customer relationships successfully in these large customer environments means learning about their habits and needs, anticipating future buying patterns, and finding new marketing opportunities that add value to the relationship. It also means using technologies that enable all of the data gathered to be used as an aid in making business decisions that will attract, retain, or motivate customers.

Successful companies make their customer relationships something the customer values more than anything else they could receive from the competition. How do companies do this? By examining their experiences with customers, including transactions and demographics, and every form of interaction — including a Web site visit, a phone call to a call center, and a response from a direct mail campaign. Building the data and information technology architecture around customers — a customer-centric approach — ensures that they enjoy a seamless and rewarding experience when doing business with a company.

This is the new marketing paradigm, placing the customer at the focal point of an organization's marketing programs.

The following two key elements of a CRM strategy will ensure the success of the process and meet the objectives of the organization to develop long-term customer relationships:

1. Build a system that allows you to track, capture, and analyze the millions of customer activities, both interactions and transactions, over a long period of time.
2. Create promotions, develop new products and services, and design communication programs that attract, reward, and retain customers (see Exhibit 3).

CRM has also been compared to viewing the customer through a single, global lens. It reflects an organization's capability to manage all interactions with its customers and to use customer information to maintain a single, long-term view of each customer across multiple channels, face-to-face, or via phone, kiosk, or Web site.

These points of interaction are often referred to as *customer touchpoints* and may involve many types of transactions. Of course, CRM includes customer billing, marketing, and other support functions that directly or indirectly interact with the customer. In fact, every department, division, and employee in an organization has a role to play in CRM (see Exhibit 4).

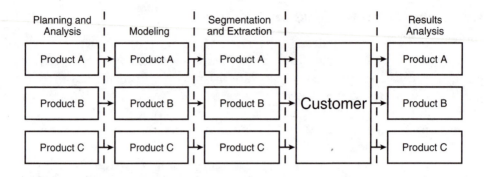

Exhibit 3. Product-Focused Marketing

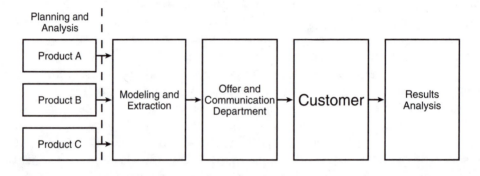

Exhibit 4. Customer-Focused Marketing

Managing customer relations using proven processes and technologies can maximize the revenue opportunity for each customer and create a foundation for satisfaction that will ultimately drive loyalty independent of the channel. CRM can enable companies to maximize profitability with their customers using measurements that quantify and qualify customers, differentiating between high- and low-value customers. CRM has the power to facilitate managing the lifetime value of a customer.

CRM Provides Answers

A successful CRM strategy can provide answers to many typical questions that every organization has about its customers:

- Who are my best customers?
- How do I attract them?
- Am I selling them the products and services that meet their specific needs and will this be profitable?
- How do I keep them coming back?
- How do I handle unhappy customers? (See Exhibit 5.)

Methods of Tracking Customer Needs

Exhibit 5.   Knowing the Customer

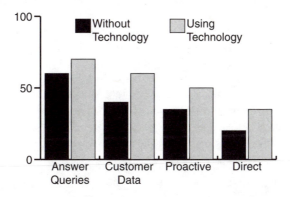

Exhibit 6.   Technology Enhances Customer Service

CRM involves centering your customers at the core of your organization with every function and department involved in serving the customer. Sales, service and support functions, as well as relationships with business partners, form a continuum, because this is the way these corporate functions are viewed by customers. When customers have a purchasing relationship with a supplier, they believe that they are relating to the complete orgànization, from sales to shipping and even to the president.

Many companies that believed technology would solve customer relationship problems learned the hard way that technology is only an enabler. CRM implementations based on this premise failed because they did not change the corporate culture to permit the technology to perform its primary function: developing and retaining loyal and profitable customers. Technology's role as an enabler is to support the strategies, tactics, and processes that result from a defined, enterprisewide CRM solution (see Exhibit 6).

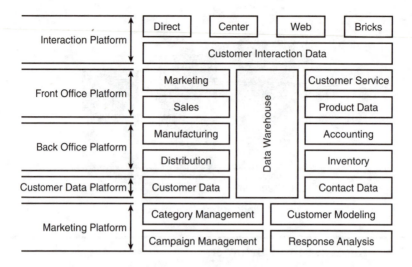

Exhibit 7. Corporate Functions and Customer Interactions

Lessons from CRM Successes

In CRM, there is no one-size-fits-all. Various industries interact differently with their customers. Even within the same industry, each enterprise has a unique approach to managing interactions with customers, one of the characteristics that differentiate one company from another. However, there are some excellent guidelines and lessons to be learned from successful CRM implementations within the same industry sectors. The information provided in Chapter 4, "Case Studies in CRM," is presented in a traditional case study format that analyzes a number of CRM projects selected from a broad range of business sectors. The lessons learned by these organizations in implementing successful CRM solutions can be translated and applied to organizations in the same business sectors (see Exhibit 7).

Because CRM applications provide functionality to enhance these interactions, it is important to match CRM strategies with the corporate business strategy. For example, a company known for its high level of customer service might use this characteristic as a starting point for implementing a CRM application. Another company may be very good at targeting profitable customers. Each organization should seek a niche on which to develop its CRM strategy, based on its existing, inherent strengths in customer relations.

Customer Data

One of the common problems many organizations share is integrating customer information. When information is disparate and fragmented, it is difficult to know who the customers are and the nature of their associations or relationships. This also makes it difficult to capitalize on opportunities to increase customer service, loyalty, and profitability. For example, knowing that other family members are also customers provides an opportunity to

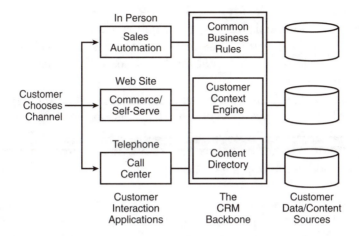

Exhibit 8. Customer Interactions in the CRM Infrastructure
(Source: CGI Group Inc.)

up-sell or cross-sell products or services, or knowing that a customer uses several sources of interaction with a supplier can also provide opportunities to enhance the relationship.

The creation and execution of a successful CRM strategy will depend on close examination and rationalization of the relationship between an organization's vision and business strategy. If the customer is not at the center of this vision, the vision must be reexamined and altered to the customer-centric position, a focal point of CRM and this Handbook. This fundamental aspect of a CRM strategy needs to be reinforced.

In building toward a CRM solution and in evaluating the use of customer data, the organization must also analyze how well it is aligned to deliver on the following core capabilities:

- Customer value management
- Prospecting
- Selling
- Collection and use of customer intelligence
- Customer development (up-selling and cross-selling)
- Customer service and retention
- Customer privacy protection

Ultimately, the success or failure of CRM implementation depends upon the capability of the organization and its employees to integrate human resources, business processes, and technology to create differentiation and excellence in service to customers and to perform all of these functions better than its competitors (see Exhibit 8).

From Product Focus to Customer Centricity

In the E-commerce business world, a customer can switch to a competitor's product with a click or two on a Web page. Customer-centricity in the new business economy — already the best means to build lasting customer relationships in traditional ways of doing business — becomes absolutely imperative. Shifting to customer centricity is not a straightforward or natural process; however, it is a process that must be initiated and instilled throughout the organization.

The reason for this is that, in general, businesses are launched because of a unique product or service. Initially, the focus is on building that product or developing that service and informing the marketplace of its availability and desirability. When another company eventually begins producing and market-ing a similar product, the original company's product focus loses its competitive edge.

At this point companies adopt other strategies to regain the competitive edge they had when they had the only product or service and begin stream-lining operations to produce the product better, faster, and cheaper. The improved enterprise performance is a short-lived advantage as the competition inevitably applies the same strategy, a leap-frogging process common to many business sectors. Customer relationship then becomes more important than simply building a good product or delivering good service. Building good products is often easier than building good customer relationships, and although product quality is still important, it is no longer the key to sustainable competitive advantage, where the competition's products are just as good. In the long term, the organization with the best customer relationship strategy will win.

Becoming customer-centric, i.e., shifting from marketing products to build-ing lasting customer relationships, is an evolutionary process. It cannot be done overnight and usually requires a major change in corporate culture. A fundamental feature of a fully customer-centric organization is the capability to successfully manage customer knowledge (see Exhibit 9).

Product-focused organizations use sales data primarily to report against financial targets. On the other hand, a customer-centric organization stores, analyzes, and uses sales, billing, service, support, and other data in an ongoing relationship with customers to accomplish the following objectives:

- *Forge* personal relationships
- *Increase* staff awareness of customer importance
- *Improve* the product development process
- *Deliver* value-added service better than competitors

Customer Value

Transforming customer knowledge into customer value can create a significant competitive advantage. For example, when high-value customers are identified, and their needs anticipated, new value is created for them where it did not exist before. Ultimately, customer-centric organizations build customer loyalty, a customer response characteristic that leads to higher profitability.

There are several determinations of customer value that organizations can use to categorize customers. Tracking revenues, cost, and profitability is not

Exhibit 9.   Sample Features Checklist for CRM Plan of Action

List #1: Essential and Mandatory	List #2: Optional Functionality
Data mining capability	Vendor input to data warehouse
Data cleansing and profiling	Departmental input
Customer touchpoints data input	Data transformation
Data from legacy systems	Advanced graphic interface
Store detail data	etc.
etc.	

Customer Marketing Implementation Phases

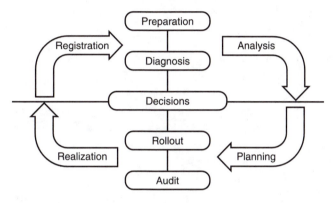

Exhibit 10.   Overview of CRM Implementation

the only way to assess customer value. Value potential, a more advanced method of evaluating customer value, is another way. It has been defined as "the willingness of customers to participate in the creation of products and services, and to what degree they are prepared to share information and other resources and control over the design and production of products and services."

The CRM Planning Phase

As noted previously, CRM is not an event but a process, evolutionary in nature, that requires a roadmap to guide organizations through the many junctions and potentially costly digressions down alternative routes. Following that roadmap needs a concerted effort from several organizational components: people, processes, culture, and technology.

There are four key elements in the development of a CRM roadmap:

1. Analysis of the current state of customer interactions
2. Predicting the future course of customer interactions
3. Developing the Plan of Action to meet the predicted future course
4. Building and presenting the business case to secure CRM project funding (see Exhibit 10)

Analyzing the current state of customer interactions and associated historical customer data will determine where the enterprise is along the path to its CRM objectives. Some of the questions about current customer relations that need to be examined include:

- Does the organization track and manage each customer as a single entity or do individual sales offices maintain their own set of customer records?
- Is customer database information accurate and up-to-date?

An early assessment of these elements of the business operation will highlight customer administration procedures that may need to be changed to take advantage of the new CRM strategy (see Exhibit 11).

The CRM Plan of Action

One of the first elements of the CRM Plan of Action is to establish priorities of functionality, by preparing two feature checklists. List 1 will consist of the essential and mandatory functionality required. List 2 will be the optional functionality that may be incorporated, budgets and time permitting. These two lists will be important elements for the business case and should be incorporated into the presentation to management for approvals of project budgets (see Exhibit 9).

If approval for both lists of features is obtained, the CRM development process may be broken into two projects: one for the essential list and the other to develop the optional features. This approach to the planning stage — adding functionality in a modular approach — coincides with a modular approach adopted by many CRM hardware and software vendors. Planning to build on earlier functionality in a building-block approach will also assist in developing the CRM Plan of Action and in the subsequent design and deployment of the CRM solution.

The following organizational elements must be included in the CRM Plan of Action:

- Employees of the corporation
- The IT department
- A selection of other resources

Participation will be required from all corporate departments and will include the user community, executive sponsors, and others who will be asked to participate actively in the project. This participation may involve providing design inputs, taking part in pilot tests of the system, or helping to train others to use the system during system rollout.

Also included in the Plan of Action will be target time frames and expected project milestones as reporting dates to meet management expectations. The Plan should mesh with the business case so that requests for resources — people, time, and money — are linked to forecast or anticipated business benefits.

The business case should describe a business rationale for investing in CRM. It should include information about the competitors, what they are doing, how such a system supports the company's strategy, as well as the expected qualitative and quantitative benefits, including return on investment (ROI). While ROI is a significant benefit of CRM over the long term (see Chapter 6, "Benefits of CRM"), financial or quantitative benefits do not represent the complete picture. Among the less tangible but equally important benefits of a well-executed CRM strategy that improves customer satisfaction and creates a base of loyal customers, are the following:

- More sales per customer
- Lower cost of sales
- More referral sales
- Higher profitability

With appropriate metrics and comparative analysis techniques in place, it is even possible to assign values to these less tangible benefits.

Selecting the Technology Solutions

As noted previously in this chapter, many enterprises believe that a large-scale enterprise CRM technology deployment is the only solution to their problems. However, the right technology enablers for an organization are those that solve the organization's business problems, as they are identified during the CRM business evaluation stage. Some of the solutions that may be identified are:

- Deploying or enhancing data warehouse or data mart information to collect and analyze customer and market data
- Web-enabling customer contact center
- Improving call center telephony infrastructure
- Improving customer relationships through customer-facing E-business

During the evolution of CRM that has occurred over the past several years, a number of CRM projects failed to deliver projected results because companies seized on technology as an immediate solution to enhanced customer relations, rather than modifying their corporate culture under the canopy of CRM. The dangers inherent in a false reliance on technology alone to produce a CRM strategy are reiterated throughout this Handbook.

Some organizations that have focused on technology as the key route to CRM were unable to produce a successful CRM because they — the people, supporting systems, the processes, as well as the corporate culture — were not ready to manage the new technology and to apply proven principles of CRM to their day-to-day operations.

Technology is a significant element in the CRM mix; however, selecting the best enabling technologies for CRM solutions must be based on solid business practices and readiness to implement. Goals and metrics must be established to measure these technology tools where selection is a critical process and decisions need to be made on vendors in several areas of technology.

Changing the Customer Focus

In the past, large and small organizations have established successful relations with their customers without the need to formalize these relationships into a definable customer strategy. In the new era, where the customer reigns supreme, businesses must change their focus to ensure that customer relationship practices maximize customer benefit.

A business must give each individual customer a reason to keep coming back. To do that, the business has to know what customers need and want.

When a business knows its clientele and targets its communications to their specific interests and shopping behaviors, the result is increased revenue and loyal, long-term customers. This is the power of one-to-one CRM. If the CRM practitioner cannot focus on individual customer transactions, both in the process of segmentation and in the contact strategy, CRM strategies will not be successful.

Tracking the transactional details of a customer's purchase allows the business to communicate with the customer in the most effective way possible. CRM has the capability to maximize the benefit of the commercial relationship with each individual customer.

Today, with practices that have evolved in the retail industry, every business can effectively define a customer's needs, without incremental cost or complexity. Using these practices enables an organization to accomplish the following objectives:

- Achieve more effective merchandise buying and planning and faster inventory turns
- Maximize return on marketing dollars by targeting customers with selected promotions
- Minimize the number of transactions at sale prices by creating customized triggers that stimulate buying at full price
- Easily attract new customers whose tastes and preferences relate to selected current customers
- Design more efficient stores with designs based on customer cross-shopping behavior
- Ensure that each customer buys more and remains a customer for life

The next phase in the CRM evolution is the era of exact transaction analysis, a customer-focused model that allows even the largest organizations to achieve the old style of customer service once again. This phase is described later in this chapter.

CRM Strategy: From Planning to Development

In the experience of many organizations, CRM is a powerful growth strategy capable of producing significant benefits and transforming both organizations and industries into customer-centric entities. However, for every company that has achieved dramatic success, there are many others that are either still struggling to realize the full potential of their customer-driven growth strategies, or have not yet realized the full potential of CRM.

For many companies, the implementation path has been filled with hurdles and the pace of implementation has been far slower and more frustrating than anticipated. However, there are proven processes and techniques that organizations can follow to provide a high probability of success.

To reinforce the validity of CRM, a corporate system that classifies as a major development project in any organization, analyzing some of the many successful implementations of CRM strategies, from a wide range of business sectors, is an extremely useful endeavor. These implementations have taken place globally, in major business organizations, many of which are household names (see Chapter 4, "Case Studies in CRM").

Over the past several years, proven development and implementation processes, as well as enabling technologies, have evolved and continue to evolve, and are available for examination and evaluation, to assist other organizations to dramatically accelerate the transition to a successful CRM solution. These case study examples also can assist organizations in avoiding some of the common errors that have resulted in unsuccessful CRM implementations.

The lessons learned by other organizations and the methodologies and technologies available today can be applied to any organization to make the change from a product or service-oriented organization to one of being customer focused, providing strong returns on the CRM investment in a matter of months rather than years.

For companies assessing a CRM strategy or in the process of implementation, there are many project-oriented issues to be resolved. Here are some of the important ones:

- *Accelerating* the overall implementation process
- *Maintaining* project momentum
- *Reducing* the risk
- *Generating* tangible returns
- *Lowering* costs
- *Minimizing* disruption to the organization
- *Establishing* a foundation for continuing gains

A Twelve-Stage CRM Strategy

The Twelve Core Stages of a CRM Strategy defined in Exhibit 11 provide a proven methodology for resolving many issues in a logical, efficient manner

Exhibit 11. Twelve Core Stages of a CRM Strategy

Develop a clear and consistent set of business objectives
Prepare a detailed Plan of Action
Build the system in stages, beginning with the most crucial area for meeting the first objectives
Provide strong leadership and mobilize the organization
Implement and follow through on a change in the corporate culture
Enlist a senior management member to support the project
Create an integrated business design
Establish a customer-driven product and service development process
Learn through action to jump-start development of organizational capabilities
Generate early wins and create a self-funding process
Focus on activities that create economic value
Establish a two-way flow of communications with customers

and are derived from successful CRM strategies. While no two companies can follow precisely the same implementation path, the stages defined below need to be a part of the process, and most of them can be carried out in parallel. Some organizations will have already moved through some of these stages, and others will need to start at the beginning.

The following paragraphs describe each stage in detail.

1. Develop Business Objectives

Defining clear business objectives is an obvious first step in any project, major or minor. However, because of the evolutionary nature and enterprisewide impact of a CRM strategy, it is extremely important to establish business objectives that will create a competitive advantage and guide the overall implementation process. These objectives relate to this fundamental concept in planning a CRM solution.

Understand how the organization wants to compete in its business environment and its corporate objectives before building the infrastructure, organizational capabilities, operations, and technologies for a CRM solution.

The business case prepared to convince senior management of the benefits of CRM should be firmly and logically based on overall corporate objectives — perhaps the corporate Mission Statement, if one exists. It should include information about direct competitors, how the system supports corporate strategies, plus expected qualitative and quantitative benefits. Return on investment (ROI), commonly used to support the development of other corporate systems, is not as significant in a CRM project, because financial or quantitative benefits are not the whole story.

As noted previously, improving customer satisfaction and creating a base of more loyal customers will have both qualitative and quantitative benefits in the long term — more sales per customer, lower cost of sales, incremental sales via referral and, ultimately, more profits. Some of these benefits are intangible; however, collectively, they are powerful motivators in support of CRM.

2. Develop a Detailed Plan of Action

It will take four to eight weeks to develop a comprehensive plan that defines the type of customer-focused initiatives that will establish the new way of doing business, the organizational capabilities, operations, and the enabling technologies that will be the driving forces behind the implementation initiatives.

Technology planning and implementation should be closely integrated with the business planning phases to create a self-correcting process. With an integrated process, the planned business objectives, capabilities, and operations define the requirements for the enabling technologies, and subsequently, the technology development process identifies feasibility issues that require adjustment to the original plans.

To structure the planning process, it is very useful to develop a framework that describes the role and interrelationship for each of the required areas of capabilities and operations. Initially, the framework for the Plan of Action provides a means for systematically planning and tracking the development process. It is also an important step toward both developing an integrated business design and managing the ongoing implementation process.

3. Build in Stages

A staged approach, where operating capabilities are developed only to the point needed to realize near-term objectives, is far more viable than one designed to meet every conceivable need for the next 20 years. Five guidelines for a staged project are:

- Build for the near-term
- Make it scalable
- Use it
- Determine the changes required to increase productivity
- Build on this knowledge

4. Provide Strong Leadership

For any major project, sound leadership is a prerequisite; therefore, the people selected as team or project leaders need to have the leadership attributes that will keep the project and the project staff on track. A balance between business and technology backgrounds is preferable for leadership candidates, because knowledge in both areas will assist at all stages of the process.

5. *Implement and Follow through on the Implementation*

The first stage of development should focus on the operations and technology needed to implement a top-priority set of CRM business objectives, as identified in Stage 1. Typically, the first stage of development can become operational in two to four months, and at a small fraction of the costs that have traditionally been incurred. Many companies use the first stage to establish a proof of concept, to demonstrate to management that CRM really works, and then follow with subsequent stages to scale up the operations and technology as well as to expand the scope of the overall program.

6. *Enlist a Senior Management Member to Support the Project*

The success of every CRM project will be dependent on several factors and the effective integration of all stages; however, the support the project receives internally is of particular value. The requirement for the support of a senior management member, (e.g., the vice-president of marketing or sales, vice-president of finance, or other member of the senior management team) is crucial to the success of the CRM strategy. This stage of the process cannot be overemphasized, and the designated senior management person must form an integral part of the CRM team, with a commitment to attend and actively participate in all project meetings and workshops.

7. *Create an Integrated Business Design*

Many companies have realized significant returns from CRM strategies simply by building systems and launching programs. Yet, to realize the full potential, CRM strategies must become a way of doing business managed through an integrated business design involving the entire organization, with every employee pulling in the same direction.

8. *Establish a Customer-Driven Development Process*

Product-driven companies have a tradition of building products based on instincts and engineering requirements rather than on customer requirements. Even when these companies agree that an outside-in, customer-driven process could remove much of the risk of product development, the transition may not be easy.

As emphasized in other chapters of this Handbook, customer-driven value proposition development — products and services, pricing, channels, and brand — is central to CRM strategies. A significant step forward in becoming customer driven is to establish a process for monitoring customer purchase rates, and then use the value proposition to quickly identify changes in customer behavior that signal a need for revitalization and new development.

It is not necessary to radically change or dismantle the product development component of an organization. The strengths of that component need to be preserved while integrating a stream of customer input. The objective is to establish a dynamic product and service development process that can adapt as quickly as the marketplace can change.

9. Learn through Action

Often, the transition to CRM strategies requires new skills and organizational processes. An ideal learning process is to learn through action, by applying new practices and processes, guided by experienced leaders.

This rapid deployment methodology enables companies to immediately launch a range of sophisticated customer programs, relying on the resourcefulness of their own staff, and to the extent needed, guidance from experienced consultants. To optimize results, the work should be carried out by cross-functional teams that have shared objectives. In addition, the teams should be focused on using innovative methodologies, and most importantly, they should be committed to producing tangible, measurable results.

At the heart of CRM strategies is a fundamental change in the decision-making process. Rigorous data analysis is replacing business instinct as a basis for both day-to-day decision making and strategic planning. And, a test and learn discipline is becoming a basic requirement for CRM success.

The test-and-learn process is much more than a measurement system. It is a way of doing business. The foundation should be a well-defined test and control-based measurement system, integrated with customer initiatives and other areas of investment to measure business outcomes in a systematic way. A key metric should be impact on customer value. In addition, the process should include a regular schedule of review sessions that brings together senior management, analysts, and key operating staff to plan refinements and steer the business, based on both internal and external (customer) feedback.

CRM leaders have demonstrated that they can utilize the test-and-learn process to continue making refinements indefinitely and to build greater and greater competitive strength. In some industries, the early adopters have reached a point where they are accelerating on the learning curves while their competitors are still working out the basics, creating a formidable hurdle for the late adopters.

10. Generate Early Wins

It is no longer necessary for companies to spend millions of dollars and years of effort before producing measurable returns. Steps can be taken to generate compelling returns within months of the launch, which in turn helps to build valuable momentum in the organization. Companies across multiple industries consistently realize dramatic gains that provide a proof of concept in the early stages of development. In addition, the gains provide a basis for developing economic projections, and in some cases, they provide companies with self-funding, self-sustaining processes.

The examples shown in Exhibit 11 illustrate the magnitude of gains realized from the first programs launched by each of the companies in various business sectors under their new CRM strategies.

11. Focus on Activities that Create Economic Value

For most companies, the formalization of a CRM strategy results in a fundamental shift in goals. Priorities are systematically established based on their potential to drive profitable growth, and the primary means for driving the growth is to grow customer value. Successful organizations in the era of the customer are placing top priority on measuring and tracking customer value in clear economic terms. Customer valuation has become a core capability that companies need to develop.

Customer value can be measured on an individual customer level. The results typically prove the rule that a large majority of the value is coming from a small proportion — often referred to as the 80/20 rule — of the customers. It may also reveal that the company has been allocating resources far too extensively to the least valuable customer segment. With this vital information in hand, a wide range of strategic and operating decisions can be made, based on the projected impact on customer value.

12. Establish a Two-Way Flow of Communications

Customer information has become a major strategic asset for corporations, creating requirements for information management and control that are just as important as managing an organization's finances. An advanced information control capability should integrate two major components of the CRM framework:

1. *Managing customer contacts* — an active control process for information exchange with customers
2. *Managing customer knowledge* — controls retention of information and accessibility.

Radial changes in the marketplace, as emphasized throughout this Handbook, mean that it is no longer sufficient to conduct periodic surveys to monitor changes in the marketplace. The marketplace changes daily and customer expectations can change significantly and quickly, often instigated by aggressive competition. The continuous and systematic capture, retention, and analysis of customer information, from virtually every point of customer contact, is an essential activity in a successful CRM strategy.

Significant advances in contact management software are being made to support ongoing information exchange between a company and its customers, and for seamless integration of multichannel communications with customers. There are several important sources of customer information available to the CRM project team:

- *Transaction systems* for detailed customer behavioral data
- *Customer contact channels* such as call centers, retail outlets, and electronic commerce Web sites
- *Outbound marketing programs* for results of promotional campaigns
- *Secondary data sources* such as credit data and compiled demographic and lifestyle data
- *Market research* for insights beyond those revealed by actual customer behavior and dialog

When properly integrated into the CRM framework, these information sources provide a continuing stream of updates from customers that enable companies to respond quickly to their evolving needs and priorities.

Applying the CRM Strategy

The goal of CRM is to evolve from a marketing-oriented model, which was based on a product-centric marketing structure, to dealing with each customer as if they were the only customer — a customer-centric model. As noted in Chapter 1, "The Customer Today," this is a new way of thinking for many companies that have thousands, even millions of customers. Managing customer relationships successfully means learning about the habits and needs of customers, anticipating future buying patterns, and finding new opportunities to add value to the relationship.

For example, in the financial sector, banks — early beneficiaries of successful CRM strategies — are using data warehousing and data mining technologies to learn from the millions of transactions and interactions with their customers to anticipate their needs. The patterns of customer behavior and attitude derived from this information enable the banks to effectively segment customers on predetermined criteria. Detailed customer data can provide answers to the following questions:

- Which communication channel do they prefer?
- What would be the risk of leaving the bank to go to the competition?
- What is the probability the customer will buy a service or product?

This knowledge assists financial institutions with CRM solutions in place to develop marketing programs that respond to each customer segment, support cross-selling and customer retention programs, and enables the staff to understand how to maximize the value of each customer's interaction.

Maximizing Individual Customer Experiences

How does an organization manage each customer relationship individually? From the corporate perspective, there are several fundamental changes in corporate functions that can be made on the way to a complete CRM solution.

Marketing departments need systems that allow employees to track, capture, and analyze the millions of customer activities, both interactions and transactions, over a long period of time. This knowledge enables the organization to create promotions, develop new products and services, and design communication programs that attract, reward, and retain customers.

A fundamental concept behind a successful CRM strategy is that only through operational excellence and technology leadership can an organization predict and maximize the value of each customer relationship.

There have been many successful, effective CRM projects initiated and implemented over the past decade, and there are numerous examples of proven implementation processes and enabling technologies available to serve as models. Examining these successful models and learning from them can dramatically accelerate the transition. A well-conceived planning phase can anticipate and resolve many of the major hurdles that typically impede implementation. By taking advantage of the sections called *Industry Checklist: Lessons Learned* in Chapter 4, "Case Studies in CRM," where proven methodologies and technologies are described, companies can realize early and tangible returns on CRM investments.

CRM Issues, Tactics, and Methodologies

Companies assessing a CRM strategy, or in the early stages of implementation, have many issues to consider. For example:

- How and where to start
- Minimizing costs
- Reducing risks
- Generating tangible returns quickly
- Accelerating implementation and maintaining momentum
- Minimizing disruption to the organization
- Establishing a foundation for continuing gains

While there is no one right CRM framework for every business sector, Exhibit 12 defines eight distinct areas of capabilities and operations that, for most companies, are core components of the required infrastructure. The specific areas of capabilities and operations noted in the framework are referred to and described in more detail in the paragraphs that follow.

CRM Workshops

It can be extremely valuable to hold CRM workshops that bring together management groups to establish an in-depth understanding of the concepts, methods, and implications of the new strategies, as well as to convey a common viewpoint. Senior management should play a prominent leadership role in this process by providing a supporting member to the CRM project team, as noted in Stage 6 above.

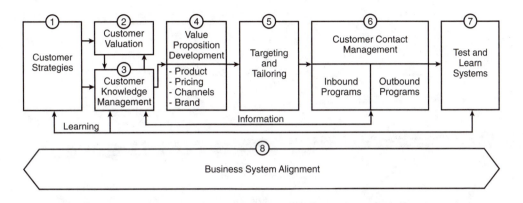

Exhibit 12. Eight Areas of Operations and Capabilities in a CRM Framework

One very important step for senior management is to meet separately in the initial planning and objective-setting stages, with key managers and groups, to establish an understanding of why the transition to CRM is needed and of the implications and opportunities for each group's area of responsibility. The leadership role remains critical throughout the implementation process, both to provide a compelling vision, driven by senior management, of where the company is going and to instill a sense of urgency and commitment to the changes that are needed.

Successful companies make relationships with customers something the customer values more than anything else they could receive from the competition. Companies can do this by examining customer experiences, not only with transactions and demographics, but also with every interaction, including a Web site visit, a phone call to the call center, and a response from a direct mail campaign. Building the data and information technology architecture around the customer will ensure that there is a seamless and rewarding experience when doing business with the company. Senior management needs to foster this process.

Exact Transaction Analysis

CRM's next evolutionary step has retraced the retail sector's original roots, where neighborhood store owners knew their customers and took special care of their interests and needs. Then came the megastore and a reduction in customer service and now CRM technology is allowing retailers to build customer relationships and to keep customers coming back, the same way as the neighborhood store did in a bygone era.

Over the past decade, CRM has evolved from being a relatively small part of marketing operations at a few forward-thinking retailers to becoming a core corporate strategy of many retail businesses, as well as businesses in other major sectors. Customer purchase history and demographic information are now used, not just in marketing programs, but in every facet of a retail business, including real estate sales and acquisitions, store locations,

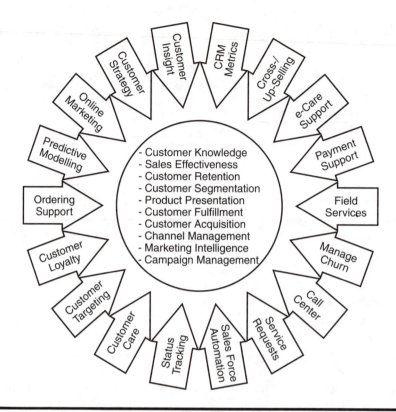

The central circle contains:
- Customer Knowledge
- Sales Effectiveness
- Customer Retention
- Customer Segmentation
- Product Presentation
- Customer Fulfillment
- Customer Acquisition
- Channel Management
- Marketing Intelligence
- Campaign Management

Surrounding labels: Customer Strategy, Customer Insight, CRM Metrics, Cross-/Up-Selling, e-Care Support, Payment Support, Field Services, Manage Churn, Call Center, Service Requests, Sales Force Automation, Status Tracking, Customer Care, Customer Targeting, Customer Loyalty, Ordering Support, Predictive Modelling, Online Marketing

Exhibit 13.   Integrating Customer Knowledge with Corporate Functions

E-commerce, and merchandise selection. There are numerous testimonials to the success of the effective application of CRM strategies in organizations from every major business sector.

As the term *exact transaction analysis* implies, this is a process of analyzing every customer transaction exactly. This process is the ultimate methodology to derive the full benefits of CRM, since this can only be accomplished if an organization has the capability to interact with each and every customer on an individual level. Only when a complete, one-on-one relationship is achieved, can an organization realize the goal of lifelong, profitable customer relationships. Access to extremely detailed customer information, down to the level of individual transactions, is the key to the full realization of CRM's potential (see Exhibit 13).

Relationship Technologies

Relationship technologies are the keys to making customer transactions more personal, more individual, and more exact. More than ever, relationship technologies have become important elements in the way an organization manages its customer relations.

A well-defined CRM solution, based on a data warehousing system, enables businesses to capture and analyze customer interactions and transactions, and reduce customer churn — a process that may be defined as "the constant and continual movement of customers from one organization to another." Properly aligned with customer needs, CRM can also help companies to better understand their requirements and changes in buying patterns and lifestyle, and build long-term relationships of value to them.

Various customer surveys have shown that people want businesses to keep in touch with them, to be responsive to their purchasing needs, even to anticipate these needs. In short, they expect a relationship that has *value*.

Every customer interaction and transaction can be used to forge and nurture a strong relationship — a phone call to a call center, a click on a Web site, or a response to a direct mail campaign. Organizations that achieve high ratings for customer relationships are those that make the relationship of value to the customer, and this factor has become a significant differentiator among organizations.

A recent survey by a major consulting firm examined the impact of technology on the delivery of improved customer practices and services. What the study found was that technology alone does not guarantee success in enhancing customer relationships, a factor that has been previously referenced in this chapter and borne out in other industry surveys.

There are two key factors that are important in the application of technology to managing customer relationships:

1. Selecting the technologies that will meet customer needs
2. Teaming up with the right partners to implement them

The application of relationship technologies to customer transactions and the implementation of a CRM strategy in stages are two more of the key elements to successful management of customer relationships.

Knowing the Customer: Another Perspective

It is important to know your customers, and most organizations have at least four different definable types of internal and external customers, as described in Chapter 1, "The Customer Today." In that chapter, four customer categories were defined: (1) *individual customers,* who buy directly from a company; (2) *businesses,* which also buy from a company; (3) *distribution channels,* which buy for resale to an end user; and (4) *internal departments*, which buy for internal consumption.

Each of these customers expects and demands customized service. Several market factors are responsible for this newly found purchasing power, including the fact that there is less differentiation in products and services and more product and supplier choices. Switching to another supplier or product is easy and requires little cost and often little effort.

Another element of customer relationships that has become a significant issue in the consumer marketplace is privacy of personal information. As organizations build large data warehouses of customer demographic and transactional information, concerns for protection of the privacy of this information become very important in developing and retaining customers and in fostering customer-centric relationships. In short, customers expect organizations to respect their privacy and are demanding to know what corporate safeguards are in place to ensure that their data is used only according to their expressed desires.

If their expectations regarding personal data are not met, customers can and will use their purchasing power to register their dissatisfaction, or in some jurisdictions where there are legal statutes in place to protect privacy, resort to the law. In Chapter 6, "Privacy Issues in CRM," the processes, protocols, and technologies available to protect the privacy of customer information, as well as legislation available in various jurisdictions, are described.

A Rationale for CRM

Clearly, transforming customer knowledge into customer value can create a significant competitive advantage. High-value customers are identified, their needs are anticipated, and new value is created for them where it did not exist before. The end-result for a customer-centric organization is customer loyalty, which translates into higher profitability.

Product-centric values — delivering functionality and quality on time and on budget — should not be replaced by a CRM solution, only augmented. In a customer-centric organization, these traditional supplier values become more meaningful when supported by effective CRM strategies.

The importance of assessing a company's current capabilities and plotting the many dimensions of the business along the continuum from product-centricity to customer-centricity, cannot be overstressed. Comparing these corporate attributes with what is happening in the marketplace should also be a part of this assessment. This process will enable the organization to benefit from the potential of CRM processes and technologies by building on an objective assessment of the company's customer-oriented capabilities, based on a defined set of projects, including investment estimates and business cases.

Two-Way Dialog: Customer Input to CRM

How can businesses maximize the effectiveness of their CRM systems to create more intimate, intelligent, and profitable customer relationships? A new approach to this marketing challenge is to give customers control over a subset of the information stored in CRM systems. A customer-directed layer in an existing CRM system enables the system to provide the customer with important, account-specific information when, where, and for whatever reason the customer specifies.

This process further reinforces the development of one-to-one relationships with customers, a major objective of CRM, as noted throughout this Handbook. By adopting the one-to-one approach, the CRM system can deliver actionable response options tuned precisely to a customer profile and relating specifically to a company's contact center infrastructure.

An additional benefit for the corporation in extending CRM systems to provide proactive outbound customer service and relevant inbound response options, is that unnecessary inbound calls will be reduced and customer satisfaction and revenue increased — without increasing staff.

When customers are forced to place calls or send e-mails to a company about their accounts, they most likely have problems with products or services. Providing an outbound CRM resource helps save customers time and effort, eliminating or reducing the voicemail syndrome that has become a facet of everyday life.

When a company proactively, or preemptively provides information that is relevant to and frequently requested by an individual customer, usually referred to as "customer alerts" — monthly account balance, shipping status, itinerary changes, etc., — the company solidifies a positive, helpful image in the customer psyche. Customer surveys reflect the fact that consumers appreciate doing business with companies that provide personalized attention and service, particularly in a proactive mode.

In one independent survey of the alert process, the survey results found that although less than 10 percent of consumers polled had actually used alerts before, nearly 70 percent said they had signed up to receive proactive alerts if companies made the service available. This statistic is a significant reflection of the importance of proactive customer relations processes and reinforces the view that more than ever before, customers are seeking consistent, personal, and results-oriented communications.

The Alert Platform

An alert platform is a concept that provides, as the name implies, an alerting mechanism for supplier companies. It enables customers to communicate with the supplier companies about their products or services (for example, to place or change an order or to advise of problems, defects, or other aspects of the supplier's product or service). To provide adequate coverage of alert/response applications to the widest market, an alerting platform must support a broad range of communication media, including:

- High-quality voice via landline telephone and cell phone
- Properly formatted text and interactive applications for e-mail, pager, Internet, fax, and wireless devices

Proactive communications from companies to customers need to be through their existing preferred communication devices. Offering only one contact mode is not enough for the media-diverse and mobile customer base that is represented in today's marketplace.

The power of the landline telephone should not be neglected. Voice alerts that are governed by detailed customer preferences are a mandatory requirement. While use of wireless text devices and e-mail is rapidly accelerating, voice is and will be the dominant communications channel for delivering timely alerts that require immediate response and interactions with the business.

An alert formatted for voice delivery reaches the broadest audience and enables the business message to rise above the flood of e-mail. Voice formatting adds a human quality and time-sensitive value to a message. Voice alerts are also the most conducive to eliciting a customer response because of their familiarity and simplicity ("press 1 to speak with a customer service agent" or "press 2 to buy"). Given the option, customers will select voice delivery for many of their alerts, and the responses associated with these alerts will be higher than any other media.

Although voice will serve the broadest customer base, many customers will insist on other media formats. With a platform that supports mixed media alert/response applications, a business may decide to include chat or "call-me-now" functionality as a feature of an outbound e-mail alert. The business could decide that certain outbound voice alerts will offer the customer options linked to a variety of services. Some customers might prefer to communicate with the company via two-way messaging or wireless text messaging. An alert/response platform should fully support all of these scenarios and continue to evolve to support the latest consumer devices.

Implementing Alert/Response Applications

The more recent evolution of CRM systems to support outbound customer contacts means that the traditional CRM hardware and software vendors may not have the products to support these applications. Today's CRM systems do not enable companies to anticipate customer calls and reach out to customers with information tailored specifically to them before they call. A sophisticated alert/response platform is the perfect companion to a company's existing systems.

If a CRM system is capable of being integrated with alerting technology, the alerts typically do not contain the customized, deep enterprise data that customers want. For example, they may only offer limited syndicated content that is individually addressed and broadcast, making the alerts more like generic SPAM messages. Or, if the information is deep and customer-specific, these systems typically support delivery via a single medium only — usually e-mail.

Those companies that have already made the initial foray into alert systems rarely include an integrated approach to managing responses to alerts. There is a critical void when it comes to solutions that deliver customer-specific information in a variety of mediums, enable intelligent two-way interaction, or make the most of a company's existing data to better serve customers and successfully involve them in one-to-one outbound interactions.

Integrating with Existing Systems

For customers to find alerts useful and to respond to them in a positive way, the alerts must be triggered on detailed, account-specific information and governed by the preferences of each customer. The data that triggers these alerts could be stored in a variety of different databases or even in multiple databases within the same organization. One of the newer computer languages and one that is rapidly becoming a developer preference for these alerts is XML. XML-based technology enables seamless integration with many disparate back-office and database systems, computer telephony integration (CTI), voice processing systems, collaboration, legacy, CRM, and Web systems. An XML-based extraction platform is a powerful, flexible way to trigger alerts.

Existing customer contact systems need to be integrated with an alert/response program. With a touch of the keypad or a click of the mouse, a customer must be able to connect easily to the business, talk to a live agent, transfer to an automated transaction system for purchasing, add personal comments, or forward the alert to others.

Armed with their exiting customer systems and the right outbound alert/response platform, companies can learn from their customer interactions in order to offer a continuously higher level of successful customer service, adding customer input to enhance their CRM system.

Configuring the Alert/Response Content

Alert content must be dynamic, easy to create, easy to manage, and appealing to the alert recipient. To maximize the application and create the highest value for the customer, administrators must be able to change alert content and create new alerts as business conditions change — via a packaged management solution, not via customer development.

Contact center management and nontechnical administrators need to be able to tune alert/response systems on an application-by-application basis. Administration elements should include the following components:

- Prerecorded voice content
- Rules for conditional use of text-to-speech, retry frequency, and logic
- Linking alert behavior to call center hours and real-time load

Given these requirements, companies strapped for IT resources will look to vendors to provide graphical user interfaces that incorporate easy-to-use, drag-and-drop alert development and maintenance. Companies are recognizing that their contact centers are a vitally important part of their overall business strategies and operations and an important and critical element in their overall CRM strategies.

As noted elsewhere in this Handbook, customer service has become a major competitive differentiator in many business sectors. By using an enterprise alert/response platform to leverage existing legacy systems, CRM systems, and Web investments, large businesses (with many thousands or millions of customers) can now engage customers in an intimate, trusted, two-way dialog that creates measurably enhanced customer loyalty and profitability.

Referrals

It is an axiom of the marketplace that satisfied customers tell their friends about a supplier that demonstrates good customer relations. One of the most powerful customer acquisition techniques is word-of-mouth referral from a friend, colleague, or family member. Businesses can quantitatively harness word-of-mouth referrals when one of their customers adds personal comments to an alert and forwards it to others who may be interested in the information or the opportunities the alert presents.

There are both operational and strategic benefits to the business, inherent in preemptive alerting. This process eliminates unnecessary, costly, nonrevenue-generating, inbound customer contact, resulting in increased customer satisfaction, dramatic cost-per-call savings, call elimination, better service levels, as well as a reduction in the number of agents required in call centers.

Testing and Evaluating CRM Solutions

Relationships with customers are constantly changing; therefore, managing CRM initiatives becomes an ongoing process. CRM operations, programs, corporate processes, and return on investment must be tested or evaluated to ensure they remain relevant to the customer and to the corporate CRM mandate.

Testing the validity of CRM solutions is a form of stress testing, analogous to performing materials stress testing in an engineering lab. CRM programs must change to remain relevant, and they must be constantly challenged, using a two-pronged approach — (1) from the customer perspective and (2) from an internal program manager perspective — that performs both internal and external evaluations.

If the components and processes involved in CRM are not managed actively, there is a strong risk that they will become irrelevant, resulting in a loss of customers and the failure of the CRM solution to accomplish the corporate goals that motivated its implementation.

The external element of the testing process involves taking a customer perspective, by stepping back from the CRM program and analyzing its performance and results, from the viewpoint of a difficult and demanding customer. Once this has been done, the evaluation process can move to the second element of the testing process by adopting the position of a demanding program manager, to determine whether the CRM strategy is being managed effectively and efficiently.

One testing methodology proposed, based on this two-pronged approach, involves the following activities:

- *The difficult and demanding customer* — reviewing and evaluating trends, issues, and solutions from the viewpoint of a customer who is not easily impressed.
  - *Discovery* — testing the company's knowledge of its customers.
  - *Dialog* — testing customer reactions to conversations.
  - *Discipline* — testing approaches, mechanisms, systems, and procedures for delivery value.
- *The demanding program manager* — assessing CRM initiatives from a program manager's perspective.

The Difficult and Demanding Customer

This test stage is so critical to the success of the CRM solution that it is recommended that a senior company executive take charge of the analysis. This process may be compared to a market research study, in which the study leader asks a specific series of questions to prepare for the launch of the corporate CRM strategy. The purpose of this test stage is to examine the CRM solution from outside the corporation, assuming that little is known about the customer, and to focus on the future of the customer relationships and the effect the CRM solution will have on them when it is implemented.

This test stage will also provide insight into how customers view suppliers. In this stage of the analysis, there is no reference to the company's CRM program. By separating this analysis from CRM, managers can determine whether the concerns of customers intersect with the solutions proposed by their CRM program, when the internal analysis is made of the existing or planned CRM solution.

Determining how CRM solutions are perceived by customers provides an opportunity to examine CRM processes from this perspective, to assess how well the processes are working and to make changes where required. One method of conducting this assessment is to meet and discuss CRM processes with customers who may have had service or product complaints and who belong to consumer groups, Internet chat rooms, or affinity groups.

To identify these customers, look for the following characteristics:

- Possible conflict between buyer and seller
- Knowledge about a variety of suppliers
- Seeking value
- Involvement in emerging markets
- Expressed interest in the future of the organization

Analyzing CRM processes from any customer perspective is obviously of value to an organization that is serious about CRM. One problem facing customers today is that they have too many options to choose from — information, advice, offers — with little time to make intelligent decisions.

Too many choices cause uncertainty on the part of customers. Are they getting the best advice? The best deal? The best service? To get objective answers to these questions, they often turn to family and friends for product and service references and opinions. This process of seeking advice provides them with some assurance that they are making the right (or wrong!) decision. They are seeking a judgment call on their choice of product or service. Unfortunately, businesses are not able to do this because they are not in the same objective position as other personal sources.

Personal referral systems are one method used by some organizations to replicate the family/friend reference — reflecting what other customers think about a product or service has good credibility and is certainly second best to a family member or friend.

For corporate CRM programs there is a lesson here: to achieve a position of credibility, suppliers need to maintain an arm's length relationship to the reference source, and this can often be accomplished by being co-participant in referral networks or enabling these networks.

In a typical business marketplace, there is an ongoing battle for a customer's attention, with shortened product manufacturing times and costs and soft product content replacing the hard product of earlier times. There are several reasons for this trend. Product manufacturing cycle times have been shortened and costs are falling due to increasing automation and more efficient production processes. Product content depends largely on software that can be easily replaced or reprogrammed, making these products easier to customize and modify. The concept of a product has changed, and some products that used to be sold — and even some services — are now offered free of charge.

As noted in Chapter 1, "The Customer Today," there is a dramatic shift in the customer's perspective on customer relationships — more is expected from suppliers on all fronts: product quality, support, service, and follow-up. "Businesses have lost any sense of treating a particular product as anything other than temporary. They hop from product to product. In such an environment, customers have a different view of customer loyalty than many enterprises. Customers used to make simple links between the product, the brand, and the company. Those links are being eroded and even broken."

Another interesting market development that further confuses the customer is the melding of brand names and products as corporate mergers create conglomerates that sell everything from stoves to stereos. Under this market umbrella, it is understandable that customers will become confused by the shifting commercial environment, one that is a hodgepodge of alliances, multiple distribution networks, and other combinations of companies under a single corporate umbrella.

Loyalty and Long-Term Relationships

With products taking on a temporary nature as far as the customer is concerned, loyalties to brand names or companies have virtually disappeared, and customers move easily from one product to another and from one supplier to another.

This evolution of products and services and the changing nature of the customer relationship provide new opportunities for building and sustaining relationships with customers as a potential impediment to progress. Many customers, especially the difficult and demanding ones, consider that the days when there was comfort in long-term relationships with a few key suppliers are either long gone or fast fading.

The move by businesses in some sectors to what are referred to as "complete solutions" is one of the approaches being used in an effort to provide more than just products. A simple example might be mortgage providers that also offer moving and relocation services. Unfortunately, these solutions may detract from the objectives of the supplier, by providing two or three related and combined services for the customer to evaluate, confusing the relationship with the supplier of the primary product or service.

Corporate CRM programs are affected by these combined offers in two ways:

1. Loyalty to one producer or brand will be difficult to deliver.
2. Organizations will seek new ways to get customers' attention.

Three Areas of Evaluation

This test and evaluation process involves the three main facets of the CRM framework — (1) discovery, (2) dialog, and (3) discipline — considered from the customer perspective.

Discovery Testing

A typical question line for discovery testing will focus on the future of relationships. A specific question might be: "Is the future of customer relationships developing in a manner different than expected?" Established corporate patterns of thought, based on the corporate culture, will need to be challenged to answer these questions accurately and completely. As noted in other chapters of this Handbook, the customer is probably way ahead of the corporation in terms of supplier expectations, so a corporation that places itself in the customer's shoes will undoubtedly discover new revelations for all participants.

To challenge the fundamental thinking of the corporation and the test team participants, particularly with respect to the future of customer relationships, several controversial customer-oriented statements, as shown below, may be used to stimulate the team participants:

- *Statement 1. We don't know who our customers are.* Most businesses think they know their customers; however, when challenged to name customers in a specific customer category, test participants will be unable to respond.
- *Statement 2. Customers expect us to know them by name. But do we really recognize them by name?* Customers often present themselves to suppliers in multiple formats — like multiple personalities — and organizations need to relate to a variety of needs and affiliations.
- *Statement 3. We don't know what customers really think about us.* With CRM, businesses spend so much time thinking about managing the relationship that no time is spent asking what customers think about them — or if their customers think of them at all. And if customers do give the subject any thought, how, when, and where?
- *Statement 4. We don't all agree on what we mean when we say "customer."* Is a customer someone who has bought something? Is it someone who might buy something? What about people who may never buy? Should they be treated as customers? What about people who may eventually own

a product that was purchased secondhand? Is a customer a person, a family, a company, the purchasing agent, or the design engineer? And what if Internet auctions become such a big business that customers become resellers?

- *Statement 5. We do not know how the Internet will change our knowledge of customers.* In this era of electronic commerce, customers deal with suppliers predominantly via electronic channels, making the supplier/customer relationship more remote than before. This new purchasing channel has had a major impact on CRM, its processes, technologies, and implementation, as well as in the way that the Internet interrelates to other channels of communication. The term coined by the industry for customer relationship processes involving E-commerce and the Internet is *E-CRM.*

- *Statement 6. We have not given consideration of demographics in our CRM solution.* Some organizations have adopted customer segmentation programs that attempt to manage the demographic aspects of the customer database; however, with new generations of consumers entering the marketplace and exhibiting a range of different purchasing habits, attitudes, and behavior patterns, customer demographics represent an important element in the CRM solution mix.

Dialog Testing

As the term implies, this element of the customer-oriented test and evaluation of the CRM program involves asking questions that a difficult and demanding customer would ask: for example, What is the value of the communications employees have with customers? Are these communications being handled effectively for maximum benefit and are they delivering some measurable value?

In this phase of the CRM test and evaluation procedure, it is important to set aside the current CRM program and look at the corporation objectively as it relates to its customers. The challenge in dialog testing is to determine why the company's communication with customers is neither effective nor relevant to the customer's needs and, therefore, of no value. Some statements that may be used by the test team to examine existing and future CRM strategies are:

- *Our organization is not mentioned or is criticized in Web-based chat group communities and consumer groups.* The Internet has increased the number of consumer advocacy groups dramatically, and they bring together the newly found purchasing power of many individual customers. These groups are major forces in the marketplace, fostering loyalty and acting as a focus for group action; therefore, companies need to learn to work with them as a part of their CRM strategy.

- *Customers access our Web site and also phone the call center.* An examination of this statement may reveal that the Web site does not provide answers to most customer questions and that customers have technical problems accessing the Web site or call center. Both of these are customer communication resources that must be conditioned to support CRM strategies effectively, or they must be changed.

- *We are not capable of one-on-one treatment of customers.* Evaluating a company's performance in meeting this objective — the concept of a one-on-one, customer-centric CRM strategy introduced previously in this Handbook — will reveal the depth of the strategy and illustrate how well the company is capable of personalizing individual customer needs.
- *The company is not managing relationships.* An analysis of this statement may lead to the conclusion that customers are managing relationships with both our organization and competitive companies. One interesting revelation that may be derived by examining this statement is that customers want exactly the opposite form of service to the one the organization is providing.
- *Analyze the marketplace — there are continual changes occurring.* Supply chains are consolidating and there are new emerging sources of supply. In the former case, businesses should consider disbanding their capabilities in these areas and handing them to companies that can perform them effectively. In the latter, perhaps there are opportunities for devising new products, or at least for regrouping suppliers.
- *We do not know how well our distribution networks are functioning.* This statement brings into focus an organization's distribution chain and is especially important where a supplier has a large network of distributors that distribute and support products. Distribution networks are an ever-changing market component, merging, disappearing, and reformatting. When they are actively involved in a business relationship with an organization, they become a customer, as defined in Chapter 1 of this Handbook, and may also function as one of the elements of the supplier's CRM strategy.

The above statements are only some examples of customer-oriented statements that can form the basis for an examination of the nature of a proposed CRM strategy from the perspective of a difficult, demanding customer and the dialog-oriented issues that might arise. Individual business sectors may develop other statements relevant to their own business sectors, which will provide the CRM management team with guidelines on which to build and strengthen the CRM program (see Exhibit 14), to achieve its objectives.

Discipline Testing

Let us now turn to the CRM strategy that has been implemented or is in the process of being implemented. Discipline testing, from a customer perspective, means asking if the CRM solutions make sense and deliver value. For example, questions such as: How do current Web-based CRM systems and procedures match customer needs for personal referral? Or, How does our organization manage information?

Managers can examine whether the CRM systems and procedures offer solutions that address customer concerns. If there is a mismatch, then these CRM systems and procedures or the programs that deliver them will need

Exhibit 14. CRM Gains for Different Business Sectors

Automobile manufacturer: 60 percent increase in the repurchase rate based on improved targeting and communication

B-to-B communications company: 50 percent gain in cross-selling effectiveness among small business customers

Pharmaceutical manufacturer: Sharply reduced product introduction and marketing costs based on channel optimization

Software manufacturer: 50 percent reduction in marketing costs associated with upgrade sales

Credit card issuer: 15 percent reduction in attrition of high-value customers based on proactive intervention

Communications company: 15 to 1 return on investment in improved customer acquisition

Property and casualty insurer: 400 percent increase in campaign response rate over forecasts

revision. Consider the following examples of statements that will create a stimulus for analyzing decisions and choices concerning CRM:

- *We don't have the right strategic goals.* Businesses need to establish a competency and begin to build initial releases of the required software that is a part of the CRM solution. This may, in turn, require a significant overhaul of the corporation's customer-facing capability within the organization. Customer-facing systems would need to enable customers to start and stop conversations about potential financial purchases without loss of comprehension.

- *Our brand has nothing to do with what demanding customers want.* In the above example, the same bank may be using its Web site to publish its extensive menu of products, or it may simply put its existing paper-based credit-card application process online. Customers may want to have conversations about financial planning, travel plans, or home ownership before deciding which product they may need. If the brand represents an extensive line of products while customers are seeking extensive conversations — advice, information, and help — then what should be done?

- *We do not have the right business partners and allies to deliver what customers want.* In this connected world, all of a company's actions, initiatives, and programs depend, more than ever, on others for their success. Organizations no longer have exclusive control of all of the elements of production and distribution. More than ever, businesses have chosen to achieve their goals through collaborations, partnerships, and alliances. And in some cases, collaborators are competitors. Defining and managing this complex interplay of resources is critical to the success of CRM programs.

Finally, here are three additional discipline-testing topics a company might discuss:

1. We are not organized to get to know customers.
2. We have hundreds of measures but none that clearly describes the value we provide to customers.
3. We are not changing quickly enough to satisfy customers.

These are only a few of the many subjects that might be addressed, from the perspective of a difficult and demanding customer, that can provide a CRM management team with some insight on the relationship futures for a CRM strategy.

Managing the CRM Program

Having fully explored the demanding and difficult customer mindset, it is time to take the insights of this outside perspective and transform them into actions — starting as soon as possible and practical.

Management has often been defined as "the art and science of getting from here to there." This description of management is most appropriate for large, complex CRM programs that touch the complete enterprise. The process of testing relationship futures up to this point has transported managers outside the enterprise to "there" — giving them a clear idea of where CRM programs need to be heading. Developing CRM program guidelines brings managers back inside the enterprise — the starting point.

CRM program management guidelines offer a sound approach to program and project management. Most large organizations have more than one CRM project. And these projects are managed by many different players — some in call centers, on Web sites, sales forces, and in a variety of different business groups. Pulling all this activity together into an enterprisewide program or into a consolidated approach is a major challenge; however, with a committed, logical, step-by-step process, it is a challenge that can be met.

A Program Manager's Perspective

The following guidelines provide a practical set of steps that can be taken to ensure that the program will work at all levels, from strategic articulation to software installation and training. The goal of these program management guidelines is to improve the success rate of CRM programs. With these guidelines, an enterprise can measure success by linking program initiatives to desired business results.

Each of the following eight steps matches a phase of CRM program design and implementation, and should be adopted as specific elements or analysis milestones:

1. Program diagnosis
2. Strategy review
3. Enterprise architecture
4. Enterprise application integration services
5. Package selection and implementation
6. Application outsourcing assessment
7. Implementation review
8. Program management

These test and evaluation elements and evaluation milestones have been proven in previous large-scale change and improvement programs — business process re-engineering, enterprise resource planning (ERP) initiatives, and other successful CRM implementations. The lessons learned from these programs can be applied directly to CRM programs to improve their success rates, as measured by the achievement of specified business results.

The eight steps in the program management guide have been referenced elsewhere in this chapter, and are detailed below, to emphasize their importance and to summarize the significant elements in each step.

1. Program Diagnosis

A diagnosis of the current status of CRM and its related programs provides an assessment of business objectives against current CRM programs and highlight areas of improvement. The diagnosis should cover several areas of CRM involvement, including:

- Relationship styles
- Conversation design
- IT infrastructure
- Organizational structure

Understanding how these compare with other organizations, with best practices, and how they fit into the enterprise's business strategy, will help identify areas for improvement.

2. Strategy Review

An organization needs to assess its CRM strategies against business objectives developed in Chapter 2. This review forms the basis for the right CRM game plan for an organization and the joint development of business and IT strategies.

3. Enterprise Architecture

The CRM diagnosis and strategy review reveals the benefits of combining all the CRM-related initiatives that may be scattered across the company into a comprehensive, enterprisewide CRM strategy that will create new conversation spaces (*dialog*). It will also transform customer information into a strategic business tool to profile, segment, target, and retain valuable customers (*discovery*), organize sales, marketing, and customer care in a consistent way (*discipline*), and integrate back- and front-office processes (also *discipline*). It is important that the CRM architecture integrates all elements — people, processes, technologies, and organization — into one cohesive strategy.

4. Enterprise Application Integration Services

One of the fundamental keys to CRM success in enterprise architecture development is the seamless integration of channels, people, and technologies into conversation spaces that deliver value to customers. This integration challenge is a difficult hurdle for most organizations and needs to be addressed in this step.

5. Package Selection and Implementation

Organizations require a system for navigating and selecting CRM services and products and assessing the effect of changes on their businesses. The selected external resources must be integrated into the IT environment, with the intention of developing a process for managing the selection, implementation, and testing of these resources, through multi-year life cycles.

6. Application Outsourcing Assessment

CRM applications require support, maintenance, and enhancement, often for several years, as upgrades and new versions of software are released to the user base. Outsourcing responsibility for this technology-intensive side of the CRM program should be considered as an option. Outsourcing contracts need to clearly define service-level agreements to allow the enterprise to focus on customer relationships and not the supporting technology.

7. Implementation Review

Organizations need to have an overview of all implementation activities to build the complete set of business and technical solutions, whether in one area of the company as a data mart or as an enterprisewide CRM solution. A coordinated approach to the design, redesign, or consolidation of CRM programs — from E-commerce initiatives to call-center operations — is essential to the ultimate success of the system.

8. Program Management

Each CRM initiative needs to be managed efficiently and effectively, and advanced program and project management methods are often required.

Program management offices should be created to ensure that CRM-related projects deliver value and fully support strategic business initiatives.

CRM Analytics in Data Mining

The CRM analytics model is an earlier concept that has evolved to meet modern-day requirements. Analytical CRM is the mining of data and the application of mathematical, and sometimes common-sense, models to better understand the consumer. By extrapolating useful insights into market and customer behaviors, companies can adjust business rules and react to customers in a relevant, personalized manner.

Although the concept has not changed much, the process certainly has become far more scientific. Because we conduct business with fewer face-to-face exchanges, getting to know and understand the customer has become even more complicated. The rise of E-business has driven the demand for more comprehensive tool sets for data mining and knowledge interpretation. For an effective CRM initiative to accomplish its goals, CRM analytics need to be incorporated in the process.

CRM analytics provide the comprehensive insight necessary for pinpointing revenue opportunities, enhancing sales channels, and mitigating cost risks. By providing meaningful insight into data, as well as transactional predictions, CRM analytics enable businesses to ensure that rules and workflow are in step with customer demands.

Analytics can be derived through several different channels, including:

- The Internet
- Retail point of purchase
- Direct marketing activities

The challenge is not in gathering data from customers but in making sense of the multitude of customer touchpoints entering the organization.

Data Mining

Analytical data-mining solutions are a significant component of most packaged CRM solutions and must be capable of providing insight into corporate data stored in the data warehouse, using process and trend analysis to isolate causes and correlations within the customer interaction model. Packaged implementations are easily installed, but few offer fully comprehensive solutions and the tight integration into existing enterprise systems that are required to meet CRM objectives.

Today's business processes are extremely complex, and strong analytics are necessary to give a functional view of data relationships. Through these dependencies, CRM can model future transactions, predict the interests and behavior of individual customers, and translate data into more traditional channels within the enterprise, such as the supply chain.

CRM analytics can perform predictive modeling of customer behavior, customer segmentation grouping, profitability analysis, what-if scenarios, and campaign management, as well as personalization and event monitoring. These functions take advantage of a customer's interactions with a business in real-time.

CRM is a highly iterative process. When data from any source is harvested and fed back into the system, it improves the personalization capability of the very next customer transaction or e-mail campaign.

More traditional marketing processes such as direct marketing often see months of lag time between a campaign's execution and the review of its metrics. With each loop of the cycle, Internet-based CRM analytics are updating, tweaking, and improving delivery of personalized, relevant sales opportunities, all in real-time. The analytics also help build a more finely tuned relationship between a business and its customers.

In addition to the personalization that benefits a customer's purchasing decision, CRM analytics will soon provide useful data that can benefit enterprisewide processes. CRM analytics will also be integrated more frequently into the general operational workflow of noncustomer systems, including financial systems and manufacturing, to provide a more singular view of customer-centric data than do the traditionally segmented departmental views offered by legacy CRM.

When all of this data can be interpreted to a variety of enterprise systems, transactional decision making and enterprise planning — from cross-selling opportunities to supply-chain and just-in-time inventory control — will be enriched.

Although several vendors are providing ad hoc, niche CRM capabilities, only a handful have emerged with the driving analytics necessary to benefit enterprisewide decision making in a meaningful way.

Data mining and analytics are not without risk. The predictability of human nature is never a sure thing, so modeling real-world transactions carries a certain degree of error which can greatly affect the quality of the data that influences decisions. CRM analytics, being more about the process than the technology, demand a degree of human interpretation for the data to yield the most beneficial results. The CRM tools merely fortify one's abilities.

Although automation can go a long way toward streamlining internal processes, technology also quickly depersonalizes the customer's experience. CRM analytics offer insight and personalization that can go a long way toward improving that experience and building customer loyalty.

CRM: Summing Up the Business Value

A CRM solution that bridges service, sales, and marketing initiatives enables businesses to realize faster problem resolution, increased sales, more effective customer acquisition, and greatly enhanced customer loyalty and retention.

In the call center, after the first customer touchpoint, there are both operational and strategic benefits to the business, inherent in preemptive alerting. This process eliminates unnecessary, costly, nonrevenue-generating inbound customer contact, resulting in increased customer satisfaction, dramatic cost-per-call savings, call elimination, better services levels, as well as a reduction in the number of agents required in call centers.

On a strategic level, proactively giving customers the information they want drives an increase in customer satisfaction and gives companies a competitive advantage. In addition, offering alerts with intelligent response options enables companies to combine sales and service initiatives that increase revenue, generate highly qualified, inbound traffic, and make the most efficient use of both customer and company time.

Chapter 3

The Technology of CRM

Mega-mergers distract management from their customers and make them easy prey to the Golden Horde of technology competent opponents.

— Anthony Hourihan
Chaired Professor in the Management of Financial Institutions
Smurfit Business School, University College, Dublin, Ireland

In business today, as has often been noted, change is the only constant, and change is occurring at an ever-increasing rate. Accelerating change has a direct effect on all aspects of business — customers, technology, organizational culture, business strategies. As a company positions itself to respond to change, information requirements also change.

A key challenge to businesses in the 21st century is implementing an information infrastructure that enables rapid responses to competitive pressures and the capability to survive into the future.

Corporate CRM strategies are dependent on an information infrastructure comprised of various technologies that enable organizations to store, access, analyze, and manipulate large amounts of customer data. Most organizations with large numbers of customers to manage, frequently in the thousands or millions, require a combination of sophisticated technologies to implement CRM. Four major areas of technology contribute to a successful CRM project:

1. Data warehousing
2. Database management systems
3. Data mining
4. Business analysis software

Within each of these major technology areas there are subsets of system and application software to handle a range of CRM-oriented functions, such as:

queries on the database, value analysis, and mathematical models for predictive analysis, as well as other mathematical data analysis techniques referred to as "analytics." All of these applications contribute to the CRM solution by enabling organizations to analyze data based on a wide range of parameters.

This chapter contains information on selected vendors of these technologies and others — data warehousing, database software, analytical software, and data transformation and cleansing software — used in the development, implementation, and application leading to CRM solutions, with Web site contact and CRM product or service information.

A central data warehouse will make the most of existing data and collect new data on an ongoing basis. Most companies have data stored in a variety of database systems — on both legacy mainframes and client/server networks — and an effective data warehouse design and implementation will enable users to mine the vast amounts of data that has been and will be gathered within the enterprise.

Data warehouses have become well-accepted in many business sectors and in companies within these sectors as a core component of doing business, as well as a building block for a corporate CRM strategy. This technology is a prerequisite for the level of one-on-one customer relations that can turn information into a company's most important resource.

Melding these technologies into a comprehensive CRM infrastructure that will meet a corporation's business needs is the challenge faced by a project team charged with the responsibility for developing the CRM strategy. This challenge begins with the data warehousing project.

An Overview of the Data Warehouse

The technology foundation of a successful CRM strategy is the development and implementation of the data warehouse. This is the technology that enables organizations to gather and store large volumes of customer transaction data in a format that enables the data to be analyzed and manipulated to provide valuable business information on the customer database (see Exhibit 1).

Many companies that have successfully implemented data warehouses discover that the implementation resulted in millions of dollars in savings, once the data warehouse was deeply integrated into their business processes to become a mission-critical system and even before it became part of a full-fledged CRM strategy.

The Healthy Centralized Data Warehouse

Most organizations engaged in a data warehousing project focus on the design and development of the warehouse. At any given time, some are busy building a data model, while others are busy selecting technology or creating the interface between the data warehouse and the legacy application environment.

No matter what approach is taken or where an organization is in its process, the primary goal of every organization is to get the warehouse up and running

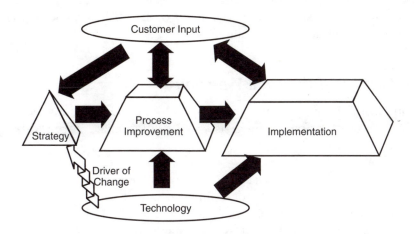

Exhibit 1. Technology as a Driver and Enabler of Change

according to established requirements. However, organizations should not ignore a secondary goal that is just as important as the first: ensuring that the warehouse can be maintained and changed as needed.

While data marts may serve as an interim solution, the data mart concept will not meet the long-term objectives of a corporatewide CRM solution.

Data warehouses are strategically too important to be treated as temporary structures. The long-term approach mandates that a real data warehouse — an enterprise data warehouse that can sustain the corporation over time — be created.

The demands of E-commerce are changing customer expectations, presenting a host of new challenges, and the data warehouse is one of the core technologies that will assist in meeting these challenges. As previous chapters of this Handbook have pointed out, managing customer relations effectively and intelligently, no matter what sales avenue the customer is using, has a significant and positive effect on customer loyalty and retention, as well as on sales revenue and profitability.

Data Warehousing Objectives

The objectives of data warehousing are:

- To produce an information infrastructure that provides the right information to the right people at the right time — and at the right cost
- To provide an architecture that yields a single, current version of customer data
- To enable the incremental deployment of subject-oriented data marts that are developed according to well-identified business needs

The value of a data warehouse as a fundamental component of CRM is in enhancing organizational insight into customer behavior. This is done by gathering and storing customer data, by revealing information on trends in the marketplace, by assisting in the dynamics of the business, and by providing a resource that will attain competitive advantage.

Characteristics of the Data Warehouse

According to Bill Inmon, often referred to as "the father of data warehousing," a data warehouse has four characteristics that differentiate it from other major operational systems:

1. *Subject-orientation* — data organized by subject
2. *Integration* — consistency of defining parameters
3. *Time-variance* — a timeliness of data and access
4. *Nonvolatility* — a stable data-storage medium

The subject-oriented database characteristic of the data warehouse organizes data according to subject, unlike the application-based database. The alignment around subject areas affects the design and implementation of the data found in the data warehouse. For this reason, the major subject areas influence the most important parts of the key structure and the selection of the database software. Data warehouse data entries also differ from application-oriented data in the relationships. Although operational data has relationships among tables based on the business rules that are in effect, the data warehouse encompasses a spectrum of time.

An operational data warehouse is also integrated in that data is moved into it from many different applications. This integration is noticeable in several ways:

- The implementation of consistent naming conventions
- The consistent measurement of variables
- Consistent encoding structures
- Consistent physical attributes of data

Operational data derived from other major systems is often inconsistent across applications. The preprocessing of information aids in reducing access time at the point of inquiry. The data store in a data warehouse is often five to ten years old, and is used for making consistent comparisons, viewing trends, and providing a forecasting tool. Operational environment data reflects only accurate values at the moment of access, although the data in such a system may change at a later point in time through updated data or inserts. On the other hand, data in the data warehouse is accurate at any moment in time and will produce the same results every time for the same query.

The time-variant feature of the data warehouse is observed in different ways. In addition to the lengthier time horizon as compared to the operational environment, time-variance is also present in the key structure of a data warehouse. Every key structure contains implicitly or explicitly, an element of time, such as day, week, or month. Time-variance is also evidenced by the fact that data in a traditional data storage facility is never updated, while operational data in a data warehouse is updated as the need arises.

Data Warehousing and Customer Relationships

Data warehousing, an information infrastructure based on detail data that supports the decision-making process, provides the capability for businesses to access and analyze data to increase competitive advantage and to manage customer relationships more efficiently and effectively. In fact, without a data warehouse, many large- and medium-size organizations could only manage customer relations in a very rudimentary manner in this competitive 21st-century marketplace.

It is the appropriate and selective use of technology that enables organizations to address customer relationship challenges posed by the newly empowered customer described in Chapter 1 of this Handbook.

There are four general categories for the application of data warehousing in a business operation, all of which relate, directly or indirectly, to the organization's capability to manage customer relations:

1. Increase speed and flexibility of business analysis
2. Provide a foundation for enterprisewide data integration and access
3. Improve or reinvent business processes
4. Develop a clear understanding of customer behavior

Building a data warehouse is a complex process and, in addition to a carefully prepared project plan, requires assembling a number of knowledgeable resources (both internal and external), including:

- Management commitment
- Collaboration of business and IT constituents on important business questions
- The right technology — database, hardware platform, software tools, and applications
- Expert consulting services

Planning, developing, and implementing a data warehouse is a process — not an off-the-shelf solution, but the complete integration of a hardware platform, a database, and business tools into an evolving information infrastructure that changes with the dynamics of the business. As the data warehouse evolves in an organization, many issues and considerations need to be discussed, resolved, and have decisions made, the result of which will directly impact the usefulness and overall success of the data warehouse and its ultimate benefit as a core component in an organization's CRM solution.

For the initial implementation of a data warehouse, as described previously, some data architects begin with a data mart approach, consisting primarily of summary data. However, the data mart approach is limited in its scope, and

Exhibit 2. Comparison of Data Marts and Data Warehouses

Data Marts	Data Warehouses
Summary data	Detail data
Deliver value to specific business area	Deliver value to the enterprise
Low cost	High cost
Less complex	More complex
Single subject-oriented, departmental	Enterprisewide, many subjects

will not meet the enterprise requirements regarding the analysis of customer data, regarding these two characteristics of that data (see Exhibit 2):

1. Breadth (data spanning the organization)
2. Depth (level of granularity and volume)

While data marts by themselves are an incomplete response to corporate CRM requirements, they can be essential and useful components of a data warehouse solution if the following features are present:

- The detail data is available in the warehouse to back up the data marts.
- The end users have access to that data.
- The data mart summaries are aggregated from the detail data.

A business rarely looks at the lowest level of data, often referred to as "atomic," except when coordinating a direct-mail campaign or to relate more closely to a customer. However, this detail data is essential to provide infinite flexibility. Summaries can be created to test end-user hypotheses to match whatever external data is brought into the warehouse and, if necessary, to view the business from a completely different perspective. Well-modeled, atomic-level data should form the basis of the data warehouse data structure, and this may require redesign of a data mart, if one is in place.

Creating a Data Mart Model

If the organization determines that the data warehouse design will begin with a data mart, here are the steps to follow:

- Create the detailed data model as if it were to be the design for a detailed data warehouse.
- Ensure that every data mart created can be summarized from that data model.
- Ensure that all other systems are capable of feeding the data mart and correlate with the detailed data model completely.

Following these steps ensures that data marts will be consistent, that is, if the same question is asked of two different data marts, the same answer will result. The data model also acts as a test for all data inputs to the data mart system.

While a data mart may not become a detailed data warehouse, properly configured data marts provide building blocks for the data warehouse that will eventually evolve.

Corporate Data — The Operational Perspective

For many organizations, corporate data is located in several different forms and locations and may come from mainframe applications or distributed systems and information-gathering devices throughout the organization. These include point-of-sale (POS) registers, automatic teller machines (ATMs), order entry, billing, financial, accounting, inventory, customer service, or logistics application systems. Regardless of its source, to be useful, this data must be collected and transformed into a consistent form, if the data warehouse is to fulfill its primary goal as a core technology in a CRM solution.

This process is called "data transformation," and it is the foundation for creating a warehouse with high-quality data. Data transformation includes a number of processes for handling and manipulating data. They are:

- Extracting
- Conditioning
- Scrubbing
- Merging
- Householding
- Enrichment
- Loading
- Validating
- Delta updating

See the *Glossary* in "Appendix A" for an explanation of these terms.

The Heart of the Data Warehouse

As described above, there are two fundamental schools of thought for designing a data warehouse. One approach is a distributed, decentralized approach, where data is stored in independent data marts, each having the data relevant to that aspect of the business. A better alternative, and more complete solution for the enterprise, is to source the data into a single, centralized data source that allows users throughout the organization to make decisions from the same consistent data.

It is also possible to combine the best features of both the distributed and the centralized approaches by using a single data store of clean, accurate detail data for the enterprise. This data is combined with dependent data marts containing subsets of data from the enterprise warehouse selected and organized for a particular set of usage requirements. The data marts can be implemented as either logical implementations or separate physical implementations. Data replication` and propagation synchronizes data between the enterprise data warehouse and the data marts.

There are a number of complex technology, resource, financial, and vendor selection issues involved in data warehousing. These include:

- Architectural configuration
- Data integrity
- Security
- Networking

According to one estimate, about 80 percent of the time spent constructing a data warehouse is devoted to extracting, cleaning, and loading data, because problems that may have been undetected for years can surface during the design phase. Finding stored data that had not been accessed previously, or data that has been altered and stored, are examples of some of the data-oriented problems that may arise during the data warehousing development stage. It is important to understand the business and all the processes that need to be modeled.

Another major consideration important to up-front planning is the difference between the data warehouse and most other client/server applications. First, there is the issue of batch orientation for much of the processing. The complexity of processes (which may be executed on multiple platforms), data volumes, and resulting data synchronization issues must be correctly analyzed and resolved.

Next, the data volume in a data warehouse, which can be in the terabyte range, has to be considered. On the hardware side, new purchases of large amounts of disk storage space and magnetic tape for backup should be expected.

It is also vital to plan and provide for the transport of large amounts of data over the network. The capability of data warehousing to support a wide range of queries, from simple ones that return only a limited amount of information to complex ones that might access several million rows of data, can cause complications. It is also necessary to incorporate the availability of corporate metadata into this thought process. The designers of the data warehouse have to remember that metadata is likely to be replicated at multiple sites. This points to the need for synchronization across the different platforms to avoid inconsistencies.

Finally, security and networking issues must be considered. In terms of location and security, data warehouse and non-data warehouse applications must appear seamless. Users should not need different IDs to sign on to different systems, but the application should be smart enough to allow access with only one password.

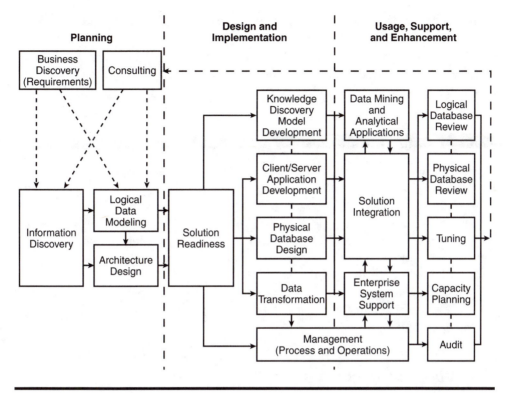

Exhibit 3. Scalable Data Warehouse

Design and Construction of a Data Warehouse

Four fundamental characteristics will guide the design and construction of a data warehouse (see Exhibit 3):

1. *The major function* — to analyze historical data, to reveal trends and correlations, and predict future outcomes
2. *Potential business insight* — valuable and unpredictable insights often result from analytical expeditions, based on information derived from the system, where starting point, routes taken, and end points were not initially known
3. *Granularity of data* — the capability to drill down into the detail data
4. *Assembling data from diversified sources* — to ensure consistency of interpretation throughout the organization

Note that a data mart containing summary data does not meet the criteria of the basic data warehousing concepts defined above, a drawback that needs to be recognized by the project team if the data mart approach is to be taken. A data mart based on summary data cannot evolve into a fully functional data warehouse and requires extensive rework to meet enterprisewide objectives. As well, summary data may obstruct the view of the business, preventing an end user from drilling down to locate the essential data required to resolve an issue.

The most effective methodology in designing a data warehouse is to acknowledge the fundamental requirement for detail data to be gathered and stored for access by business users.

Data in Data Warehouses

The concept of data and its categorization in a data warehouse leads to a second set of fundamentals regarding this data:

- The detection of trends is related to the amount of historical data stored — the more history, the better. (Most companies keep fifteen or twenty-seven months [one or two years, plus one quarter] of historical data, depending on the business sector).
- The most significant factor in delivering a successful data warehouse application is an understanding of the business purpose driving the need for information.

Restrictions of Summary Data

In the real world, summary data can restrict the view of a business, if it does not have the parameters that allow it to synchronize with other data inputs, as demonstrated by the following examples:

Example 1. Retail

A retail organization using a data mart based on summarized data for each stock keeping unit (SKU), by store and by week for 15 months of history, runs printed advertising every Wednesday and Saturday. With sales aggregated weekly, the retailer is unable to identify the one-day impact on sales created by that ad. If the retailer were to access detail data at the store level, the retailer could then determine the sales pulled through by the ad, in addition to the product purchase affinities in each store.

Additionally, a store-level aggregation would enable matching internal sales data with data purchased from any external source.

Example 2. Consumer Goods Manufacturer

A consumer goods manufacturer summarized data in the same manner as the retailer, but neglected to segregate the numbers by distribution channel. This firm could not determine the volume of product, number of returns, or profitability by channel. This same manufacturer stored historical sales data by month within calendar quarter, and the three months within each quarter were defined as five-week, four-week, and four-week periods, respectively.

Syndicated sales data was also available from a vendor by month within a calendar quarter, but the vendor had defined the months as four weeks, four weeks, and five weeks, respectively, in reverse order. If the consumer goods manufacturer had kept sales data by week, the firm could have aggregated to match any syndicated data.

A data warehousing system should not be structured to answer only preconceived questions. Users need complete freedom to conduct analytical expeditions, to achieve the full benefits of the system, which will be provided by a well-planned and implemented data warehouse that will impact significantly on the ultimate success of a CRM strategy.

Finally, an enterprisewide data warehouse, as the name implies, should always be built using the lowest level of data (detail data), which allows the greatest flexibility to summarize data. Detail data is essential in answering the complex questions of the business; however, a level of summarization may also be required. Data aggregation is often required to enable a view of the data that end users require or to match the level of aggregation of data acquired from an external source.

Data Marts in the Real World

Although data marts do not meet all of the requirements of an enterprise data warehousing system, as noted above, they can provide many decision support capabilities without incurring the cost and complexity associated with the larger system. As an entry capability to the data warehousing world, data marts may be the starting point for many organizations. With proper planning, they can be gradually consolidated and expanded to create a centralized warehouse that meets and leverages improved technologies and will provide the basis for a corporate CRM solution.

Data marts may be a more cost-effective option for many enterprises. They are more manageable data warehousing projects that can be focused on delivering value to a specific business area and to provide credibility and proof of concept to the corporation.

In today's global economy, enterprises are challenged to do more with less in order to compete successfully with a host of competitors, big and small, new and old, domestic and international. With fewer people and financial resources with which to operate, enterprises need to leverage their information resources more efficiently and effectively. This requires improved access to timely, accurate, and consistent data that can be shared easily with other team members, decision makers, and business partners.

It is currently acknowledged that data warehousing is the most effective way to provide this business decision support data. Under this concept, data is copied from operational systems and external information providers, then conditioned, integrated, and transformed into a read-only database that is optimized for direct access by the decision maker. The term *data warehousing* is particularly apt in that it describes data as being an enterprise asset that must be identified, cataloged, and stored using discipline and structure, and categorized to ensure that the user will always be able to find the correct information when it is needed.

Data Marts versus Data Warehouses

The term *data warehousing* can be applied to a broad range of approaches for providing improved access to business decision support data. These approaches can range from the simple to the more complex, with many variations in between. However, there are two major approaches that differ greatly in scale and complexity. They are the data mart and the data warehouse.

A data mart is a subject-oriented or department-oriented data warehouse. It is a scaled-down version of a data warehouse that focuses on the local needs of a specific department such as finance or marketing. A data mart contains a subset of the data that would be in an enterprise's data warehouse because it is subject- or department- oriented. An enterprise may have many data marts, each focused on a subset of the enterprise.

A data warehouse is an orderly and accessible repository of known facts or things from many subject areas, and it is used as a basis for decision making. In contrast to the data mart approach, the data warehouse is generally enterprisewide in scope. Its goal is to provide a single, integrated view of the enterprise's data, spanning all the enterprise's activities. The data warehouse consolidates data marts and reconciles the various departmental perspectives into a single enterprise perspective.

Advantages and Disadvantages

As noted previously in this chapter, there are advantages and disadvantages to both data marts and data warehouses. These two approaches differ in terms of the effort required to implement them, in the way that they use technology, and in the way the business and the users utilize these systems.

One of the advantages of the data mart is that the effort required to implement it is considerably less than that required for a data warehouse. The scope of a data mart is a subject area encompassing the applications in a business area versus the multiple subject areas of the data warehouse, which can cover all major applications in the enterprise. As a result of its reduced scope, a data mart typically requires an order of magnitude (1/10) less effort than a data warehouse, and it can be built in months rather than years.

Another advantage of the data mart is that it costs considerably less than a data warehouse — tens or hundreds of thousands of dollars versus the millions of dollars necessary for a data warehouse, because of its considerably-reduced complexity — fewer subject areas, fewer users, and less data transformation.

By contrast, a data warehouse is cross-functional, covering multiple subject areas having more users, and is a more complex undertaking because it requires establishing a centralized structured view to all data in the enterprise.

Since it is a much larger project, it is much more costly to develop and implement and also requires significantly more resources.

Comparison of Data Requirements

From a data perspective, a data mart has a reduced requirement for data sharing because it has a more limited scope than a data warehouse. It is simpler to provide shared data for a data mart because it is only necessary to establish shared definitions for the business area or department. In contrast, a data warehouse requires common data, which necessitates establishing identical data definitions across the enterprise — a much more complex and difficult undertaking.

Generally, it is easier to provide timely data updates to a data mart than to a data warehouse. The data mart is smaller (megabyte to low gigabyte versus gigabyte to terabyte for a data warehouse), requires less-complex data transformations, and the enterprise does not have to synchronize data updates from multiple operational systems. Therefore, it is easier to maintain data consistency within the data mart but difficult to maintain data consistency across the various data marts within an enterprise.

The smaller size of the data mart enables more frequent updates (daily or weekly) than is generally feasible for a data warehouse (weekly or monthly). This enables a data mart to contain near-current data in addition to the historical data that is normally contained in a data warehouse.

Supporting Technologies

From a supporting technology perspective, a data mart can often use existing technology infrastructure or lower-cost technology components, thus reducing costs and complexity. A data mart often resides on an Intel-based computer running Microsoft NT operating systems. A data warehouse, by contrast, often resides on a RISC-based (Reduced Instruction Set Computer) computer running the UNIX operating system or on a mainframe computer running the MVS operating system, to support larger data volumes and larger numbers of business users.

Frequently, a data mart can be deployed using a lower-cost workgroup relational database management system, while a data warehouse often requires a more costly and more powerful database server.

Business Application

In addition to their different data requirements and supporting technologies, the business applications of these systems by users are also different. For example, there are fewer concurrent users in a data mart than in a data warehouse. These users are often functional managers, such as sales executives or financial executives, focused on optimizing activities within their department or business area. On the other hand, users of a data warehouse are often analysts or senior executives making decisions that are cross-functional and require input from multiple areas of the business.

Because of these differences in data handling, technologies, and business applications, the data mart is often used for more operational or tactical decision making, while the data warehouse is used for strategic decision making and some tactical decision making. In summary, a data mart has a more short-term, timely, data delivery mechanism, while a data warehouse has a reliable history or archive of enterprise data, with a longer-term delivery cycle.

From Data Mart to Data Warehouse

An enterprise's data warehousing strategy can progress from a simple data mart to a complex data warehouse in response to user demands, the enterprise's business requirements, and the enterprise's maturity in managing data resources, including their application to an enterprisewide CRM strategy. An enterprise can also derive a hybrid strategy that utilizes one or more of these base strategies to fit its current application, data, and technology architectures. The right approach is the data warehouse strategy that is appropriate to the business needs and the perceived benefits.

For many enterprises, a data mart is often a practical first step to gaining experience in building and managing a data warehouse, while introducing business users to the benefits of improved access to their data and, generally, demonstrating the business value of data warehousing. These data marts often grow rapidly to hundreds of users and hundreds of gigabytes of data derived from many different operational systems.

Planning for its eventual growth to a data warehouse should be an essential part of a data mart project.

Data Marts, Data Warehouses, and Marketing Campaigns

In every business with a marketing department, there are always requirements for direct mail or telephone campaigns, or even for product sales offered by salespersons. Data marts and data warehouses have an important role to play in these marketing activities. Sales history, demographics, and psycho-graphics are evaluated and the target market segment is determined.

In order to execute the campaign, detailed customer or prospect information must be available, including the appropriate attributes of each individual. Depending upon how the target segment is defined, this could include sales history, demographics, and psycho-graphics. Without this information it would not be possible to determine which individuals match the target market, and generate mailing labels or prepare phone lists, or conduct other customer-related marketing activities.

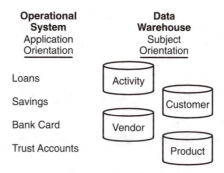

Exhibit 4.   Typical Enterprise Infrastructure — Operational System versus Data Warehouse

Avoiding the Pitfalls of Data Warehousing

It is important for organizations involved in developing CRM strategies to understand fully what a data warehouse is, how to specify and apply this technology, and how to use the interfacing hardware and software solutions that make it function as a core component in the CRM solution.

Implementing a data warehouse is a major project in itself, and it is the first significant step along the road to a CRM solution, whether or not it evolved from a number of data marts or on its own. This project may take a few to several years to complete and to gather the data that will form the basis for the CRM solution. Data warehouse project teams must remain focused on a definition of the data warehouse that addresses the real business issues of their organizations (see Exhibit 4).

The secret of data warehouse success is in collecting, storing, and applying detailed transaction data.

The experience of some of the world's largest organizations in implementing CRM strategies indicates that there are at least seven major, identifiable pitfalls in the data warehousing development process, all of which can be avoided if the project team is aware of them before beginning the project:

1. Paralysis by analysis — a long evaluation period and a focus on technology versus business issues
2. Political issues between IT and the business users — who controls the project?
3. Lack of well-defined short-term goals — no clear set of definitions of the end product
4. Reliance on untested or unproven hardware or software
5. Too much emphasis on benchmarking and price/performance evaluation
6. A belief that self-education programs will teach developers how to build a data warehouse
7. No definition of a query tool methodology or of the tools business users need to use the data warehouse effectively

Exhibit 5. Ten-Point Checklist: DEFINITION

Define a specific query tool based on real needs of users.
Establish clearly defined and consistent goals.
Focus on a core technology that will serve as the foundation for the data warehouse.
Identify a data warehouse champion to support the project.
Nominate the right levels of corporate sponsorship.
Initiate a plan for future growth.
Take an iterative approach.
Install detailed transaction data.
Only use proven vendors and service providers.
Needs of users are paramount.

How can an organization avoid these pitfalls and improve the chances of implementing a successful data warehouse project? The planning process developed for this Handbook with the acronym D E F I N I T I O N provides a ten-point checklist for implementing a successful data warehousing project. The checklist defines a step-by-step approach that will minimize problems and enable a successful data warehouse project to be delivered to the organization (see Exhibit 5).

The evolution of CRM has made data warehousing a high-profile technology. As a result, many IT vendors and consultants offer products and services specific to data warehousing and CRM. A selection of vendors offering CRM products or services is provided at the end of this chapter.

Data Warehousing Processing Environments

There are two interrelated processing environments in a data warehouse:

1. Repetitive
2. Iterative

In repetitive processing, the same functions are executed repeatedly. All factors are known ahead of time, including the amount of data required to fulfill the request, the amount of processing power required, and the expected response time. This is the traditional data processing environment, and because all factors are known, this environment is very predictable and easy to manage. Applications that support repetitive processing are generally written and tuned by IS professionals to meet specific performance requirements and to fully leverage the company's investment in hardware.

Iterative processing (also referred to as "ad hoc processing") often leads to unexpected new questions from a single posed question. The general starting point is known in advance, as well as the universe of data involved. This environment may be new to many organizations, and its successful application is measured by the ability to immediately adapt and answer any question needed to support the business. In this environment, end users often write the applications or use intelligent software tools to make the first level of decisions.

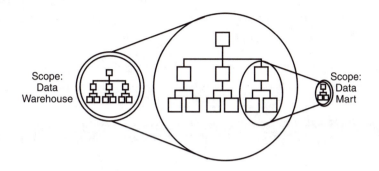

Exhibit 6.   Scope of the Data Warehouse

Data Granularity and Performance Comparison

The two data warehousing environments described above have different objectives. For the repetitive environment, the primary goal is to obtain maximum performance; therefore repetitive processing relies heavily on summarized data. Data may be provided in summary form to meet the requirements of a department, an application, or a specific analysis tool. Summarized data stores (the data marts previously described) are also known as departmental summaries.

Flexibility is the primary goal of the iterative environment; therefore iterative questions may draw on any combination from the universe of corporate data and may do so in some unexpected ways. Iterative processing relies primarily on detail data.

In general, a data warehouse contains both summary and detail data, because data is gathered and stored in both formats. Strategic and tactical decisions will be based on this data, requiring that detail and summary levels of data must be in total agreement. Note that while summary data may serve a useful purpose for some applications, detail data must be the foundation for the data warehouse, and all summaries must be derived directly from the detail data (see Exhibit 6).

The Data Warehouse Development Process

As noted previously in this chapter, the development of a data warehouse is quite a different process than the development of IT applications for other major applications, because of its complexity and its involvement and dependency on data input from many corporate departments.

The following two statements compare a traditional IT development project and a data warehousing development project:

1. In an IT development project, it is relatively easy to map a set of user inputs to a set of desired outputs, based on known business processes and user interviews.

2.   In a data warehouse, the primary objectives are to support unanticipated questions, identify new opportunities, and respond to business tactics that are often completely unknown.

These two fundamental differences between traditional IT projects and the data warehouse provide challenges to both the IT departments and the business departments of an organization.

Data warehouse developers need to have two strong characteristics: (1) business skills and (2) technical skills. These skills are required to anticipate new areas of business concerns that may arise in the future and to apply appropriate technologies to the implementation process.

Data Warehouse: Business Contents

Data in a data warehouse should replicate the business characteristics of the particular business and the transactions that make the business work. Here are some examples of the structure required of a data warehouse for some specific business sectors:

- If there are plants, warehouses, and suppliers, then the data warehouse should have plants, warehouses, and suppliers.
- If insurance policies have an arbitrary number of participants and coverage, then the data warehouse should match these characteristics.
- If several subsidiaries sell product to a specific customer, this customer should be represented in the data warehouse.

The data warehouse must be an accurate model of the business, not of the applications. The process of interfacing legacy systems and applications is another phase in the development of a CRM solution that must be addressed, because these systems were not designed to work together. However, the historical data stored in these legacy systems will be an important contribution to the data warehouse project and to the CRM solution.

Information stored in a data warehouse must be user friendly. Balancing accuracy of data with ease of use can be a challenge for the development team. The data warehouse may used for more than one kind of operation within an organization, and the data stored in the warehouse is mission-critical. However, the applications built to use that data should not necessarily have the same level of corporate criticality.

A significant factor affecting the quality of data that feeds a data warehousing system is that the data warehouse becomes the victim of data errors from all other systems that provide data inputs. These inputs come from existing systems designed independently to accomplish functions other than supporting the data warehouse and were never designed to work together. Also, data comes from several sources outside the company — from suppliers, customers, or data vendors — and may be corrupted before, during, or after the transfer process.

Every piece of data in the data warehouse needs to be edited for applicability to the business objectives. If the data does not adhere to the documentation, users will have difficulty using the information.

Bad Data

Bad data poses another problem, because the data warehouse must accept all data it receives — customer, warehouse, product, order, claim, payment, or shipment — to balance with the official company results. Values that do not pass the edits need to be converted to universal values that will:

- Prevent reports and graphics from containing unusable values
- Prevent the system from dropping transactions with no product, customer, or sales organization match
- Assist management in understanding the extent of a reporting error so they may take appropriate action to improve data quality

Many CRM deployments are thwarted by faulty, inconsistent data sets that prevent user sites from having a clear, unified profile of each customer, when they require this information. Some software vendors have developed solutions for these problems, and products are available that will profile, clean, and organize data prior to its storage in the data warehouse.

An effective CRM solution is dependent on knowing the customer, a requirement that can only be met through accurate customer information. Most front-end systems that deal with customers do not have accurate information about customers. Specific data errors that are often encountered include disjointed data and blank areas in critical fields. Also, in some data warehousing installations, many business rules intended for databases have been broken, resulting in data integrity problems.

Even such seemingly small errors as being one digit off on a customer's street address can plague datasets. For example, this type of problem can result in a company sending out multiple direct mailings to the same customer, because the address is listed in two different ways in company databases.

Data quality problems are a hindrance to successful CRM deployments. The well-known industry analyst firm, The Gartner Group, has reported that more than 75 percent of enterprises engaged in CRM initiatives cannot combine a comprehensive view of a customer with actionable, personalized advice to customer service and sales agents.

In a typical bank or insurance company, for example, there could be 50 to 150 different systems containing customer data, and to obtain a single view of each customer and the value of that customer and their needs, the data must be combined.

Assembling this data involves addressing several database issues, including:

- Different data stores
- Data of varying ages

- Data on different databases
- Multiple programming languages and data formats
- Poor data quality

Cleaning up the data is a task that can be performed manually; however, the activity is tedious, time-consuming, and not accurate. There is vendor software available that can automate the data assessment process up-front, providing the structure of the data and an assessment of its quality. These products are designed to find different relationships in customer data in multiple sources, as well as providing information on restructuring and cleaning the data and on its functionality, and developing an enhanced repository for automated profiling.

The Operational Data Warehouse

An operational data warehouse (ODW) is a data-centric architecture, which enables an organization to react in real-time to changing customer needs, supply-chain demands, and financial concerns. In this configuration, the data warehouse is updated in real-time rather than periodically (usually overnight or weekly).

One of the underlying technologies that supports an ODW and real-time data warehousing is parallel processing; however, this technology must be supported by an organizational structure that takes advantage of the technology and applications that are designed to feed information back to the data warehouse in real-time (see Exhibit 7).

The new challenge is to assess customer trends, recognize customers, and act on the information in real- time — whether in-store, via the World Wide Web, phone, or mail. This is where an ODW can play an important role in CRM.

A benefit of the operational data warehouse is that it allows new systems to be created and populated, based on the data warehouse, in a very short time frame (less than 24 hours). Another key real-time capability of the ODW is the capability to react to warehouse information in real- or near-time rather than waiting for periodic reports, a drawback of earlier data warehouse designs.

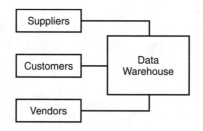

Exhibit 7. Data Sources

Three main types of ODW have evolved as data warehouses have become more advanced, and as organizations have realized the benefits of real-time data storage, extraction, and manipulation:

1. *Customer-based* — contains product profiling and customer profiling, allowing cross-selling of related products in real time by querying the data warehouse product subject areas for related sales opportunities. E-business also uses statistically determined customer profiles to personalize the online customer experience.
2. *Supply chain/manufacturing* — aggregated customer information serves as a middleman between sellers and buyers.
3. *Financial/asset management* — managing financial assets for a financial institution, including fraud detection.

An ODW that uses just-in-time (JIT) systems and enables active warehousing applications to be used needs to have several additional elements as part of its technology and human resource infrastructure, including:

- An infrastructure that serves a multi-application environment
- A problem-solving approach
- A metadata system based on current standards
- Staff technologists and business analysts with vision

A process called "data mining," described later in this chapter and refer-enced in Chapter 2, is used in many organizations to analyze customer data. As the name implies, this process refers to the activity of "digging out" customer information from the vast amounts of detail data stored in a data warehouse.

Components of the ODW

The ODW represents an evolution from a traditional, application-centric data warehouse. In the ODW, the infrastructure acts like the central nervous system, coordinating access to information in all parts of the organization. The fol-lowing subsections describe the components of an ODW.

JIT Applications

Most data warehouses are so tightly integrated with the applications they serve that there is no distinction between data and function. In the ODW, built with a data-centric rather than application-centric approach, the data warehouse provides data to individual application functions, enabling it to operate as a multi-application environment, in the same way that an operating system is made up of a kernel with many functional parts. It also provides future proofing by separating data from function and allowing companies to prolif-erate JIT applications, which are important because they free employees to take advantage of standardized data in an unstructured way.

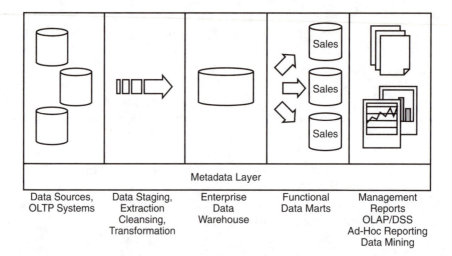

| Data Sources, OLTP Systems | Data Staging, Extraction Cleansing, Transformation | Enterprise Data Warehouse | Functional Data Marts | Management Reports OLAP/DSS Ad-Hoc Reporting Data Mining |

Exhibit 8. ODW in the Enterprise Infrastructure

RAD Tools

An ODW acts as a central source to supply information to operational systems, operational data marts, and analysis tools. It does this by providing a standardized set of protocols to enable access. Regardless of how a third party tool stores information internally, it can access warehouse data through this interface. Rapid application development (RAD) tools, such as Microsoft Access and Lotus Notes, as well as other data analysis tools, can obtain a single consistent version of data through this interface.

The capability to access the information in the data warehouse, using these tools, is the key to a successful ODW.

Instead of each tool defining profit, for example, the tools draw on a common definition of profit from the metadata repository, ensuring that the value of profit used for the business tools is the same as the value of profit used by any other tool.

The two main components of the ODW infrastructure are (see Exhibit 8):

1. *Operational system* — including current online transfer protocol (OLTP) feeder systems for handling transactional information in the organization and demographic data purchased from third parties.
2. *Data warehouse* — specifically, a normalized, centralized data warehouse containing detail-level data — not aggregated online analytical processing data (OLAP) — and not application-specific. The data warehouse may provide data to other applications or systems, for example: operational, application-focused data marts, JIT systems that solve a single business problem, or a single business problem category for a whole department.

OLAP Generator

The OLAP generator is a module that creates OLAP data, such as star schemas, multidimensional databases, and hypercubes, for individual analysis tools. The ODW provides a decentralized data warehousing environment where analysis tools can be applied. The OLAP generator produces the particular type of data storage these products need.

Metadata Repository

Metadata is defined as "the detailed properties and characteristics of the information within the database or systems." The metadata repository stores the analysis tool profiles that allow the OLAP generator to produce OLAP data for individual tools, the business definitions used by the business information directory (BID*)*, and information on data warehouse changes over time.

Programming API

The application programming interface (API*)* is an object linking and embedding (OLE) automation interface into the data warehouse that allows any RAD tool with a programming language to interface directly to the data warehouse. The tool interface allows the individual analysis tools to interrogate both OLAP data marts and the normalized data warehouse. Like the API, this interface allows third-party tools to access the data warehouse without regard to the format of the tools used to store the data internally.

Business Information Directory

The business information directory (BID) allows users to navigate the data warehouse in a context-sensitive mode similar to the Help function in Microsoft Windows. It delivers data in the correct format for a desktop application or departmental server, scheduling the data delivery to ensure that data center concerns are addressed.

ODW: Problem-Solving Approach

Much data warehousing takes place at a departmental level to implement a solution to a particular business problem. It is a fundamental economic relationship in business that "profit equals sales minus costs." For example, an airline might approach the challenge of increasing profits by seeking ways to reduce the number of empty seats on flights. Although this problem affects the organization as a whole, the sales or marketing department probably has the primary responsibility for accomplishing this objective.

Solutions Using JIT Applications

Unfortunately, the departmental approach fosters the development of islands of information that block the synergies and data relationships required in an enterprisewide CRM strategy. Instead of islands, the ODW approach creates temporary peninsulas of information connected to the data warehouse but individual in their function. JIT applications provide the solution.

JIT applications are created and used to solve a particular problem. Once this problem is solved, any information the system captured is fed back into the data warehouse to be used for analysis or for other applications, and the JIT system is discarded.

JIT systems deliver solutions using RAD tools such as spreadsheets, personal databases, and third-party applications. Line managers and others responsible for producing sales and profit require software tools that give them a competitive edge.

A JIT application can meet these business requirements because it may furnish a simple problem-solving application that provides competitive advantage using a RAD tool, a Web page, or an off-the-shelf package populated by information from the data warehouse. JIT systems can be developed in hours rather than weeks, and produce results very quickly.

Typically, the requirement for these business tools precludes a long, drawn-out application development cycle. Sales and marketing user requirements are straightforward; they simply want to retain or attract customers, increase sales, and improve their performance related to their functional responsibilities.

With the proliferation and migration of office suites and collaboration tools to the desktop, users already have most of the tools they need. These tools can be augmented with additional functionality on an as-needed basis.

The ODW in Action

The ODW contains a data modeling and design layer component representing the creation of a logical data model to support the business information needs and the physical design of the database to support the logical model.

Also located in this layer is the data dictionary for providing consistent data definitions and the metadata for establishing an efficient directory and usage of the data. The development of standards for metadata is an ongoing process, and as accepted standards become available, it will be easy to populate tools from different vendors with identical information from a metadata repository. Until this occurs, companies will have to use proprietary standards that do not allow data migrations from one vendor's tool to another.

Metadata standards will help prove the benefit of the ODW by providing rapid response to user needs. Corporate departments that are skeptical about the benefits of a data warehouse and the business value of the project will be able to easily create their own data marts from the centralized warehouse, and will be able to apply the system to their own business problems. Rapid and successful application of the ODW in its early stages, for resolving business issues, will generate credibility and alleviate any skepticism associated with the project.

XML Facilities in Search Engines

The BID is an integral part of the metadata repository and the data warehouse infrastructure. It is the user's interface to the data warehouse where the user seeks information, and it needs to be developed around standards. Where BIDs acquire the features of popular search engines, the development process will be easier. Also, the increasing adoption of intranets and the inclusion of XML facilities in search engines will mean that XML can be used to create BIDs that are essentially enhanced XML-based search engines.

XML will assist in proving the value of metadata, enabling users to understand what metadata is and what it can do for them. Presenting metadata on an HTML page makes it less esoteric, enabling nontechnical users to understand what metadata is and how it can be used in business analysis applications.

The key to a successful ODW is to encourage IT managers to understand the importance of giving users access to the data and letting them solve their own problems. The ODW will also provide the capability for risk managers to create new risk simulations and assessments, allow marketing personnel to find new market segmentations from existing customer databases, and enable salespeople to make last-minute offers to the appropriate customers so that everyone benefits.

When implemented to meet enterprisewide corporate objectives and linked with an effective CRM strategy, the ODW facilitates new types of information delivery applications, including trend analysis and data mining, customer profiling, consolidated marketing systems, and management information systems.

Data Warehousing Computer Platforms

There are two basic computer mainframe configurations used in data warehousing systems:

1. SMP (symmetrical multiprocessing)
2. MPP (massively parallel processing)

Selection Criteria

In selecting the type of configuration to employ, there are only two critical issues involved:

1. Scalability
2. Price/performance

Vendors have an important responsibility in the selection process and need to provide specific responses to questions regarding the state-of-the-art of their proposed data warehousing systems. Vendor responses to requests for proposals should include a full range of answers to evaluation-based questions on their products or services, including the following:

- When was the system first installed at a customer site?
- How many sites are in production?
- Can existing customers be contacted?
- What elements are included in a production-ready package?
- What is the total cost of the package?

Other information provided in vendor proposals — number of orders received, number of implementations, number of implementations currently under way, or consultant community evaluations — is irrelevant to the success of the data warehousing project and should be viewed as vendor promotion. These elements are not a part of the evaluation process.

It is important to verify that the data warehouse selected will operate in a production environment. A typical production-ready system package will include:

- Systems management software
- Performance and capacity planning tools
- Operations support software to effectively load and back up the data warehouse

Evaluating and selecting hardware and software technology for the data warehouse is a time-consuming process, and there are recognized, effective processes leading to a final selection of products and services. Some of these processes are described in the following subsections.

Benchmarking

Benchmarking is a technique that has been used since the early days of computer systems to evaluate competing hardware and software, particularly with respect to combined price/performance criteria. The object of benchmarking to implement a data warehouse is to determine which vendors have the best price/performance mix and then to select those vendors. The key issues addressed in benchmarking are:

- What performance yardstick can be used and trusted?
- Is it a sound strategy for an organization to develop and conduct its own benchmark?
- Should a consultant be hired to direct the evaluation process?
- Will a consultant be completely unbiased?

Although benchmarking was a commonly used selection technique by internal IT departments for mainframe system selection and for major software acquisitions, such as databases, it has largely disappeared as an evaluation tool, because of its prohibitive costs and manpower requirements. Even when it was a popular evaluation process, the results of a benchmark often did not correlate well to real-life processing workloads and may have been completely inaccurate.

Benchmarking has always had limitations to its evaluation capability because it can only simulate some of an organization's IT processes, and critical activities often were not included. While benchmarking for data warehouses may still form a part of the selection process, if an organization is comfortable with the pros and cons, it is more commonly and effectively performed by outside consultants selected for their experience and objectivity.

In many organizations, a data warehouse project is often implemented as the first nonmainframe-based project undertaken. For those organizations that do not have core competency in UNIX-based systems, there are consultants who specialize in various aspects of data warehousing, and the following consulting specialties with the credentials of experience can be a valuable resource for the selection team:

- Data warehouse management consultants
- Data warehouse technical/database consultants
- Hardware/RDBMS performance/benchmarking specialists

Some of these resources are included in the vendor descriptions at the end of this chapter.

Where consultants are retained, a competitive data warehousing procurement process should be followed, including a modified comparative price/ performance benchmarking process that uses the services of the consultant to create, referee, and report on the results of the benchmark.

The Mentor Approach to Building a Data Warehouse

A methodology for building a data warehouse that may be appropriate for some organizations is a hybrid approach, where an experienced data warehousing consultant is hired and provides an apprenticeship or tutorial program for the internal project team. The consultant is used as a mentor and provides overall project management and accountability to ensure the data warehouse project is delivered on time and on budget.

The corporate staff works as team implementation members and, eventually, takes over full responsibility for the data warehouse project, phasing out the consultant.

For the mentor approach to be successful, it is essential that the consultant retained for the project have verifiable hands-on experience in designing and implementing a data warehouse.

Accessing the Data: Query Tool Methodology

Data warehouse access tools are an important component of a CRM strategy, and data access is probably one of the least understood areas. Bill Inmon, commonly referred to as "the father of data warehousing," has written extensively on the issue of access of data. One of his books concentrates on data warehouse basics and building the data warehouse; however, it also contains some excellent advice for CRM project leaders, which helps them to understand how to derive answers to business questions and how to use the data warehouse effectively.

The key issues to be addressed for the different types of business users (explorers, miners, developers, and managers) who will access the data warehouse include:

- Does the query tool scale along with the hardware and RDBMS being used?
- Is it meaningful to view a single tool as the standard for the company?
- What are the top-ten business questions?
- Is there a tool strategy that will provide answers to these questions?

It is important for the data warehousing project team to fully understand the complexities of a data warehouse and know what the scheduled deliverables will be. Most importantly, the team needs to have a clear definition of the value to the business in the overall implementation of a CRM solution.

Data Warehousing: Processing Methodology

Data warehousing is an iterative process, and it is not a "product" that can be purchased as an off-the-shelf item because it has a number of elements that typically are not part of a single technology package. The following primary activities are involved in the data warehouse, from the beginning of the project to its final launch:

- *Planning* — determination of business and information requirements, selection of technologies, and logical modeling
- *Design and implementation* — physical design and implementation and data acquisition
- *Support and enhancement* — operations, capacity planning, tuning, and auditing of results
- *Future planning* — enhancements and upgrades

For the success and credibility of a CRM project, it is important to adhere to a basic business practice during the technology selection and implementation stages and throughout the CRM project: keep corporate management informed through a regular reporting process. It is quite appropriate for a senior management group that has approved the investment of a few to several million dollars to ask questions about whether their investment is providing measurable business value and to have these questions answered.

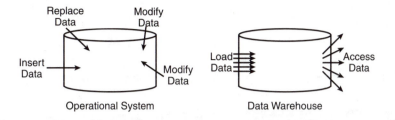

Exhibit 9. Operational System versus the Data Warehouse

Data Warehousing and CRM: Managing the Project

At the data warehousing stage, and throughout the technology selection and implementation process, the objectives of the CRM project need to be aligned with traditional management processes through the following analysis activities:

- Identifying applications with large benefit opportunities and exploiting those opportunities
- Identifying the return on investment (ROI) of each application
- Identifying applications that are not cost-justified, and improve, move, or eliminate them
- Measuring the total cost of ownership (TCO)
- Reporting quarterly and annually on the results of the corporation's investment

The ultimate value of the data warehouse and its contribution to a CRM strategy will be determined by its usefulness to business users in decision making. Information access tools help provide business users with improved access to data, enhancing their decision-making ability. Data mining tools facilitate the process of sifting through large amounts of data to uncover meaningful trends, correlations, or patterns (see Exhibit 9).

A data warehouse project is a major undertaking and should demonstrate business value early and often to corporate management to ensure high visibility and justification of the immense resource commitment and costs associated with the project.

To determine business value in the implementation of a data warehouse that will be the foundation of the CRM solution, the following criteria are useful guidelines:

- *Cost reduction* — Effectively utilize assets, through the identification of idle time, for people, planes, production equipment, rail cars, etc., depending on the business sector and the significant contributors to the revenues and profitability of the business.
- *Opportunity identification* — Provide input to corporate programs to develop new products and new markets.

- *Customer retention* — Utilize loyalty and other incentive programs that identify frequent purchasers to offer premiums and rewards for their business.
- *Business management* — Provide comparisons of current performance against prior periods, or between like organizations, or against a competitor (market share), and furnish comparisons of performance against goals or budget in volume, profit, costs, etc.
- *Diagnosis* — Assess spending on advertising, merchandising, temporary price reductions, coupons, etc., for effectiveness in improving volume and profit, and failure sourcing to evaluate systematic and component failure against source.
- *Fraud detection* — Analyze corporate data to highlight potential fraudulent transactions based on matching characteristics from prior successful investigations.

Data Warehousing: The Planning

As noted in other chapters of this Handbook, technology can support a data warehouse, but it cannot make it successful. Different technology choices can make the warehouse easier to operate, provide freedom from application and content compromises, or provide integration with the existing infrastructure. However, the most outstanding choice of products can only affect the cost of ownership; it cannot create a data warehouse that will become valuable to the enterprise.

The connotation of the term *data warehousing* may be responsible for the misdirection of some organizations that attempt the development process. Too often project teams begin the project by looking for a technology that will store a large volume of data. The experience of organizations with successful data warehousing installations is that technology is really the last step in the planning stage, not the first. This means that the individuals involved in planning, developing, and implementing the data warehouse in the early stages are the most important contributors to its success, and they must realize how and when technology issues must be considered and resolved.

The focus of data warehousing is not just the storage of data, but more importantly, the effective utilization of data to drive business results.

Project Scope and Resources

The sponsor of the project generally states whether the warehouse's scope is for the sponsor's business area or for the enterprise. If the sponsor's scope is below the total corporate level, the data warehouse project team should seek opportunities to align with other departments to coordinate implementation of components that can provide business value to other business areas. Initially, a sponsor may resist this process because it could compromise the content or timing of the project.

While the potential benefits of a major data warehousing project are significant, if the sponsor and systems professionals lack the power or skill to resolve the organizational issues, it may be wiser to implement a more limited data warehouse, or data mart, that is designed with future expansion in mind.

The total number of systems professionals required for planning and implementation of the data warehousing project is dependent on the number and complexity of the source systems, the size and cleanliness of the data, and the setup and support required by tools. For example, some database management systems can require five to eight times as much effort to build, tune, and operate as others.

The other key ingredient in the project is the involvement, and the extent of this involvement, of people from the business side of the company. They will be valuable in the initial collecting, analysis, and definition of the business requirements and system justification, especially toward the end of each phase in coordinating with user organizations for content validation, user documentation, user training, and analysis of business value achieved.

For large user populations, at the point of user training it is beneficial to select a number of lead users to test the training and then have them deliver a portion of the training for the balance of the users. Training delivered by colleagues from the business side will often speed acceptance of new technology and establish additional support for the program.

Business Discovery: Analyzing Business Issues

The objective of business discovery is to understand and gain consensus on key business issues, and its objectives are accomplished through a structured set of interviews and workshops with key executives within the company.

When the business discovery stage is completed, business issues are prioritized, quantifiable benefits to these issues are resolved, and there is a bottom-line analysis of the impact to the business. Additionally, business discovery can help foster cooperation across functional lines within a business at an executive level.

Data Warehouse Consultants

There are numerous decisions that the sponsor and the IS professionals will need to make during the course of the project. Getting experienced implementers of data warehousing from the consulting environment to provide a base level of education, support, and advice is a valuable aid to developing informed decisions.

A data warehousing consultant with the requisite experience can work with members of the project team to help them evaluate and understand the advantages and disadvantages of the major components of the system, which are:

- System architecture (centralized versus distributed)
- Database
- Application/access methods

- Management of data
- Operational organization
- Information discovery

In this stage of planning for the data warehouse, the requirements of the solution are refined and solidified by validating and focusing critical business needs or issues. These issues or needs are captured in the form of business questions, usually those that have been derived from the business discovery stage. The activities in this stage may benefit from the resources provided by an outside consulting firm that can bring a level of objectivity to the process.

Once the business needs are focused, a form of data modeling is used to show how data can be turned into useful information and how that information can be used to address critical business issues. A high-level data model that supports business needs is also developed during this stage, and it may later be used as a basis for the technical solution.

Data Warehouse Logical Modeling

This activity will produce a logical data model that can be used to begin the construction of the data warehouse. This model will be based on the information obtained during the information discovery stage and may be referred to as an "Enterprise Logical Data Model." It contains all the attributes necessary to begin the implementation of the data warehouse. The specific deliverables from this stage are:

- A validated business solution model
- Documented business rules
- Entity definitions
- Identification of data sources

With this activity completed, the company is ready to create the metadata describing the data warehouse.

Data Warehouse Architectural Design

Once all the business requirements are known and defined, the technology and architectural design elements of the data warehouse can be configured. During this stage, multiple structured design processes will be developed, leading to a comprehensive data warehouse specification. In this stage, final decisions will be made on the following aspects of the project:

- Data warehouse location and configuration (centralized, distributed, data marts)
- Sources of data, integrity of data, business rules, and data relationships

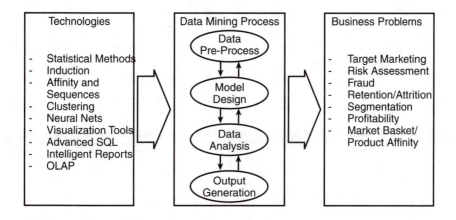

Exhibit 10. Matching Methods to Business Issues

- Warehouse management — hardware, software, network, support, restore, archive, and refresh requirements
- Application tools and loads, access methods, and types of applications
- Mathematical modeling needs and opportunities

The data warehousing design specification resulting from this stage will meet the business needs of the company and can be used to implement the solution (see Exhibit 10).

Project Implementation

The project should be structured to produce results in about three months, but no more than six months, to ensure that a tangible solution can be identified and reported on to management. Ideally, the biggest business values should come first, but before reporting on the first release to obtain the best visibility and recognition for the project, be wary of the dangers of losing credibility by missing target dates.

The data warehouse will create changes in the business and the way it is conducted, providing users with greater knowledge and understanding of their business requirements and opportunities. It is a good development and notification strategy to provide users with small increments of the data warehouse before the business changes, and before user requirements and priorities change.

Marketing the project and its benefits to users and senior management is another strategy that can benefit the data warehouse project and encourage its acceptance. Users will be enthusiastic about the project and its contribution to CRM if they are kept informed about the significant changes that will result, improving their ability to perform their job responsibilities and adding new dimensions to their careers. There are several practical steps that can be taken to reinforce the benefits of the project:

- *Remind organizations frequently of the value they will receive* — to keep them interested and ensure their participation in meetings and as trial users.
- *Keep the warehouse project in their plans* — so other departments will have difficulty launching competing projects.
- *Create excitement through noting the significant changes to come in their job functions* — they should want the system at start-up!

Generally speaking, it is simply good business practice to promote the data warehousing project and its resultant CRM strategy throughout the organization. An effective and active internal marketing strategy will benefit the project over the long term, develop user acceptance, and make it more difficult for the project to be sidetracked by other corporate priorities.

Initiating the Data Warehousing Project

As noted previously, a data warehousing project is a major undertaking for any organization and is more complex than a straightforward, mainframe selection and implementation project, because it involves and impacts many more departments, numerous input and output interfaces, and is a part of the core CRM business strategy. Once implemented and operational, the data warehouse with all of its access tools and business applications will become a mission-critical, enterprisewide resource.

The most successful data warehouse development projects are based on an enterprise view of the data-handling requirements, in combination with the long-term objectives of the organization. The project team will begin by performing a quick analysis of the information needed to support all requirements, and then focus on one area to build the first increment of what will be the enterprise data warehouse. The scope of each increment of the data warehouse should be configured to deliver results in *less than six months,* so that there is a relatively rapid payback to demonstrate the business benefit to management.

To make the most of IT expenditures in the creation of a CRM solution, it is important to review the number of key components involved in this process:

- A customer data warehouse or data mart
- Analytical tools
- Links to operational systems
- A customer-oriented front-end interaction system
- Staff to manage the implementation

Many companies overspend on their IT investment without deriving benefit, because they have not included all of the vital elements of a CRM system.

Select a Scalable Product

A product's limitations will quickly become handicaps; however, its capabilities will grow into opportunities for the organization. As a guideline to capacity, consider a product that can easily handle databases from two million to more than 20 million entries. The product should also be capable of handling very high levels of activity, including simultaneously managing multiple, complex campaigns.

Scalability is an extremely important product feature. If the services provided by the data warehouse become affected by query volumes, for example, as users and data expand, then users will abandon the system. If it is not scalable and fast, it will quickly become redundant.

Measurable Results

The technology layer — and its integration with the emerging business processes — is the key to the successful implementation of a data-driven CRM strategy. Technology that can monitor the results from marketing campaigns will assist in evaluating the benefits of the CRM solution. For marketing departments, there are several aspects of customer response that need to be tracked and measured — history of contacts and purchases, time frames, frequency, and monetary value of transactions — to assess both current and future profitability of the relationship.

The data warehouse and its associated software tools need to be flexible enough to handle all possible sales channels, both present and future, to ensure that the system continues to be a multifunctional, enterprisewide facility.

It is important to present the internal IT organization with a problem-free implementation process for the CRM solution that begins with the data warehousing project. Take the appropriate steps to ensure that the underlying operational system, tools, interfaces, and all other elements are functional before implementing the CRM solution.

Avoid installing a CRM solution at the same time as any other in-house system is being installed or upgraded. This seems logical when the complexities and resources required for the CRM solution are considered. Mixing this process with any other changes within the IT structure is not recommended practice.

Departmental or Enterprisewide

An effective CRM solution should be able to handle enterprisewide marketing initiatives and deal with multichannel campaigns; therefore, as noted previously, an enterprisewide solution is usually the best option. Deployment across an entire organization can be done via the Internet, or an intranet, with all information provided via a standard Web browser. This process eliminates high application deployment and maintenance costs. In addition, implementing a Web-based architecture means the CRM solution is instantly and dynamically accessible by every knowledge worker in the enterprise, as well as by partners and customers throughout the extended enterprise.

Data Warehouse Development: One Vendor's Methodology

One methodology that the CRM project team can follow in the development of a data warehouse is a process developed by NCR Corporation, which recommends the following major steps in the implementation process:

- *Solution readiness* — Ensure that the plans and the environment are complete.
- *Physical database* — Implement the data model into the database management system.
- *Data transformation* — Build the applications for initial loading and on-going maintenance of the data warehouse.
- *Client server application* — Prepare the tools needed to access the data warehouse.
- *Data warehouse management* — Prepare the tools and procedures needed to manage the system.

The following subsections provide a brief overview of each of the steps in this methodology.

Solution Readiness

Solution readiness (see Exhibit 11) validates the impact of the identified data warehouse solution within a customer's environment, based on range-of-readiness parameters. Solution readiness examines those elements that are necessary to support the implementation and determines the status of each one, as follows:

- Data readiness
- Technology readiness
- Functional readiness
- Support readiness
- Infrastructure readiness

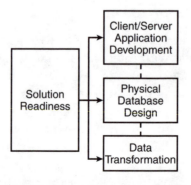

Exhibit 11.   Solution Readiness

The purpose of solution readiness is to avoid implementing a solution for which the organization is unprepared or that might impact other functional areas within the company that were not included in the planning. In addition to readiness evaluations, implementation project plans can be adjusted as required, based on the results of the assessments.

Physical Data Modeling

This process provides a physical database design and database implementation optimized for an organization's particular data warehousing solution. The database is designed and constructed using the project plan, logical data model, and data warehousing architecture design plan. The primary activities in this process are:

- Translating the logical data model to a physical database design
- Database construction and design optimization
- Functional testing of the constructed database

The physical database design service provides design guidelines appropriate for the environment and for the specific database platform used within this project.

The physical data model should follow the logical model because it maximizes the number of business questions that can be asked. One violation of the logical model that may occur in a database is denormalization of information. An example of denormalization is putting the name of the salesperson, sourced from the salesperson's record, onto their accounts and transactions. With some vendor databases, it is often possible to avoid denormalization.

For organization and storage of data in the data warehouse, the following sales-oriented example illustrates the impact of denormalization on the database design:

- When placed on the *account,* if the salesperson is reassigned, then all accounts with that name will need to be updated, or the entire table of accounts would be reloaded with the current month's salesperson's assignments. Because this is a table of less than a million rows, the cost is probably minor.
- When placed on the *transaction*, if the salesperson is reassigned, all transactions with the salesperson's name may need to be updated to provide historical reporting for the new salesperson. This could involve many millions of updates, and reloads could take days.
- Denormalizing information into tables with huge numbers of rows increases the width of those rows, impacting the amount of storage space and decreasing the number of rows transferred on each input/output operation.

On the other hand, with some database technologies, in order to get acceptable retrieval performance, the developer may violate the logical model at the cost of greater maintenance effort. However, the denormalized model may take so many maintenance hours that the size and scope of the data warehouse may need to be constrained to provide normal workday availability.

The nonvolatility of the warehouse means that there is no inserting, deleting, replacing, or changing of data on a record-by-record basis, as is the case in the operational environment. At the design level, for example, there is no need to be cautious about update anomaly. It follows that normalization of the physical database design loses its importance, because the design focuses on optimized access of data. Other issues that simplify data warehouse design involve the nonpresence of transaction and data integrity as well as detection and remedy of deadlocks, which are found in every operational database environment.

Effective and efficient use of the data warehouse necessitates that the data warehouse run on a separate platform from other major systems. If it does not, it will slow down the operational database and reduce response time significantly.

Data Transformation

In this stage, utilities and programming software are developed, which will enable the data warehouse database to be loaded and maintained. Data is located, extracted, conditioned, scrubbed, and loaded onto the target platform. The time required for performing the data transformation function will vary and is based on the amount of data, the source of the data, and its condition.

A transformation tool may be used to make the transformation easier and less time-consuming; however, there are some transformations and quality checks they will not perform. There is also a significant amount of construction and testing required for the programs that run these utilities. These programs need to use the correct generations of source data, execute on the timing when that data is available, and have the capability to recover from reruns. Additional quality control may be required.

Before data loading can be performed, the physical database design must be in place, and the operation planning that allows the reloading or incremental loading of the data warehouse on a periodic basis must be available.

Client/Server Application Development

This development process provides the implementation of applications for the query interface for a data warehousing solution, utilizing the prototypes, specifications, recommended tool-sets, and other outputs of the application design. The applications that allow end users to access the data and information they need to perform their business functions will also be developed.

Training and documentation that describes the tools and data content being made available to solve business problems are provided to users at the same time. Business members of the project team can assist in developing and documenting the productive methodologies for utilizing this new business information and analysis resource.

Data Warehouse Management

Planning the data warehouse management function is an important element of the overall planning process that implements the data, network, systems, and operations management procedures necessary to manage the environment successfully, and includes the following action items:

- Emergency operating procedures
- Administration of users and database space allocation
- Back-up and archiving of system and applications tables
- Security maintenance and auditing
- Procedures for restoring/recovery of individual tables, databases, or the entire system
- Usage reporting
- Operation of in-box and out-of-box replication
- Application and table/view version control
- System and application error analysis and resolution
- Establishing service level goals and reporting performance versus goals
- Monitoring tools and procedures for identifying service level issues such as tables locked by applications and runaway queries

During the initial construction of a data warehouse, a procedure should be established for setting up, documenting, and testing each of these processes, to ensure that they will provide the management functionality to maintain an active, well-managed data warehouse.

Elements Of Database Technology

Database software has been a rapidly evolving technology and is another key component of the data warehouse, and ultimately a CRM strategy. There are a number of vendors with proven products that will run in a data warehouse environment, enabling organizations to access and manipulate customer data. This latter process is the second major stage in the implementation of a CRM strategy and one that brings the CRM solution closer to meeting the corporate objectives described in detail in Chapter 2 of this Handbook.

Although there are several viable database management systems that can be used, as with most software products, vendors typically market and sell the product that is in the final development stages and ready for its first release. There are always implementation glitches, or even worse, code that just does not work. To avoid a data warehouse project failure, it is important to exercise extreme care in the selection of the database technology and the vendor that will support it.

Every method of verifying the status of a database product under evaluation should be utilized in the selection process — benchmarking (as applicable), reviewing other active, successful customer installations, conducting independent research analyses, meeting with user groups, and analyzing independent consultant reports.

The selected database vendors listed at the end of this chapter have established credentials in data warehousing and CRM over a number of years, and can provide customer testimonials to support the successful application of their products. The case studies in CRM analyzed in Chapter 4 include solutions provided by some of these vendors.

Determining Database Requirements

Determining database requirements is one of the critical areas of data warehousing. Selecting a database with the rationale that it is the company standard is a criterion sometimes used by organizations for two simple reasons: (1) it is expedient, and (2) it eliminates the need for support staff to learn another database.

This process should be avoided, and the database software should be selected on its merits, because it meets the objectives of the data warehouse and subsequent delivery of the CRM solution.

A second aspect of the database selection process is to understand the limits of the requirements for the relational database management system (RDBMS). Most of the RDBMSs available are based on online transaction processing. These products can handle operational data warehouse (ODW), a data warehousing architecture described previously, and typically have short but high transactional volumes, a response time requirement, and a very limited amount of historical data.

These characteristics contrast very clearly with the informational data warehouse (IDW), which has long, low transactional volumes, no real response time requirement, and a large amount of historical data. The access characteristics of these two different data warehouse environments are completely different from one another. Database management systems need to differentiate between an ODW and an IDW, and it is important in selecting the RDBMS to be aware of how it is architected to provide effective data access to either or even both data warehouse configurations.

Because a data warehouse is subject oriented, the first design step involves choosing business areas to be modeled and based on the following characteristics:

- The business process that needs to be modeled
- The facts that need to be extracted from the operational database
- The level of detail required
- Characteristics of the facts (e.g., dimension, attribute, and cardinality)

After each of these areas has been thoroughly investigated and more information about facts, dimension, attributes, and sparseness of data has been obtained, still another decision must be made. The question now becomes which *schema* to use for the design of the data warehouse database. There are two major options: (1) the classic star schema and (2) the snowflake schema.

The Star Schema

In the star design schema, a separate table is used for each dimension and a single large table is used for the facts. The fact table's indexed key comprises the keys of the different dimension tables.

With this schema, the problem of sparseness of data, or the creation of empty rows, is avoided by not creating records where combinations are invalid. Users are able to follow paths for detailed drill-downs and summary roll-ups. Because the dimension tables are also relatively small, precalculated aggregation can be embedded within the fact table to provide extremely fast response times. It is also possible to apply multiple hierarchies against the same fact table, which leads to the development of a flexible and useful set of data.

The Snowflake Schema

The snowflake schema is best used when there are large dimensions such as time. The dimension table is split at the attribute level to provide a greater variety of combinations. The breakup of the time dimension into a quarter entity and a month entity provides more detailed aggregation and also more exact information.

The Business Tools: Analytical CRM

Data mining and analytical tools are the third major technology components of the CRM solution, as noted in Chapter 2. In combination with the data warehouse and database technology, these software tools assist in increasing the return on investment (ROI) on the data already stored. In addition, they allow organizations to target customers based on behavior patterns, rather than just grouping or segmenting them according to products they buy, age, or other personal characteristics, highlighting cross-selling opportunities and pinpointing the most profitable client profiles. Moreover, analytical applications are critical for optimizing collaborative interactions, not only with customers, but also with employees, suppliers, and partners, and ensuring improvements throughout the entire supply chain.

Integrate Front- and Back-Office Systems

It is important for the project development team to be able to act on the intelligence gained from the data through integration with front-end systems. The results of automated data mining processes should feed into marketing and sales force automation programs through one or another communication channel.

Conversely, customer information gained at the front office should be continually fed back into the data repository. The more integrated the process, the closer the organization is to achieving one of the key objectives of the CRM solution: a single view of the customer throughout the organization.

Necessary Data

The most sophisticated, visionary, and strategic direct marketing campaign will fail at the first hurdle if it applies customer data that is not relevant. Analysts and marketers must agree on the data needed to resolve current business issues. Extraction and cleansing of data is a costly and time-consuming exercise, so it is vital to get it right the first time.

Business templates built up from experience over time, e.g., a template view of the data needed for a churn campaign, are valuable starting points. They will differ greatly from that for a cross-selling campaign. In some cases, it may be necessary to supplement internal consumer data with external data — income, household information, and life stage details, all of which help to complete the customer profile.

These templates must be amalgamated to provide one unique view of the customer, and continually updated by ongoing inputs from all points of customer interaction. The ideal is to have data that is as up-to-date as possible so that the customer profile contains real-time information. Once this central repository has been established, data mining tools and techniques can be used to analyze the data and create different data models for specific, defined business issues.

Establish Data Standards

Set standards for the format of data in the warehouse — consistent formatting reduces complications for data extraction. Insist on the highest quality data from the beginning of the data input stage, to ensure the data warehouse becomes populated with valid data. Apart from the obvious advantages, accurate data promotes acceptance of the new CRM system by delivering reliable and actionable results.

Many CRM deployments are thwarted by faulty, inconsistent data that prevents users from having a clear, unified profile of each customer. Disjointed data, blanks in some of the critical fields, and broken business rules are a few of the ways in which data can be corrupted, resulting in data integrity problems.

Integrating customer datasets is a challenge for any organization that wants to achieve a single view of the customer, with inputs from various departments — ordering, shipping, manufacturing — that have customer contact and therefore customer data to contribute to the database. In a typical financial institution or insurance company, there could be 50 to 150 different systems containing customer information, and to have a single view of each customer to establish value levels and meet customer needs, this data must be combined.

This process of combining and integrating data to obtain a complete, current customer profile requires assembling different data stores with data of varying ages and on different databases, and usually involves multiple programming languages and data formats. There is vendor software available that can assist in assembling and analyzing data before it gets stored in the data warehouse. Typically, these products locate different relationships in customer data from multiple sources, irrespective of source code and documentation, and provide information on how to clean and restructure the data.

Automate the Decision-Making Process

Automate as much of the decision-making process as possible, from the extraction of the data to campaign management. For example, intelligent agents can be used to monitor variances in customer's behavior to predict key customer events. Intelligent agents can inform the marketing department when the customers are likely to leave, based on existing characteristics and changed behavior.

A typical direct mail campaign generates a response rate under three percent, making the cost per contact extremely high. A better understanding of customer behavior can have a dramatic impact on the response to a direct mail campaign. For example, a Netherlands-based bank has used a CRM system to increase response to an impressive and cost-effective 50 percent, thanks to data mining, a key component of analytical CRM.

Data Clustering Offers New Insights

Cluster analysis is an exploratory data analysis tool that uses statistical algorithms to identify distinct groups of customers that may not traditionally group together. It is used not only in segmentation for independent validation of business assumptions, but also to discover new interrelationships between variables that were previously not available.

These clusters act as virtual account managers, pinpointing changes in an individual customer's behavior likely to lead to a specific outcome regarding future behavior patterns. The true power of these intelligent agents lies in their capacity to be deployed on a large scale. Many agents continuously and independently monitoring the behavior of each and every market segment can deliver more valuable results than detailed studies of individual segments.

Data Warehouse Support and Enhancement

Once all the components have been developed and acquired, turning these components into an enterprisewide resource for a CRM solution is the next step. This phase establishes the blueprint for ongoing support and operation of the data warehouse.

Just as the building of the data warehouse is an iterative process, the integration of new applications and tools into the production environment is also an ongoing process. This phase has the following major components and can be conducted by an outside consultant or an internal support team that may be independent of the data warehousing project team:

- *Solution integration* — final testing and installation of tools and applications warehouse
- *Data warehouse management* — administration of users, space, backup/ recovery, and usage reporting
- *Enterprise system support* — coordination with other company operations
- *Data warehouse capacity planning* — growth projections in system utilization and budgeting for upgrades
- *Logical database review* — periodic review to validate the physical data model
- *Physical database review* — periodic review to validate the physical data model
- *Modifying performance* — resolve performance issues with specific applications or queries
- *System audit* — identify business value and recommend changes

The following subsections describe the activities of each component in detail.

Solution Integration

Where there is an existing data warehouse, this activity will integrate the new application components and tools with the existing system, and will involve these functions:

- *Duration of table maintenance activities of the new system* — processing may need to contend with other applications in the overnight batch windows and if 24-hour access is required, an alternate table may be built and brought online
- *Dependencies on the processing of other systems* — establishing correct scheduling information in the system's automatic job scheduler
- *Host software installation* — moving jobs and executable programs from development areas to production areas
- *Capacity impact* — monitoring and scheduling new jobs with critical storage and processing requirements
- *Client software installation* — testing to ensure that installing and removing software is properly managed, and that network setup enables users to access the data warehouse
- *Final documentation revisions* — ensuring that user and systems documentation are current and accurately define processes
- *Identification of change procedures* — verifying system procedures for maintaining the system
- *Establishment of help desk procedures* — providing ongoing user support

This solution integration process is executed jointly by the development team and data warehouse support personnel.

Enterprise System Support

This support activity involves integrating the hardware operations into the IT department operation and includes procedures for start-up and shutdown of data warehousing hardware, maintenance of support accounts, and identification of hardware problems such as the failure of a disk drive, a power supply, or other hardware component. If goals are not being met, steps to correct the problem need to be documented. A central organization should monitor the space allocated and used by the different databases in conjunction with capacity planning activities.

Depending on the database product selected for the data warehouse, striping of physical disks may be required, as well as establishment of table spaces across the stripes, and allocation of permanent, temporary, log, and index areas across different table spaces.

When space requirements change, the database may need to be recreated and reloaded. During normal operations, the table and indexes may need to be rebuilt to get the entries back into logical = physical sequence. Depending on the size of the tables and the speed of the system, this could mean coordinating a process that makes the system unavailable for hours or even days, and requires careful scheduling to avoid impacting users.

Logical Design Review

A logical design review examines and analyzes the requirements with the user, along with their execution, and offers analysis and suggestions for improvement. This review validates and examines the data warehouse design for correctness of technique and the ability to meet performance, quality, and business requirements.

Physical Database Design Review

A physical database design review is performed to review user requirements, along with their execution, and to offer analysis and suggestions for improvement where the physical database is involved.

Data Warehouse Tuning

For organizations with an existing production environment, this activity may be required when performance problems are encountered or perceived. In this situation, a detailed analysis needs to be done to pinpoint the source or sources of the problem. This analysis will examine the network, applications, users, and structure of the database, utilization of the system, and other areas. Detailed analysis is necessary to accurately tune the actual operating environment.

Data Warehouse Audit

The organization may bring in an independent consultant to provide another point of view and experience, and to audit the performance of the system, as well as examine and report on other specific functions of the system. The purpose of the audit is to ascertain the business value of the data warehouse by validating the current state of the system against best practices and recommending changes where necessary, that will ultimately maximize and rebalance the system, if required, to ensure business value.

The areas of assessment include:

- Flexibility and extensibility of the database design
- Data richness, consistency, and consumer access
- Use of third-party extraction and conditioning tools
- Use of summary tables
- Audit of the operational aspects of the data warehousing environment

Data Warehousing Architectures: Options

Data warehousing has evolved from a relatively simple concept involving the collection and storage of data that could be used by organizations to gain knowledge about their customers, to a much higher-level, more complex, core corporate business strategy. This strategy envisions a system that not only collects and stores information, but also provides the tools to enable businesses to use this information to manage customer relationships in a manner that will benefit both the customer and the corporation. This enterprisewide capability enables organizations to gain competitive advantage in their individual markets, through improvements in all aspects of customer relationship management.

The original concept of a data warehouse was a single, enterprisewide system that stored all corporate data for access by users throughout the organization. However, the real world of data warehouse and data mart system implementation has evolved to a point where the technology is being applied in several different forms to meet different application requirements and varying corporate objectives.

This Handbook focuses on the planning, development, and implementation of the enterprise data warehouse (EDW) option, because this is the data warehousing technology that has been demonstrated to provide the broadest and most effective CRM solution. The EDW is the repository for data from enterprisewide sources, as well as from any other source of customer data, and in its final form represents the totality of up-to-date customer data — demographic, transactional, and current, real-time information from all customer touchpoints.

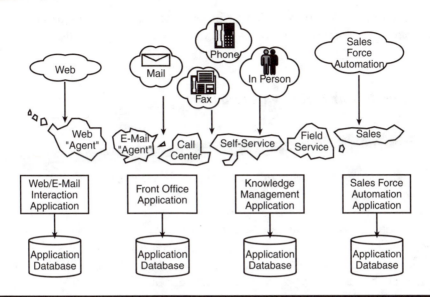

Exhibit 12. The First Wave of CRM: Information Islands

Another definition of the EDW is that it is a common and unique repository for enterprise information. It is a read-only environment made up of detailed and aggregated data that is fully cleansed and integrated; and it includes an extensive detailed history of transaction level data. Architecturally, the enterprise data warehouse delivers a single, integrated version of customer data, primarily through subset, or dependent, data marts (see Exhibit 12).

The advantages of EDW architecture are as follows:

- Presents a single version of customer data
- Provides one set of extraction processes and business rules
- Uses common semantics
- Offers a centralized, controlled environment
- Enables easy creation and population of subset data marts
- Designed with a single metadata repository

The disadvantages of EDW architecture are:

- Extremely resource intensive
- High cost to implement
- Requires enterprise-scale systems and resources
- Risk of storing all corporate data in one system

An overview of some of the other categories of specialty data warehouses, with a brief description of the pros and cons, is also provided in this section. The purpose of the overview is to indicate the range of data warehousing technology and applications that have evolved over the past several years, and to introduce IS professionals to these optional data warehousing architectures.

In addition, two different development scenarios — (1) top-down and (2) bottom-up — are described, as are the advantages and disadvantages of each one.

Special Function Data Warehouses

Two of the special-function data warehouses, with brief descriptions of the advantages and disadvantages are described below:

1. Federated Data Warehouse/Data Mart (FDW/FDM)
2. Incremental Architected Data Mart (ADM)

Other specialized data warehouses that have evolved and been implemented in some organizations are not included in this Handbook, because they do not meet the criteria required for full implementation of the CRM solution by maximizing the use of customer data throughout the enterprise. These other data warehouses include the data stage/data mart (DSDM) and the distributed data warehouse/distributed data mart (DDW/DDM) architectures.

Federated Data Warehouse/Federated Data Mart (FDW/FDM)

In many organizations, multiple teams undertake data warehouse projects, resulting in multiple data warehouse systems across the enterprise. Although there can really be only one enterprise data warehouse, with all other entities being subsets or incremental data marts, few organizations have strictly defined their systems in these terms, so that many enterprises around the world will have two, six, or a dozen or more data warehouse systems.

One of these specialty warehouses, the next evolution of the EDW architecture, is a federated system of data warehouses or data marts (FDW/FDM), a data warehousing solution that offers many of the features of the EDW. The FDW/FDM architecture is marked by the characteristics of sharing common data points among multiple data warehouse or data marts, eliminating redundancy and ensuring a consistent and unique version of complete customer data throughout the organization.

Advantages of FDW/DM architecture are as follows:

- Common semantics and business rules
- A single set of extraction processes
- Decentralized resources and control
- Parallel development process

The disadvantages of FDW/DM architecture are:

- Difficulty in coordinating efforts
- Political and ownership issues among departments
- Agreement required on architecture, business rules, and semantics
- Complex technical environment
- Need for multiple metadata repositories

Non-Architected Data Marts

The goal of achieving a true EDW is a challenging one, and as a result, organizations often take short-cuts in an effort to deploy some form of data warehouse and to derive business benefit from the capabilities of these systems. Unfortunately, as noted throughout this chapter, these short-form data warehouses are not capable of providing the full functionality of an EDW, because they do not gather and store all customer data, are not capable of being integrated with other data resources, and often do not operate in real-time.

These quick and dirty data marts are not architected in a structured manner, and typically their development and implementation do not follow a recognized, formal process. They quickly become legacy systems — single, stand-alone sources of information that frequently add to business problems and do not provide solutions. These legacy data marts, or "legamarts" as they are often referred to in the literature, are marked by multiple extraction processes, multiple business rules, lack of architecture, and multiple versions of customer information.

Advantages of legamarts are as follows:

- Rapid deployment
- Low cost

Disadvantages of legamarts are:

- Several versions of semantics
- Multiple versions of data
- Multiple extraction processes
- Many and varied business rules
- Difficult to integrate with source OLTP systems

To overcome the defects of the EDW/FDW, and at the same time avoid the problems inherent in a legamart, an alternative architecture has evolved, referred to as "incremental architected data marts" (ADM). The ADM is constructed data mart by data mart in the context of an enterprise data mart architecture (EDMA). It is typical that a modern, enterprise-class tool is used to facilitate an "extract once, populate many" strategy of populating the incremental ADMs.

Advantages of the ADM are:

- Common semantics and business rules
- Single set of extraction processes
- Practical project scope
- Inherently incremental

Disadvantages of the ADM are:

- Most effective when using an enterprise class tool
- Requires enterprise data mart architecture (EDMA)
- Requires compliance with EDMA by all teams

Implementing the Enterprise Data Warehouse

As mentioned above, the two basic routes to the goal of the EDW are top-down or bottom-up. In a top-down scenario, the EDW is architected, designed, and constructed in an iterative manner. In a bottom-up scenario, a series of incremental architected data marts is created, which form the basis of the resulting EDW.

Top-Down EDW

An EDW is composed of multiple subject areas, such as finance, human resources, marketing, sales, and manufacturing. In a top-down scenario, the entire EDW is architected, and then a small slice of a subject area is chosen for construction.

Subsequent slices are constructed, until the entire EDW is complete. The typical EDW project, from the perspectives of time and cost, is illustrated as follows: a typical project will take from three to four years to complete from initial conception to final launch date, and the cost for a mid-size organization will be in the $3–4 million range. Larger global organizations should expect to spend $10–50 million to build the initial EDW, which will most likely be FDW architecture.

EDW Phased Subject Area Development

While the top-down approach was the first method to be used in the development of data warehouses, and remains the best and most sophisticated design process for a data warehouse, there are many challenges in the successful completion of such a large project.

There are several factors contributing to the challenges involved in this process, including:

- Competing internal business requirements
- Tight deadlines
- Out-of-date source systems
- Varying and conflicting user demands
- Ineffective or faulty business analysis tools
- Instilling changes in corporate culture

These challenges need to be addressed and managed in the decision-making stages, where the future of an organization's data warehousing and ultimate CRM strategy is decided. There is no technical reason for avoiding a full-scale EDW implementation — proven technologies are available to ensure its success, if reasonable and rational planning, evaluation, selection, and development processes are followed.

In addition to the major challenges listed above, the EDW project has an all-pervading aspect, because it is enterprisewide, and by its nature requires that the EDW team cross many corporate boundaries: departmental, political, functional, departmental, process, ownership, organizational, and geographic.

Meeting these challenges successfully requires a tremendous level of technical, business, and political acumen, characteristics that need to be represented in the makeup of the EDW team.

Despite these challenges, a top-down approach provides two key advantages from an implementation perspective:

- Coordinated environment
- Single point of control and development

The disadvantages of a top-down approach are:

- Time required to analyze problems and complete project
- Difficulty controlling the project
- Enterprisewide nature of the project
- High risk

Bottom-Up EDW

To achieve the significant benefits of data warehousing and avoid the challenges inherent with the top-down model development process, some corporate data warehousing teams developed a bottom-up approach to achieve the objectives of an EDW. In the bottom-up approach, an EDMA is developed to provide a context and foundation for further development.

While it takes in the entire system scope at a high level, it is not as detailed as an EDW system architecture, so the long and time-consuming emphasis on analysis (often referred to as "analysis paralysis"), so common to many top-down processes, is avoided.

Once the EDMA is complete, an initial pilot project is undertaken with one business department or group, for the first incremental ADM, to validate the process. The EDMA is expanded in this area to include the full range of detail required for the design and development of the incremental ADM. Subsequent phases fill in the EDMA, until the team and the organization is ready to construct the EDW.

This bottom-up approach has an important benefit to the organization, because its allows the project team to develop the skills and techniques required for data warehousing in a much lower-risk and lower-exposure environment than a full-scale EDW project. Incremental ADMs are much quicker to develop than EDWs, and it typically takes only six to nine months to develop the first ADM, while the first phase of an EDW project may take twelve to eighteen months. The reduced time to market is especially important to demonstrate the return on investment (ROI) and intrinsic value of data warehousing to an organization.

From the project management standpoint, incremental ADMs greatly assist in keeping the team focused, whereas EDW teams tend to attempt to solve tomorrow's problems today, building generalist systems that may lead to many project delays and slipped deadlines. In contrast, incremental ADMs are built to solve specific problems for the business, focusing on one business problem at a time.

Cost is rarely a deciding factor once an organization has committed to a data warehouse as an initial stage in moving toward a CRM solution. However, incremental ADMs are less costly to develop than an EDW; a scalable, industrial-strength ADM can be constructed for about 20 to 30 percent, or less, of the cost of a full EDW.

Advantages of a bottom-up approach are:

- Lower risk and exposure
- Incremental design
- Lower-level, shorter-term political will required
- Quicker delivery
- More focused
- Faster ROI

Disadvantages of a bottom-up approach are:

- EDMA required to integrate incremental data marts
- Success may swamp allocated resources
- Needs multiple team coordination

Analyzing the Organization

In considering the design and development approach to take in initiating a data warehousing project, it is important to recognize that there is no one best solution or architecture that will meet every organization's requirement and fit the corporate culture and environment. Undoubtedly, because of the differences in organizational cultures, even within the same business sectors, there will be different approaches from one organization to another. Therefore, before an organization makes a decision on which particular approach to follow in the data warehousing development process, the characteristics and corporate objectives of that organization must be fully understood — including the following high-level aspects:

- Business objectives within its market environment
- Level of technology competence
- Capability and corporate will to adopt a CRM solution

One approach to analyzing an organization, to determine its characteristics in the development of a data warehouse and subsequent CRM strategy, is to categorize the organization as to thinking and acting. Does the organization Think Globally — Act Globally? Or does it Think Globally — Act Locally? Or, alternatively, does it Think Locally — Act Locally?

The first pioneers in data warehousing were in the Think Globally — Act Globally camp. These organizations made huge investments in technology and realized important competitive advantages or productivity gains. Early EDW adopters skewed the perceptions of analysts and some vendor organizations, which believed the entire data warehousing market would move in this direction.

However, as the market has developed, it has become apparent that a majority of organizations are in the Think Globally — Act Locally group. The entry of major software providers into the data warehousing market, with very low price points, scalable, packaged solutions, has expanded this segment of the market.

Once the nature of the organization has been determined, the next step is to evaluate specific criteria: time, cost, risk, impact, resources, ROI parameters, and the scale and politics of the business problems that need to be solved. These criteria can be ranked to develop a weighted score based on priorities and internal political realities. In developing this weighting, it is critical to recognize that internal political issues and other soft issues are more critical to long-term success or failure than any hard, technology issues associated with the data warehouse or data mart system. These issues are also important to the success of the ultimate CRM strategy which evolves from the selected top-down or bottom-up process.

The top-down data warehousing development process will be more successful if the organization has the following characteristics:

- Management acceptance of the long-term ROI benefits from major projects
- Appropriate level of human and technology resources

On the other hand, the bottom-up, incremental ADM development process will be most successful where the evaluation reveals an organization with these characteristics:

- Management with short-term goals
- Small-scale, corporate culture
- Need to demonstrate measurable ROI very quickly

Challenges for the EDW Project Team

The project team, empowered with the decision-making authority as to which method to adopt, must be objective in its decision. While both approaches are viable and have been proven in thousands of sites around the world, the opportunities for success will be slim if the approach selected does not match the organization's characteristics.

The bottom-up approach breaks down the task and delivers only a small subset of the data warehouse. New pieces are then phased in until the entire organization is modeled. The bottom-up approach lets data warehouse technology be quickly delivered to a part of the organization. This approach is recommended because its time demands are not as rigorous. It also allows development team members to learn as they implement the system, identify bottlenecks and shortfalls, and find out how to avoid them as additional parts of the data warehouse are delivered.

The development of an EDW is a major corporate undertaking, and as has been emphasized elsewhere in this Handbook, requires a complete commitment from senior management, as well as a significant commitment of funds and human resources.

These systems take a long time to develop — a few to several years, and may not demonstrate an ROI for some years. To fend off competing initiatives, maintain resources, funding, sponsorship, and the commitment of the organization, the project must be supported by political will at the CEO/managing director level. The sustaining of political will, in the face of ever-changing executives, the shifting sands of corporate priorities, and constantly growing demands for resources, often prove to be challenges as significant as any technology challenges faced by an EDW project team.

Decision Support Systems and Data Warehousing

Many vendors offer decision support system (DSS) products, and information on how to implement them abounds; therefore, some insight into the different technologies available is useful in the analysis of data warehousing/data mart requirements leading to a CRM solution. Three concepts should be evaluated in terms of their usability for decision support and relationship to the so-called "real data warehouse." They are:

1. Virtual data warehouse
2. Multidimensional online analytical processing (OLAP)
3. Relational OLAP

Virtual Data Warehouse

The virtual data warehouse promises to deliver the same benefits as a real data warehouse but without the associated amount of work and difficulty. The virtual data warehouse concept can be subdivided into the surround data warehouse and the OLAP/data mart warehouse. In a surround data warehouse, legacy systems are surrounded with methods to access data without a fundamental change of the operational data. The surround concept negates a key feature of the real data warehouse, which integrates operational data in a way that allows users to use it to meet business analysis objectives.

In addition, the data structure of a virtual data warehouse does not lend itself to DSS processing. Legacy operational systems were built to ease updating, writing, and deleting, and not with simple data extraction in mind. Another deficiency with this technology is the minimal amount of historical data that is stored, usually only 60 to 90 days of information. A real data warehouse,

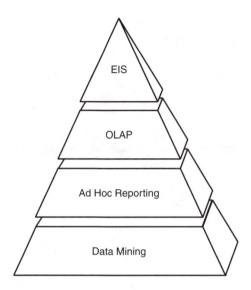

Exhibit 13.   User Access to the Data Warehouse

on the other hand, with its two to five years of stored data, provides a far superior means of analyzing trends.

In the case of direct OLAP/data marts, legacy data is transferred directly to the OLAP/data mart environment. Although this approach recognizes the need to remove data from the operational environment, it too falls short of being a real data warehouse. If only a few, small applications were feeding a data mart, the approach would be acceptable. The reality is, however, that there are many applications and thus many OLAP/data mart environments, each requiring a customized interface, especially as the number of OLAP/data marts increases.

Because the different OLAP/data marts are not effectively integrated, different users arrive at different conclusions when analyzing the data. In this situation, it is possible for the marketing department to report that business is doing fine and another department to report just the opposite. This drawback does not exist with the real data warehouse, where all data is integrated. Users who examine the data at a certain point in time will all make the same decisions because they will all be using the same data (see Exhibit 13).

Multidimensional Online Analytical Processing (OLAP)

Multidimensional database technology is a definite step up from the virtual data warehouse. It is designed for executives and analysts who want to look at data from different perspectives and have the ability to examine summarized and detailed data. When implemented together with a data warehouse, multidimensional database technology provides more efficient and faster access to corporate data. Proprietary multidimensional databases facilitate the organization of data hierarchically in multiple dimensions, allowing users to make advanced analyses of small portions of data from the data warehouse. The technology is understandably embraced by many in the industry because of its increased usability and superior analytical functionality.

As a stand-alone technology, multidimensional OLAP is inferior to a real data warehouse for a variety of reasons. The main drawback is that the technology is not able to handle more than 20 to 30 gigabytes of data, which is unacceptable for most larger corporations, where data storage needs range from 100 gigabytes to several terabytes.

Furthermore, multidimensional databases do not have the flexibility and measurability required of today's decision support systems because they do not support the necessary ad hoc creation of multidimensional views of products and customers. Multidimensional databases should be considered for use in smaller organizations or on a departmental level only.

Relational OLAP

Relational OLAP is also used with many decision support systems and provides sophisticated analytical capability in conjunction with a data warehouse. Unlike multidimensional database technology, relational OLAP lets end users define complex multidimensional views and analyze them. These advantages are only possible if certain functionalities are incorporated into the relational OLAP.

Users must be removed from the process of generating their own structured query language (SQL). Multiple SQL statements should be generated by the system for every analysis request to the data warehouse, so that a set of business measurements (e.g., comparison and ranking measurements) is established, a process that is essential to the appropriate use of the technology. The shortcoming of relational OLAP technology works well in conjunction with a data warehouse. However, by itself, the technology is limited.

An analysis of the three preceding decision support technologies leads to the conclusion that the data warehouse is still the most suitable technology for larger firms.

Integrated, cleansed data from legacy systems, together with historical information about the business, makes a properly implemented data warehouse the primary choice for decision support.

Database Management Systems

In a repetitive processing environment, most relational database management system (RDBMS) tools can perform the functions required, because of the ease of predictability of results. However, iterative processing tends to be more unpredictable and requires a much more sophisticated database management system that is designed to handle the real-time data query environment of an operational data warehouse.

Many performance decisions traditionally made by database designers, administrators, and application developers are made by untrained users and automated tools. Detailed data demands a much larger online environment than for these traditional situations and adds another level of complexity to the selection and implementation of an RDBMS that will meet the objectives of the CRM system.

The capability of the RDBMS to handle the business information workload will depend on four characteristics:

1. Complexity of the data model
2. Number of concurrent users
3. Data volumes
4. Complexity of the processing environment

Complexity of the Data Model

Iterative processing is capable of running against any data in the warehouse. Therefore, the data must be modeled to match the business, rather than for a specific set of applications. The database model that results from this condition is referred to as a "third-normal form" model, and is very complex, placing considerable stress on a DBMS.

In a data warehousing environment, every data modeling concession made for performance will leave some questions unanswered. Unanswered questions mean unaddressed business issues and a more difficult support environment.

Number of Concurrent Users

A data warehouse may have a mix of iterative and repetitive users at any given time, and the number and mix of users are important characteristics from a system performance perspective. In the discussion of product selection methodologies, it was pointed out that benchmarking has some limitations, and one of them is that it does not adequately simulate the case where there are multiple users of different types.

Data Volumes

Data volume is a critical element affecting the selection of the database management system, because some products may have bottlenecks that do not show up at lower data volumes. The amount of data may significantly impact the capability of the system to load data within a batch window. For example, the inability to meet batch windows with a normalized model may require one table to be split into several smaller tables. Parsers have distinct limits, which vary by DBMS product, in determining how many tables can join in one query.

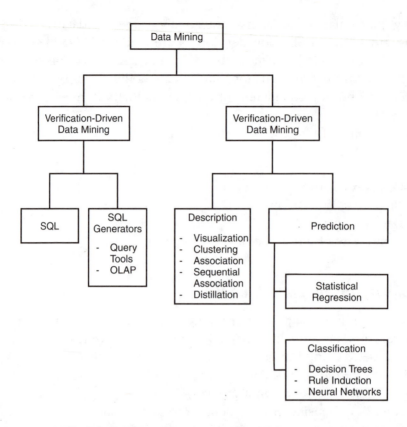

Exhibit 14. Elements and Processes of Data Mining

Complexity of the Processing Environment

The DBMS processing capability is affected by the iterative processing and detailed data, which present a more complex processing environment, particularly when the user mix may include both iterative and repetitive types. The number of users and the workload mix are crucial components of the data warehouse. Combinations of large amounts of data and large numbers of users often cause failure in a data warehouse environment and definitely increase the complexity of the processing environment.

From Data Warehousing to Data Mining

The technology of data mining is closely related to that of data warehousing and is interwoven with the database management system. Data mining involves the process of extracting large amounts of previously unknown data and then using the data to make important business decisions. The key phrase here is "unknown data," meaning data that is buried in the huge mounds of operational data that, if analyzed, provides relevant information to organizational decision makers (see Exhibit 14).

Significant data is sometimes undetected because most data is captured and maintained by a particular department. What may seem irrelevant or uninteresting at the department level may yield insights and indicate patterns important at the organizational level, in particular, customer behavior and purchasing patterns. Determining the effectiveness of sales promotions, detecting fraud, evaluating risk and assessing quality, and analyzing insurance claims are some of the areas where this information can assist decision making.

Often, data that is needed is located on several different systems, in different formats and structure, and may even be somewhat redundant. This data provides no real value to business users without some method of accessing it. This is where the data warehouse comes into play as a better source of consolidated and cleansed data, facilitating analysis much more effectively than regular flat files or operational databases.

Three steps are needed to identify and use hidden information:

1. Captured data must be incorporated into other data instead of in only one department's data store.
2. Information must be specially organized to simplify decision making.
3. Data must be analyzed or mined for valuable information.

Data Mining Techniques

Several analysis methodologies are used in data mining operations. Among the most common are the following:

- Classification
- Association
- Sequence based
- Clustering
- Estimation

Classification is the most-often employed data mining technique. It involves a set of instances or predefined examples to develop a model that can classify the population of records at large.

The use of classification algorithms begins with a sample set of preclassified example transactions. For a fraud detection application, this would include complete records of both fraudulent and valid transactions, determined on a record-by-record basis. The classifier-training algorithm uses these preclassified examples to determine the set of parameters required for proper identification. The algorithm then encodes these parameters into a model called a "classifier," or "classification model." The approach affects the decision-making capability of the system. Once an effective classifier is developed, it is used in a predictive model to classify new records automatically into these same predefined classes.

In the fraud detection case above, the classifier would be able to identify probable fraudulent activities. Another example would involve a financial application where a classifier capable of identifying risky loans could be used to aid in the decision of whether or not to grant a loan to an individual.

Association is an operation performed against a set of records — a collection of items and a set of transactions, each of which contains some number of items from a given collection. The operation returns affinities that exist among the collection of items.

Market basket analysis is a common application that uses association techniques. It is used by retailers to determine affinities among shoppers. For example, in an analysis of 100,000 transactions, association techniques could determine that 20 percent of the time, customers who buy a particular software application also purchase the complementary add-on software pack.

Association tools discover rules based on items that occur together in a given event or transaction. Another example of the use of association discovery would be an application that analyzes the claim forms submitted by patients to a medical insurance company. The goal is to discover patterns among the claimants' treatment. Assume that every claim form contains a set of medical procedures that were performed on the given patient during one visit. By defining the set of items as all medical procedures performed on a patient, and the records to correspond to each claim form, association technique can be used to find relationships among medical procedures that are often performed together.

Sequence-based analysis· is often used as a variation of the association technique when there is additional information to tie together a sequence of purchases, an account number, a credit card, or a frequent shopper number.

Rules that capture these relationships can be used to identify a typical set of precursor purchases that might predict the subsequent purchase of a specific item. In the software example above, sequence-based mining could determine the likelihood of a customer who purchases a particular software product to subsequently purchase complementary software or a hardware device such as a joystick or a video card.

Sequence-based mining can be used to detect the set of customers associated with frequent buying patterns. Use of sequence-based mining on the set of insurance claims discussed earlier can lead to the identification of frequently occurring medical procedures performed on patients. This information can then be harnessed in a fraud detection application, also discussed earlier, to detect cases of medical insurance fraud.

Clustering segments a database into different groups. The goal is to find groups that differ from one another, as well as similarities among members. The clustering approach assigns records with a large number of attributes into a relatively small set of groups or segments. This assignment process is performed automatically by clustering algorithms that identify the distinguishing characteristics of the dataset and then partition the space defined by the dataset attributes along natural boundaries. There is no need to identify the groupings desired for the attributes that should be used to segment the dataset.

Clustering is often one of the first steps in data mining analysis. It identifies groups of related records that can be used as starting points for exploring further relationships. This technique supports the development of population segmentation models, such as demographic-based customer segments. Additional analysis using standard analytical and other data mining techniques can determine the characteristics of these segments with respect to some desired outcome. For example, the buying habits of multiple population segments might be compared to determine which segments to target for a new marketing campaign.

Estimation is a variation on the classification technique. Essentially, it involves the generation of scores along various dimensions in the data. Rather than employing a binary classifier to determine whether a loan applicant, for instance, is approved or classified as a risk, the estimation approach generates a credit-worthiness score based on a prescored sample set of transactions. That is, sample data (complete records of approved and risk applicants) are used as samples in determining the worthiness of all records in a dataset.

Data Mining: Exploring Corporate Assets

Data mining is a process that is very dependent on the underlying technologies — data warehouses, data marts, database management systems, business analysis tools — and is used to uncover previously obscure or unknown patterns and relationships in very large databases. The ultimate goal is to arrive at comprehensible, meaningful results from extensive analysis of information. For companies with very large and complex databases, discovery-based data mining approaches must be implemented in order to realize the complete value that data offers. True data mining tools automatically uncover trends, patterns, and relationships.

The success of data mining depends on having correct, up-to-date data. The most advanced data mining tools and algorithms will not compensate for data that is incomplete, outdated, or inaccurate.

Companies today generate and collect vast amounts of data, which they use in the ongoing process of doing business. Transaction data such as that produced by inventory, billing, shipping and receiving, and sales systems is stored in operational or departmental data stores. Although companies know that this data represents a significant competitive advantage, realizing its full potential is not a simple task. Decision makers must be able to interpret trends, identify factors, or utilize information based on clear, timely data in a meaningful format. For instance, a marketing director should be able to identify customers 18 to 24 years of age, who own notebook computers, who need or may purchase an upcoming collaboration software product. After identifying them, the director sends out advance offers, information, or product order forms to increase product presales. This is just one example of how data mining can be used to fine-tune marketing campaigns

Data Mining versus Other Business Tools

Data mining differs from other business analysis methods in several ways. One difference is in the approach that each method uses in exploring the data. Many tools support a verification-based approach in which the user hypothesizes about specific data relationships and then uses the tools to verify or refute those presumptions.

This verification-based process stems from the intuition of the user to pose the questions and refine the analysis based on the results of potentially complex queries against a database. The effectiveness of this analysis depends on several factors, the most important of which are the following:

- Ability of the user to pose appropriate questions
- Capability of tools to return results quickly
- Overall reliability and accuracy of the data being analyzed

Other available analytical tools have been optimized to address some of these issues. Query and reporting tools, such as those used in data mart or warehouse applications, let users develop queries through point-and-click interfaces. Statistical analysis packages are used by many insurance or actuarial firms to explore relationships among several variables and determine statistical significance against demographic sets. Multidimensional OLAP tools enable fast response to user inquiries through the ability to compute hierarchies of variables along dimensions such as size, color, or location.

Data mining, in contrast to these analytical tools, uses discovery-based approaches in which pattern matching and other algorithms are employed to determine the key relationships in the data. Data mining algorithms can look at numerous multidimensional data relationships concurrently, highlighting those that are dominant or exceptional.

As noted above, many other types of analytical methods rely on user intuition or on the ability to pose the right questions. Analytical methods — query tools, statistical tools, and OLAP — and the results they produce are all user-driven, while data mining is data driven, a significantly different process.

Data Mining Supports CRM Solutions

Traditional methods of data analysis involve the decision maker hypothesizing the existence of "information of interest," converting that hypothesis to a query, posing that query to the analysis tool, and interpreting the returned results with respect to the decision being made. For instance, using the previous example, a marketing director may hypothesize that notebook-owning 18- to 24-year-old customers are likely to purchase the upcoming software release. After posing the query, it is up to the individual to interpret the returned results and determine if the list represents a good group of product prospects. The quality of the extracted information is based on user interpretation of the posed query results.

The intricacies of data interrelationships, as well as the sheet size and complexity of modern data stores, necessitate more advanced analysis capabilities than those provided by verification-based data mining approaches.

The ability to automatically discover important information hidden in the data and then present it in the appropriate way is a critical complementary technology to verification-based approaches. Tools, techniques, and systems that perform these automated analysis tasks are referred to as "discovery based."

Discovery-based systems applied to the marketing director's data store may identify many groups. These groups might include 18- to 24-year-old male college students with laptops, 24- to 30-year-old female software engineers with both desktop and notebook systems, and 18- to 24-year-old customers planning to purchase portable computers within the next six months. By recognizing the marketing director's goal, the discovery-based system can identify the software engineers as the key target group by spending pattern or other variable.

Verification-based approaches, although valuable for quick, high-level decision support, such as historical queries about product sales by fiscal quarter, are insufficient for direct marketing to customers or prospects on a one-on-one basis. For companies with very large and complex databases, discovery-based data mining approaches must be implemented to realize the complete value that data offers.

Data Mining Processes: Selection and Extraction

Constructing an appropriate database to run queries against is a critical step in the data mining process. A marketing database may contain extensive tables of data from purchasing records and lifestyle data to more advanced demographic information such as census records. Not all of this data is required on a regular basis, and it should be filtered out of the query tables. Additionally, even after selecting the desired database tables, it is not always necessary to mine the contents of the entire table to identify useful information under certain conditions and for certain types of data mining techniques. For example, when creating a classification or prediction model, it may be adequate to sample the table first and then mine the sample. This is usually a faster and less expensive operation.

There are several potential sources of data that may be useful in a data mining application, including:

- Census data
- Sales records
- Mailing lists
- Demographic databases

These sources should all be explored before performing an analysis of the data. The selected data types can be organized along multiple tables. Developing a sound model involves combining parts of separate tables into a single database for mining purposes.

Data Cleansing and Transformation

Once the database tables have been selected and the data to be mined has been identified, it is usually necessary to perform certain transformations and cleansing routines on the data, as discussed previously in this chapter. Data cleansing or transformations are determined by the type of data being mined and by the data mining techniques being used.

Transformations vary from conversions of one type of data to another, such as numeric data to character data, or currency conversions, to more advanced transformations such as the application of mathematical or logical functions on certain types of data. Cleansing, on the other hand, is used to ensure reliability and accuracy of results. Data can be verified or cleansed, in order to remove duplicate entries, attach real values to numeric or alphanumeric codes, and omit incomplete records.

The clean and transformed data is subsequently mined using one or more techniques in order to extract the desired type of information. For example, to develop an accurate classification model that predicts whether or not a customer will upgrade to a new version of a software package, a decision maker must first use clustering to segment the customer database. Next, rules are applied to create a classification model automatically for each desired cluster. While mining a particular data set, it may be necessary to access additional data from a data mart or warehouse and perform additional transformations of the original data.

So-called "dirty" or inaccurate data in the mining data store must be avoided if results are to be accurate and useful. Many data mining tools include a system log or other graphical interface tool to identify erroneous data in queries, but every effort should be made prior to this stage to ensure that it does not arrive at the mining database.

There are various techniques for cleansing and transforming data to ensure its consistency, accuracy, and format, prior to inputting it into a data warehouse or data mart. Software that automates these processes is also available from vendor organizations and software developers specializing in data handling software. Some of these vendors are profiled at the end of this chapter.

Mining, Analysis, and Interpretation

In a data mining environment, data warehouse, query generators, and data interpretation components are combined with discovery-driven systems to provide the capability to automatically reveal important yet hidden data. The following tasks need to be completed to make full use of data mining:

- Create prediction and classification models
- Analyze links
- Segment databases
- Detect deviations

Creating Models

The first task, creating models, makes use of data warehouse contents to generate a model that automatically predicts desired behavior. In comparison to traditional models that use statistical techniques and linear and logical regression, discovery-driven models generate accurate models that are also more comprehensive because of their sets of if–then rules. For example, in an investment environment, the discovery-driven model can predict the performance of a particular stock to assess its suitability for an investment portfolio.

Analyzing Links

The goal of the links analysis is to establish relevant connections between database records. An example is the analysis of items that are usually purchased together, such as a washer and dryer. Such analysis can lead to more effective pricing and selling strategies.

Segmenting Databases

When segmenting databases, collections of records with common characteristics or behaviors are identified. One example is the analysis of sales for a certain time period, such as Presidents' Day or Thanksgiving weekend, to detect patterns in customer purchase behavior. For reasons discussed earlier, this is an ideal task for a data warehouse.

Detecting Deviations

The fourth and final task involves detecting deviations, the opposite of data segmentation. In this process, the goal is to identify records that vary from the norm or lie outside of any particular cluster with similar characteristics. The discovery from the cluster is then explained as normal or as a hint of a previously unknown behavior or attribute.

Modeling Techniques

There are several modeling techniques that aid data mining efforts. These techniques include:

- Creation of predictive models
- Performing supervised induction
- Association discovery
- Sequence discovery

Creating Predictive Models

The creation of a predictive model is facilitated through numerous statistical techniques and various forms of visualizations that ease the user's recognition of patterns.

Supervised Induction

With supervised induction, classification models are created from a set of records, which is referred to as the "training set." This method makes it possible to infer conclusions from one set of descriptors of the training set to the general. In other words, a rule might be produced which states that a customer who is male, lives in a certain zip code area, earns $25,000 to $30,000 per year, and is between 40 and 45 years of age, listens to the radio more than he watches TV. Therefore, he might be a possible buyer for a new camcorder. The advantage of this technique is that the patterns are based on local phenomena, whereas statistical measures check for conditions that are valid for an entire population.

Association Discovery

Association discovery allows for the prediction of the occurrence of some items in a set of records if other items are also present. For example, it is possible to identify the relationship among different medical procedures by analyzing claim forms submitted to an insurance company. With this information the prediction could be made, within a certain margin of error, that for a specific treatment protocol, the same five medications are usually required.

Sequence Discovery

Sequence discovery aids the data miner by providing information on a customer's behavior over time. If a certain person buys a VCR this week, he or she usually buys videotapes on the next purchasing occasion. The detection of such a pattern is especially important to catalog companies, because it helps them target their potential customer base more effectively with specialized advertising messages.

Data Mining Tools

The four main analytical tools used in data mining are (see Exhibit 15):

1. Neural networks
2. Decision trees
3. Rule induction
4. Data visualization

Neural Networks

A neural network consists of three interconnected layers: an input and output layer with a hidden layer between. The hidden processing layer is like the brain of the neural network because it stores or learns rules about input patterns and then produces a known set of outputs. Because the process of

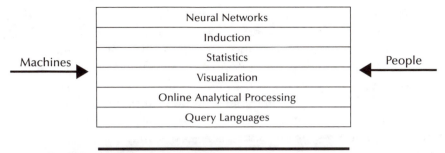

Exhibit 15. Data Mining Layers

neural networks is not transparent, it leaves the user without a clear interpretation of the resulting model.

Decision Trees

Decision trees divide data into groups based on the values of different variables. The result is often a complex hierarchy of classifying data, which enables the user to deduce possible future behavior. For instance, it might be deduced that for a person who only uses a credit card occasionally, there is a 20 percent probability that an offer for another credit card would be accepted. Although decision trees usually are faster than neural networks, they have drawbacks. One of these is the handling of data ranges as in age groups, which can inadvertently hide patterns.

Rule Induction

The method of rule induction is applied by creating nonhierarchical sets of possibly overlapping conditions. This is accomplished by first generating partial decision trees. Statistical techniques are then used to determine which decision trees to apply to the input data. This method is especially useful in cases where there are long and complex condition lists.

Data Visualization

Data visualization is not really a data mining tool; however, because it provides a picture for the user with a large number of graphically represented variables, it is a powerful tool for providing concise information. The graphics products available for data visualization make the detection of patterns much easier than when more numbers are analyzed.

Because of the pros and cons of the varied data mining tools described above, software vendors today incorporate all or some of them in their data mining software packages. Each tool is essentially a matter of looking at data with different means and from different angles.

The final step in the data mining process is analyzing and interpreting results. The extracted and transformed data is analyzed with respect to the user's goal, and the best information is identified and presented to the decision maker through the decision support system. The purpose of result interpretation is not only to represent the output of the data mining operation graphically, but also to filter the information that will be presented through the decision support system. For example, if the goal is to develop a classification model during the result interpretation step, the robustness of the extracted model is tested using one of the established methods.

If the interpreted results are not satisfactory, it may be necessary to repeat the data mining step, or to repeat other steps. This situation relates directly to the quality of data. The information extracted through data mining must be ultimately comprehensible. For example, it may be necessary, after interpreting the results of a data mining operation, to go back and add data to the selection process or to perform a different calculation during the transformation step.

Data Mining Applications

Data mining is being applied in a variety of industries ranging from investment management and retail solutions to insurance companies, and in marketing, manufacturing, and healthcare applications. It has been pointed out that many organizations, due to the strategic nature of their data mining operations, will not even discuss their projects with outsiders. This is understandable, due to the important and potential competitive benefit these successful solutions offer organizations. However, there are several well-known applications that are proven performers across the business spectrum.

In customer profiling, for example, characteristics of good customers are identified with the goal of predicting which other customers will become good customers, and of assisting marketing departments to target new prospects. Data mining can find patterns in a customer database that can be applied to a prospect database so that customer acquisition can be appropriately targeted. For example, by identifying good candidates for mail offers or catalogs, direct-mail marketing managers can reduce expenses and increase their sales generation efforts. Targeting specific promotions to existing and potential customers offers similar benefits.

Market basket analysis helps retailers understand which products are purchased together by an individual over time. With data mining, retailers can determine which products to stock in which stores and how to place them within a store. Data mining can also help assess the effectiveness of promotions and coupons.

Another application of data mining is fraud detection, which is of great benefit to credit card companies, insurance firms, stock exchanges, government agencies, and telecommunications firms. The aggregate total for fraud losses in today's world is enormous, but with data mining these companies can identify potentially fraudulent transactions and contain damage.

Financial companies use data mining to determine market and industry characteristics as well as to predict individual company and stock performance.

Another interesting niche application is in the medical field. Data mining can help predict the effectiveness of surgical procedures, diagnostic tests, medication, and other services.

As the previous examples indicate, data mining has numerous applications across a broad spectrum of business sectors, and with a data warehouse installed and operational, the elements for applying data mining techniques are present. However, unlike the plug-and-play, out-of-the-box business solutions that are popular, data mining is not a simple application. It involves considerable forethought, planning, research, and testing to ensure a sound, reliable, and beneficial project. It is also important to remember that data mining is complementary to traditional query and analysis tools, data warehousing, and data mart applications. It does not replace these useful and often vital solutions.

Data Mining: Summing Up

Data mining enables organizations to take full advantage of the investment they have made and are currently making in building data stores. By identifying valid, previously unknown information from large databases, decision makers can tap into the unique opportunities that data mining offers.

For those organizations that have adopted data mining and integrated the required processes into their corporate environments as a component of their CRM strategies, the benefits have proven to be significant, fully justifying the investment of time, money, and resources these companies have committed.

Data Consistency and Quality

The economic benefits of the data warehouse are linked directly to the quality of data that is stored and will be stored over the years to come. Unfortunately, some data warehouses have become data pits into which data disappears, never to be seen again.

This is not surprising, because in many companies the concern for data quality in regard to legacy and transaction systems is not a priority. Accordingly, when it comes to ensuring the quality of data being moved into the warehouse, many companies continue with their old practices.

This can turn out to be a costly mistake and has already led to many failures of corporate data warehousing projects. As more and more companies are making use of these strategic database systems, data quality must become a high priority for all parties involved with the data warehousing project.

Data: A Corporate Asset

Poor quality of data held within organizations appears to be quite common and indicates that many technology managers have generally ignored the issue of quality. This is caused in part by the failure to recognize the need to manage data as a corporate asset. Data managers cannot allow just any type of data to be moved into a data warehouse, or it will become useless. To avoid data inaccuracies and their potential for harboring disasters, there must be a corporatewide awareness of data quality.

Unreliable and inaccurate data in the data warehouse causes numerous problems. First and foremost, the confidence of the users in the validity and reliability of this technology will be seriously impaired. Furthermore, if the data is used for strategic decision making, unreliable data affects the entire organization, and will affect senior management's view of the data warehousing project.

An excellent example of the damage that can be caused by erroneous data occurred in the early 1980s when the banks had incorrect risk exposure data on Texas-based businesses. When the oil market slumped, those banks that had many Texas accounts encountered major losses. In other cases, manufacturing firms scaled down their operations and took actions to eliminate excess inventory. Because they had inaccurate market data, they overestimated the inventory and sold off critical business equipment.

As emphasized previously in analyzing the characteristics of data required for data warehousing and data mining applications, the quality of the data is of extreme importance in a data warehousing project, and the challenge for data managers is to ensure the consistency of the data entering the system. In some organizations, data is stored in flat, VASAM, IMS, IDMS, or SA files and a variety of relational databases. In addition, different systems designed for different functions contain the same terms but with different meanings.

If care is not taken to clean up this terminology during data warehouse construction, misleading management information results. The logical consequence of this requirement is that management has to agree on the data definition for elements in the warehouse. Those who use the data in the short term and the long term must have input into the process and know what the data means.

Erroneous data should be captured and corrected before it enters the warehouse. Capture and correction are handled programmatically in the process of transforming data from one system to the data warehouse. An example might be a field that was in lowercase that needs to be stored in uppercase. A final means of handling errors is to replace erroneous data with a default value. If, for example, the date February 29 of a non-leap year is defaulted to February 28, there is no loss in data integrity.

Separation of Warehouse Data

One aspect of data warehouse growth that must be monitored and corrected is data separation. As data warehouses grow in volume, the data inside the warehouse begins to separate, a natural result of the way data is used. The separation occurs as data divides into two classes: (1) data that is actively being used, and (2) data that is infrequently used. For example, a terabyte of data may have 50 GB that are actively used and 950 GB that are accessed perhaps only once a month or once a quarter. The organization pays the same for the data regardless of how frequently it is used. The data warehouse administrator can either archive the inactive data or place it in near-line storage. Accessing the inactive data, moving it to near-line storage, and then deleting the data from the data warehouse makes the separation.

While it is true that all data warehouses face separation, the degree of separation varies among warehouses, based on these factors:

- Size of the warehouse
- Type of business the warehouse supports
- Who uses the warehouse
- What kind of processing is being done
- Level of sophistication of end-user analysts

Critical Success Factors

There are three critical success factors that each company needs to identify before moving forward with the issue of data quality:

1. Commitment by senior management to ensure quality of corporate data
2. Definition of data quality
3. Quality assurance of data

The senior management commitment to maintaining the quality of corporate data can be achieved by instituting a data administration department that oversees the management of corporate data. The role of this department will be to establish data management standards, policies, procedures, and guidelines pertaining to data and data quality.

Data quality, in addition to referring to the usefulness of the data, has to be defined as being data that is complete, timely, accurate, valid, and consistent with the degree of quality that is required for each element being loaded into the data warehouse. If, for example, customer addresses are stored, it might be acceptable that the four-digit extension to the zip code is missing. However, the street address, city, and state are of much greater importance. This parameter must be identified by each individual company and for each item that is used in the data warehouse.

A third factor that needs to be considered is the quality assurance of data. Because data is moved from transactional/legacy systems to the data warehouse, the accuracy of this data needs to be verified and corrected if necessary, and this will often involve cleansing of existing data. And because no company is able to rectify all of its unclean data, procedures must be put in place to ensure data quality at the source.

This task can only be achieved by modifying business processes and by designing data quality into the system. In identifying every data item and its usefulness to the ultimate users of this data, data quality requirements can be established. One might argue that this is too costly, but is has to be kept in mind that increasing the quality of data as an after-the-fact task is five to ten times more costly than capturing it correctly at the source.

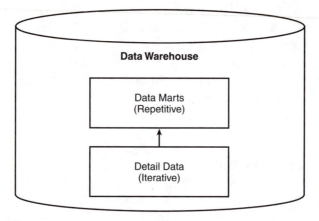

Exhibit 16. Accurate Detail Data Is the Foundation of the Data Warehouse

If companies want to use a data warehouse for competitive advantage and reap its benefits, the issue of data quality is extremely important. Only when data quality is recognized as a corporate asset by every member of the organization will the benefits of data warehousing and CRM initiatives be realized (see Exhibit 16).

Managerial and Organizational Impacts of Data Warehousing

The development of the data warehouse is an ongoing process. Once the first iteration is built, it will be refined; then a second iteration is built, and the process goes on. The following sections describe how to manage and organize the data warehouse after the first iteration of data is captured and loaded.

Adding New Data to the Warehouse

The data warehouse administrator's first consideration after building the initial iteration of development is the addition of new data. The questions to ask before adding new data include:

- What is the business justification for the addition of new elements of data?
- Do the new elements of data conform to the data model that governs the structure of the data warehouse?
- If there is a relationship between the new data to be placed in the data warehouse and the data that already exists there, does the introduction of the new data conform to data already recognized in the data model?
- Does the new data participate in a key relationship?
- How much volume will the new data add to the data warehouse?
- How much time will it take to load the new data on an initial load basis and on an ongoing basis?
- Will existing data have to be reconfigured in any way?

Monitoring the Data Warehouse

The data warehouse collects historical data at a detailed level. The inevitable result of collecting detailed historical data is that the volumes of data grow at a rapid rate. To accomplish any form of rigorous and believable capacity planning in the data warehouse environment, growth must be measured regularly, beginning with the first input of data.

Measuring warehouse volume is just one aspect of monitoring. It is equally important to monitor warehouse activity. This can be accomplished with a data warehouse activity monitor, software designed to capture a variety of actions going on inside the data warehouse, such as:

- Size of the queries
- What data the user base is looking at
- What queries are being submitted
- Which users are submitting queries
- What data is not being used by the user base
- Workload schedule — daily, weekly, monthly
- Average daily workload

In the formative stages of data warehousing development, corporate managers will be anticipating the arrival of the new technology and awaiting the opportunity to avail themselves of the business tools that it will provide. However, before these expectations can be realized, many issues must be resolved.

Data Warehouse Provides New Tools

Data warehousing affects management and organizations in a general way that enables the organization to meet the tenets of the modern business motto: "work smarter, not harder." Data warehouse users will become more productive because they will have the tools to analyze the large volumes of data they store, instead of just collecting it.

Some organizations believe that implementing data warehousing technology simply consists of integrating all pertinent existing company data into one place. However, managers need to be aware that data warehousing implies changes in the job functions of many people in an organization. For example, when an organization implements a data warehouse, data analysis and modeling become much more prevalent than simple requirements analysis. They also become an important component of the corporate CRM strategy.

The role of the database administrator involves more than the critical aspect of efficiently storing data. This individual takes on the central role in the development of the application. Furthermore, because it is a data model-oriented methodology, data warehouse design requires a development life cycle that does not follow traditional development approaches: the development of a data warehouse essentially begins with a data model, from which the warehouse is built.

Data warehouses are high-maintenance systems that require their own support staff. In this way, experienced personnel implement future changes in a timely manner. It is also important to remember that users will probably abandon a technically advanced and fast warehouse that adds little value from the start, reiterating the importance of storing only clean data, useful to the user community, in the data warehouse.

Armed with the information derived from the data warehouse activity monitor, a data warehouse administrator can do many things, such as:

- *Tune the data warehouse* — As end-user patterns of usage become apparent, the data warehouse administrator can improve performance for common queries.
- *Ensure that end users are taking advantage of the data warehouse in the manner originally envisioned* — If not, determine whether they have discovered a new and beneficial way of using the data warehouse.
- *Watch end-user queries become increasingly sophisticated* — Progression from simple to sophisticated queries should be apparent in the mix of queries submitted over a period time.

Exploration Warehouses

In general, applications used by nonpower users of the warehouse environment are most applicable to the phenomenon of separation. When explorers use the warehouse, they tend to access large amounts of obscure data.

Explorers are out-of-the-box thinkers who may want to submit 72-hour queries. If there are only a few 72-hour requests, or if exploration processing is not a priority item, then these queries can be handled in the enterprise data warehouse.

But if the 72-hour query becomes a regular feature and if exploration becomes a regular occurrence, then it may be expedient to create an exploration warehouse. An exploration warehouse is easily created from the enterprise data warehouse, assuming the enterprise data warehouse has been created at the proper level of granularity. If the enterprise data warehouse contains very detailed data, then it is a straightforward process for an explorer to create an exploration warehouse by placing a subject of data peculiar to his or her analytical needs into the exploration warehouse.

Creating exploration warehouses can be a regular part of data warehouse life. By creating the exploration warehouse, the data warehouse administrator provides a positive way to handle the workload disparity between high-power explorers and regular users.

The Metadata Infrastructure

Another important activity that is a part of the ongoing management of a data warehouse environment as the data warehouse matures, is the creation and population of a metadata infrastructure. In most cases, data warehouse administrators are so busy during the initial design and population of the warehouse that little or no attention is paid to the metadata that resides inside the data warehouse. Issues to address when creating a metadata environment include:

- Is there support of both business and technical metadata?
- Will metadata reside at every server in the decision-support environment, at each enterprise data warehouse, and at each operational data store?
- Can the metadata at each server communicate and share metadata with every other server?
- Is there a system of record in which any unit of metadata is owned by exactly one server?

Organizational Growth

When a data warehouse grows and matures, so too does the data warehouse administrator function. There are several signs of growth within the data warehouse administrator organization. They include:

- An increase in the number of people doing data warehouse administration work
- A transition from data warehouse administrator generalists to data warehouse administrator specialists
- An increased understanding of data warehouse administration tasks

The administration requirement of the warehouse environment may grow for several reasons, including:

- *Complexity* — As the different types of data grow, the complexity of managing them also grows.
- *User demands* — As the number of users grow, their demands for data grow, creating challenging and ever-expanding administrative work.
- *Age* — As data ages, its structure changes and requires administrator work.

Proactive Administration

Meeting the requirements of ongoing administration and management of the data warehouse, as described above, are key issues in maintaining the health of a centralized data warehouse. It is important to broach these considerations as early in the warehouse's life cycle as possible — optimally at the design stage. Once the warehouse is built and is being administered, it is too late to go back and reengineer the warehouse.

Ensuring Stability

There are several steps the development team should take to ensure the proper management, stability, and viability of the data warehouse, the data stored in it, and the technologies that support the corporation's CRM strategy.

First and foremost, as noted previously in this chapter, the data warehouse must be designed to store data at the lowest level of detail (granularity) feasible. In doing so, the designer sets the stage for flexibility and change in the warehouse architecture. By designing the data warehouse at the lowest level of granularity, the designer prepares for future contingencies without needing to know future requirements. The mere fact that the data exists at the lowest level of detail allows the granular data to be reshaped and recombined to meet any future requirement.

Second, a designer can ensure that the interface between the applications and the enterprise data warehouse is as automated as possible. When the interface is created and maintained manually, changes to the warehouse can only occur slowly. It is very difficult for the data warehouse administrator to appear responsive to the end users' changing needs when the changing requirements must be constantly hand crafted. There are many tools designed for automating code for an integration and transformation interface. It makes no sense for an organization to have to rely on manual intervention every time a user requirement changes.

Third, a designer should create the enterprise data warehouse in an integrated manner. If the same data appears in five different formats with five different structures, the end user will have difficulty accessing and understanding the data inside the warehouse.

And finally, to support exploration warehouses, a designer should provide end users with access to a wealth of historical data in the data warehouse.

As can be noted, there are many definable management and administrative tasks the data warehouse administrator needs to carry out as the data warehouse goes from development to operational state. Preparing for these tasks as part of a transition strategy is as important as any other aspect of the design and development of a data warehouse.

User Training

Training for users of a data warehouse will involve the introduction of new concepts for these users, covering a number of topics and business analysis techniques, many of which will not be familiar to these staff members. Topics for the training syllabus will include:

- Introduction to processes and capabilities now available
- Introduction to new business elements in the data model
- Validating answers
- Documenting analyses
- Using the data warehouse — when enough analysis is enough
- Analyzing the value being generated from the data warehouse
- Sharing tools with others
- Learning about information in the data warehouse

Vendors with CRM Technology

The information provided on vendors in this chapter is not intended to be a complete list of all vendors of CRM technologies. In a rapidly evolving world of technology, it is impossible to present all of the major participants at any given time.

However, the selected list of CRM vendors (see Exhibit 17), and the brief corporate and product data provided with each vendor, are representative of the products and services available from technology vendors, many of them offering their services on a global basis. While the list is not intended to be definitive, it does reflect the reputation and credibility established by these vendor organizations through successful CRM implementations, many of them described in Chapter 4.

Mergers and acquisitions will impact the CRM vendor market; however, at publication date for this Handbook, the vendors listed below offered hardware, software, or consulting services to support the technologies required to implement CRM solutions.

The vendor selection process, particularly in the area of packaged software, must be conducted with corporate priorities as a key criterion, coupled with the desired functionality.

Checklist for Vendor Selection

Technology choices should be based on a structured and detailed comparison between a reasonable number of qualified vendors, by following these basic steps:

- Identify internal IT issues first.
- Assess requirements of technology with all departments.
- Prepare invitation to tender with details on functionality, capacity, and scalability.
- Based on responses received, prepare an initial short-list of suppliers.
- From this list, select two or three to develop a prototype to demonstrate operational functionality.

Conclusion

The value to an organization of data warehousing and the supporting technology tools that are components of a CRM solution is multidimensional and multifaceted. An enterprisewide data warehouse serves as a central repository for all data used in an organization and, therefore, simplifies business relationships among departments by using one standard. Users of the data warehouse get consistent results when querying this database and understand the data in the same way without ambiguity.

Exhibit 17. A Selected List of IT Vendors with CRM Products or Services

Vendor	Area of CRM Specialization
CGI (www.cgi.ca)	A range of IT services, consulting, systems integration, and management of IT and business functions, including CRM; specialized experience in these sectors: financial services, telecommunications, manufacturing, government, healthcare, and public utilities.
Delano Technology Corp. (www.delanotech.com)	Enables multichannel, intelligent interactions between an organization and its customers and trading partners; provides the analytic and interaction management software needed for E-business interactions, including CRM.
DWL Inc. (www.dwl.com)	Provides products that consolidate disparate E-business systems into unified industry solutions.
Epiphany Inc. (www.epiphany.com)	A provider of intelligent customer interaction software for the customer economy; special experience in E-commerce and CRM applications for financial services, communications, consumer-packaged goods, and technology sectors.
Evoke Software (www.evoke.com)	Specializes in data profiling software that restructures and data cleansing software that automates the process of cleansing and transforming data prior to inputting it into a data warehouse.
Kana Communications (www.kana.com)	Software solutions to businesses to assist them to understand their customers and to better manage customer and partner relationships.
IBM (www.ibm.com)	Hardware platforms for data warehousing and database management systems; consulting services in CRM solutions.
Metagenix (www.metagenix.com)	Metarecon software provides data profiling and analysis, code generation, and online analytical processing specifications.
Microsoft (www.microsoft.com)	A range of customer relationship management software products.
NCR (www.ncr.com)	Data warehousing platforms and database management systems for a range of business sectors.

Exhibit 17.   A Selected List of IT Vendors with CRM Products or Services   (Continued)

Vendor	Area of CRM Specialization
Norkom (www.norkom.com)	Software and services that help organizations to proactively identify and nurture the optimal customer base, addressing client retention, cross-sell, up-sell, acquisition, churn, channel migration, and optimization.
PeopleSoft (www.peoplesoft.com)	CRM solutions that provide seamless integration among customer, financial, supply chain, and employee management systems.
Pivotal (www.pivotal.com)	eRelationship suite provides sales, marketing, and service capabilities that track, capture, and consolidate all customer data, enabling office employees in sales, marketing, and customer support and service to manage relationships with customer and partners.
SAP (www.sapag.de)	Products for E-business, including E-CRM, that support databases, applications, operating systems, and hardware from almost every major vendor.
SAS (www.sas.com)	Decision-making software tools for CRM and ERP applications, and E-intelligence software and services, to assist organizations in transforming data into information to support decision-making processes.
Seibel Systems (www.Seibel.com)	Multichannel E- business applications and services that enable organizations to create a single source of customer information that facilitates selling to, marketing to, and servicing customers across multiple channels — Web, call centers, field, resellers, retail, and dealer networks.
Triversity's (www.triversity.com)	CRM solutions for the retail marketplace, designed for retailers with multiple channels.
Vality (www.vality.com)	Specializing in software products and services for enterprise data quality management, data cleansing, standardization and matching.

Data warehousing has evolved rapidly and continues to be a very fast-moving, fast-changing market segment. At one time, there were no tools to support a data warehousing application, never mind a CRM solution, and only one way to design and architect a data warehouse system. Now there are myriad tools and technologies to choose from and a variety of viable data warehouse system architectures.

Where the top-down approach to the design of the data warehouse was once the only option, we now have a viable architected bottom-up approach that greatly enhances the chances of success for those sites not well suited for the top-down approach.

Given an appropriate architecture and a suitable approach to the goal of the enterprise data warehouse, a data warehousing project team can deliver a high-impact, high-value, and high-ROI data warehouse system. This will provide the basis for a CRM solution that will enable the enterprise to benefit significantly from improved customer relationships and a CRM strategy that places the customer first.

Chapter 4

Case Studies in CRM

Knowledge itself can be defined as detailed awareness of unsolved problems.

— **New York Times, 1976**

One of the best methods for learning how to implement customer relationship management systems in a specific business sector is to analyze CRM implements in that sector to determine the factors and processes that have contributed to success, as well as the benefits that organizations have derived from their CRM solutions.

By analyzing these successful examples and reviewing the "Industry Checklist: Lessons Learned" guidelines developed for this Handbook, IS professionals, business analysts, and senior managers in similar business sectors can develop their own CRM solutions with a high level of assurance that they will meet their objectives.

These selected CRM implementations represent a series of real-life CRM solutions that have met their design objectives, presented in traditional business school case study format. For each case study, the methodology employed by the organization to implement a CRM solution to meet defined objectives is described and analyzed, with emphasis on the following aspects of the development process:

- Project objectives
- Technologies
- Vendor products and resources used

The following 38 selected case studies represent businesses in every major business sector from the worldwide business community and are representative of the importance these organizations place on CRM as a core business strategy. The sectors and organizations represented are:

- Automotive
  - A1: General Motors
  - A2: Saturn Corporation
- Communications
  - C1: AT&T Wireless — Southwest Region
  - C2: Access Integrated Networks
  - C3: Canada Post
  - C4: Pele-Phone Communications
- Energy
  - E1: Enbridge Consumers Gas
  - E2: ENMAX Energy
- Entertainment
  - Ent1: BMG Entertainment
  - Ent2: Harrah's Casinos
- Financial Institutions
  - F1: Alberta Treasury Branches
  - F2: Guaranty Bank
  - F3: National Bank of Canada
  - F4: The Royal Bank of Canada
  - F5: Union Bank of Norway
- Fund-raising
  - Fund1: United Way of Greater Toronto
- Healthcare
  - H1: Anthem Blue Cross Blue Shield
  - H2: Apotex Group
  - H3: TLC Laser Eye Centers
- Insurance
  - Ins1: Zurich Kemper Life Insurance
- Investment
  - Inv1: Yorkton Securities
- Packaging
  - P1: Tipper Tie
- Recruiting and Training
  - RT1: Eagle's Flight
  - RT2: Global Interactive and Workopolis
- Retail
  - R1: Home Depot
  - R2: M&M Meat Shops
  - R3: Migros Cooperatives
  - R4: RadioShack Canada
  - R5: Wal-Mart
- Technology
  - T1: Canon Canada
  - T2: Hewlett-Packard
  - T3: Western Digital

- Transportation and Travel
  - TT1: AeroXchange
  - TT2: Burlington Northern Santa Fe Railway
  - TT3: Canadian Pacific Railway
  - TT4: Delta Airlines
  - TT5: Travel Unie
- Wholesale
  - W1: Clearwater
  - W2: Fujifilm France

Note: Where applicable, the industry source for each case study can be found in the References/Bibliography section of this Handbook.

Each CRM case study is divided into five stages that take the project from the statement of objectives to the benefits and finally to a summary of the important aspects of each CRM solution. These stages are defined as follows:

- CRM Project Objectives
- Corporate Background
- The CRM Solution
- The Benefits
- Industry Checklist: Lessons Learned

Automotive

Case Study A1: General Motors (GM)

CRM Project Objectives

To enable customers to readily access information on a range of GM automobiles.

Corporate Background

Historically, GM dealers have been separated from one another across the automaker's different product divisions. As a result, there has been very little cross-selling among the divisions. There were many disparate pieces of information among the divisions, making it difficult for customers to obtain specifications, pricing, etc., on automobiles they wanted to evaluate.

The CRM Solution

GM launched cross-divisional shopping capabilities for a group of 250,000 customers, to assist them in accessing information on a variety of new vehicle models, through the company's Web site. Content was changed to enable customers on one division's Web site to view product information from another division.

The Benefits

The key benefits achieved by General Motors as a result of implementing a CRM solution include:

- Easier customer searches for vehicle information on GM Web sites
- An increase of eight percent in purchase rates
- Increased revenue and profitability

Industry Checklist: Lessons Learned

An automotive manufacturer can implement a CRM solution by:

- Combining automotive industry legacy systems with current data warehousing and Internet technologies
- Providing customer access to Web site information

Case Study A2: Saturn Corporation

CRM Project Objectives

To support increased sales and consumer interest in Saturn vehicles without decreasing service levels.

Corporate Background

Saturn is one of America's newest car companies, created through a unique partnership between General Motors and the UAW, formed as a wholly owned subsidiary of General Motors in 1985.

Saturn entered the automotive market in 1990, bringing a new level of customer service to automotive retailing. Over the years, Saturn has sold more than 2.2 million vehicles, valued at more than $20 billion. Saturn's Tier One Customer Care Consultants regularly assisted people who contact Saturn for general product, service, and feature and option information. These agents often functioned more as "traffic controllers," directing calls to the next level — customer-assistance managers who provided tier-two support to owners needing additional assistance.

To provide world-class service, the Saturn Customer Assistance Center team needed to rethink how it handled customer contacts. This required faster, better service, and increasing the number of calls resolved in the first contact — without adding personnel, significantly increasing wait time, or increasing costs.

The CRM Solution

Saturn selected EDS, a vendor with CRM consulting services and experience in CRM solution implementation. EDS identified better methods of handling callers to Saturn's contact-center operation. Together, Saturn and EDS scrutinized and evaluated the current customer-assistance process and developed the "One-Call Resolution" strategy, which empowered customer care consultants to resolve inquiries in the first contact, instead of referring them to a tier-two manager.

The Benefits

The CRM solution implemented by Saturn has resulted in the following benefits:

- Customer care consultants resolved 95 percent of customer inquiries in the first contact and fewer calls are referred to managers.
- Service levels have remained above 90 percent — with the same staffing levels.
- Customer care consultants have a challenging career-development path, an expanded role, and stronger relationships and rapport with the staff at Saturn's retail facilities.
- Significant cost savings were realized.

Industry Checklist: Lessons Learned

A well-conceived CRM strategy for customer service in the automotive sector can be accomplished through the following processes:

- An analysis of customer contact strategies
- Contracting with an outside resource to assist in revising the customer assistance process

Communications

Case Study C1: AT&T Wireless Services — Southwest Region

CRM Project Objectives

To improve customer retention using a data warehouse, customer profiling, and predictive modeling.

Corporate Background

AT&T Wireless Services is one of the world's largest wireless services providers and, like other companies in the highly competitive, rapidly changing communications environment, faces several challenges in terms of customer retention. AT&T Wireless offers cellular and digital voice, data, and messaging communications services to more than seven million customers worldwide.

In this sector, as in other business sectors, customers can and do change suppliers regularly — customer churn — as described in Chapter 1 of this Handbook.

In an earlier data warehousing project, the company had established a database environment to address sales and marketing initiatives. At one of the AT&T Wireless' five U.S. regions — Southwest region — staff realized that it needed more detailed results than anticipated with an earlier legacy system. The legacy data warehouse met the basic needs, but limited the region's capability to expand it to an enterprisewide system capable of answering complex queries. Easier access to more detailed customer information was required.

The CRM Solution

To reduce high levels of customer churn, which are common characteristics of the communications sector, AT&T Wireless decided to focus on customer loyalty and retention. The company initiated and built a scalable data warehouse for planning and product implementation and used it to improve customer profiling. This feature of the data warehouse enabled it to serve existing customers, as well as approaching prospects with more targeted information based on predictive modeling.

The Southwest Region established the following three key goals for the CRM project, all of which were accomplished:

- Build better customer profile information for improving service to customers and prospects.
- Retain customers and reduce churn through predictive modeling.
- Improve direct-marketing capabilities.

The Benefits

AT&T Wireless Southwest Region has achieved the following benefits from its CRM solution:

- The region is able to analyze information to help continually improve customer satisfaction and retain its lead in the wireless market.
- Easy access to customer profiles enables AT&T staff to have a much better understanding of customer needs and how to meet them.
- New promotions help retain existing customers and attract new customers in cost-effective ways.

- Accurate predictive models determine which customers are most likely to switch to a competitor.
- Profitability of customers can be determined, enabling the company to take action to retain profitable customers, while unprofitable customers are allowed to switch to other carriers.

Industry Checklist: Lessons Learned

In the communications sector, a CRM solution can be successfully implemented by applying the following methodology:

- Build scalable data.
- Combine legacy system data with current data warehousing technology.

Case Study C2: Access Integrated Networks

CRM Project Objectives

To integrate back-office functions and a new billing system with existing customer data, and to quickly and reliably increase capacity for processing new business orders.

Corporate Background

Access Integrated Networks is a fast-growing telecommunications company providing service in nine of the southeastern United States, with a focus on customer care and the delivery of innovative communications solutions for small- and medium-sized businesses. In addition to local service, Access supplies long distance, paging, calling cards, and other communication services, all wrapped up in packages tailored to individual client needs.

The CRM Solution

Access retained the services of CGI to develop new methods to process and store information to support the growth trajectory and establish a Web site that clearly communicates the Access value proposition to customers. CGI designed and built an E-business system, which allows sales agents to log onto a secure Web site and create new accounts that flow easily through customer support and into the billing system.

The Benefits

The benefits to Access included:

- Enhanced competitive advantage based on a customer-centric E-business model
- Improved customer service

Industry Checklist: Lessons Learned

Regional telecommunications companies can benefit from a CRM strategy by:

- Integrating back-office functions with billing and customer data
- Improving access to and functionality of Web sites

Case Study C3: Canada Post

CRM Project Objectives

To deliver on a commitment to universal access, communication, and security, and to adapt to changing customer needs in the fast-paced Internet marketplace.

Corporate Background

Canada Post provides a range of communication services to Canadians — governments, businesses, and citizens — through the secure delivery of information and parcels to some 13 million addresses in Canada, including 900,000 businesses and public institutions.

The Canadian postal system differs from other communication and distribution organizations because of its capacity and mandate to provide secure and accessible service across the country. With the new Internet economy forcing changes in communications trends and practices around the globe, the role of Canada Post is continually evolving.

The CRM Solution

Canada Post chose SAP — a provider of inter-enterprise software solutions — to implement its corporatewide business transformation initiative. The program, enabled by mySAP.com, SAPs E-business solutions platform, has streamlined information flow both inside and outside the company, delivering E-business solutions.

In addition to streamlining business processes, mySAP.com has enabled Canada Post to move into E-logistics, E-procurement, and other new revenue-generating opportunities in both the physical and electronic worlds. Business transformation will support Canada Post's five major strategic priorities: (1) enhanced customer satisfaction, (2) reduced operation costs, (3) improved commercial sales, (4) growing commercial distribution, and (5) expanded E-commerce capability.

The CRM solution is the major focus of the first phase of the implementation. It enables employees, partners, suppliers, and customers to collaborate and leverage integrated information from, throughout, and beyond an organization, linking CRM functionality with E-commerce and supply-chain management for a holistic network of collaborative businesses.

The Benefits

Canada Post, a major national postal and communication service, has achieved the following benefits through its CRM solution:

- Enabled customers to pay invoices online, 24 hours a day, at convenient, secure locations
- Provided new revenue-generating services
- Streamlined business processes
- Enabled the organization to move into E-logistics and E-procurement

Industry Checklist: Lessons Learned

A public-sector corporation offering a range of communication-oriented services can improve its customer service and transform it to an electronic business environment through a CRM strategy that:

- Links CRM functionality with E-commerce and supply-chain management
- Uses outside resources and technology that enable it to transform its business to an E-commerce environment

Case Study C4: Pele-Phone Communications

CRM Project Objectives

To track customer needs, usage, and network capacity to develop new services and product packages to meet customer needs and to retain customers.

Corporate Background

Pele-Phone Communications of Israel is the largest of three cellular communications providers and was established as a joint venture between Motorola and Bezeq, the Israeli Telecommunications Corporation. Pele-Phone was the first cellular company in Israel and has close to one million subscribers. The company has approximately 50 percent of the market for cellular communications in a country where almost half the population has cell phone service.

Pele-Phone has over 1000 employees, a corporate headquarters in Tel-Aviv, and maintains 14 service centers in Israel.

Faced with strong competition, the company decided that it needed to use the large volume of customer data to develop a better understanding of customer usage patterns to direct marketing campaigns based on this knowledge.

The CRM Solution

The company upgraded its data warehouse installation and extended its traditional database management system, designed for transaction management for its more than ten million customers, to a data warehouse application that has enhanced its customer relationship capabilities. These changes in managing customer relationships enabled the company to confirm that between 50,000 and 70,000 customers remained loyal rather than move to the competition.

The Benefits

Several benefits have resulted from the successful upgrading of the data warehouse to support a CRM solution:

- All detailed customer data can be scanned.
- Customer service loyalty has been improved.
- Multiple customer models can be developed.
- Customer "churn" has been reduced.
- New customers are offered a range of services.
- Known, tangible paybacks have been demonstrated.
- The right customers are targeted for communication services.

Industry Checklist: Lessons Learned

In a highly competitive environment, a telecommunications company can successfully upgrade its traditional data warehouse to one that supports a CRM solution, by:

- Implementing an enterprisewide data warehouse
- Providing sophisticated business analysis tools to leverage customer data
- Developing a range of additional information resources to increase revenue and profitability, while enhancing customer loyalty and increasing the customer base

Energy

Case Study E1: Enbridge Consumers Gas

CRM Project Objectives

To implement a major organizational change to a natural gas company, a transition that involved a new provincial regulatory environment, strong competition, and transformation of over three million customer records from a legacy system.

Corporate Background

The utilities industry is one of the largest industries in North America, with revenues approaching $500 billion. The customer experience required in a competitive environment is becoming a cross-industry issue. Companies can no longer concentrate on the competition in their vertical segment. They must meet and exceed the experience a customer has, based on the best-in-class customer care solutions being developed across industries, to stay ahead of the competition. Utility industry reform is motivated by the emergence of a customer-based energy business, new technology, and deregulation, shifting decision and execution to the customer.

In accordance with Ontario Energy Board guidelines, Enbridge Consumers Gas filed with the intention to separate into a deregulated service entity and a regulated utility, with certain criteria, including the development of a stand-alone company requiring its own IT infrastructure.

The following activities were completed over a 15-month timeframe:

- Definition of the re-engineered processes to meet the future state deregulated environment
- Selection of vendor partners
- Design and construct of application suite and IT infrastructure architecture
- Testing, training, and deploying the application suite
- Converting over three million customer records from a legacy system

The CRM Solution

To comply with Ontario Energy Board regulations, the following components were required:

- CRM application
- Billing system
- Financial system
- Supply-chain systems (logistics and warehouse management)
- Human resource system
- Technician scheduling system
- 150-seat call center
- IT infrastructure (network, desktops, telecoms, servers, databases)

To "go live" required deployment of a number of resources, including installing voice and data networking capabilities to 27 locations, deploying 700 configured desktops, training 800 end users, and testing and deploying 25 integrated applications.

Dedicated team members, with strong vendor partnerships, implemented on time and under budget the CRM solution-effective management of all processes and rigorous testing of applications for volume and breadth of functionality.

The Benefits

The new organization was able to accomplish the following:

- Integrate its operation with the previous gas supplier in compliance with energy regulations
- Successfully transfer customer files to its new IT infrastructure
- Establish a competitive organization within a tight timeframe

Industry Checklist: Lessons Learned

CRM solutions for energy companies can be implemented by:

- Applying appropriate technology to the process
- Planning and managing resources effectively
- Converting legacy records to new technology

Case Study E2: ENMAX Energy

CRM Project Objectives

To transform the ENMAX business model by focusing on the needs and desires of its customer base.

Corporate Background

ENMAX Energy, a wholly owned subsidiary of ENMAX Corporation, distributes electricity to more than 400,000 residential and commercial customers in Alberta. Like many other power providers in North America, the company faces industry competition and consumer choice for the first time because of government deregulation.

The company realized that to remain competitive, it had to build customer trust and satisfaction by providing a proactive, one-on-one experience every time a customer makes contact with the company.

As a $530-million provider of electrical energy, ENMAX has a lot of business to protect. Prior to deregulation, the company had been tracking its customer records on a series of disparate databases that contained redundant and, in certain cases, outdated information. The company had formed few relationships with its residential customers and had only select ties to its top-tier commercial clients.

The CRM Solution

ENMAX initiated its companywide re-engineering effort by establishing a new corporate vision that focused on excellence and core values such as innovation, customer focus, and employee support. To assist in achieving this corporate vision, the company turned to Onyx and its enterprisewide, Internet-based CRM product line.

The ENMAX customer base included individual residential clients and small- to mid-size businesses to large commercial clients. Because sales are one of the most critical areas in its business model, ENMAX opted to roll out its CRM system in the sales department first. To encourage quick adoption, the company assigned its top sales executive to champion the solution, realizing that this implementation would turn the company into a customer-centric organization and fundamentally change the business processes.

ENMAX is able to engage each customer individually because its Internet-based CRM solution tracks information each time the customer contacts the company, no matter which door the customer enters. Customers can access service representatives by phone, the Internet, or directly at the company's offices, and can expect the same level of service. If a customer makes a product or service recommendation, it is recorded for follow-up and the customer is kept informed.

The Benefits

ENMAX Energy has experienced a number of significant benefits as a result of implementing a CRM solution:

- Considerable cost savings have been achieved on promotional campaigns.
- Sales representatives have been able to sell more efficiently and effectively, recording every win and loss with supporting reasons.
- Sales managers have been able to determine where sales are lost and assist pricing managers to set rates and discounts.
- Marketing efforts have been enhanced by tracking and managing the company's branding and messaging efforts.
- Sales-cycle times and the volume of service-related telephone calls have been decreased.
- Dramatic improvements have been achieved in the capture and application of customer information, and a number of multimillion-dollar contracts were signed as a result of the CRM solution implementation.

Industry Checklist: Lessons Learned

An energy-based company can implement a CRM solution by adopting the following processes:

- Refocusing its core values to customer-centric positions
- Consolidating customer records
- Appointing a senior executive to champion the process
- Selecting a CRM product to meet its specific business process requirements

Entertainment

Case Study Ent1: BMG Entertainment

CRM Project Objectives

To manage the influx of information and increased demands of its customers more effectively through all channels in the organization.

Corporate Background

BMG Direct is part of BMG Entertainment, the global music division of Bertelsmann AG, one of the world's leading media companies. Headquartered in New York City, BMG Entertainment is home to more than 200 record labels in 54 countries, including Arista Records, BMG Music Canada, BMG Classics, BMG Direct, BMG Distribution, BMG Music Publishing, BMG Special Products, RCA Music Group, RCA Label Group Nashville, and the Windham Hill Group. It also has regional operations in Asia-Pacific, the United Kingdom, Europe, and Latin America, and markets artists' music over the Internet.

BMG's success relies on its ability to retain and attract music members. As the world's largest group of music clubs, including BMG Music Service, Classical Music Service, Jazz Club, Sound & Spirit, and Ritmoy Caliente, BMG Direct depends on its ability to communicate appealing and appropriate promotions to over 11 million members with a variety of requirements.

BMG manages several marketing channels — direct mail, telemarketing, e-mail, and its Web site — to reach its customers. Helping customers sort through a large collection of various magazines, flyers, and other promotional materials to find the music they want is a major challenge at BMG. Effective marketing of those opportunities is key to the company's success.

The music field has changed considerably over the past several years. New listening preferences occurred, and these specific music genres needed new, tailored magazines. BMG had also established telemarketing programs to target members whose interest and purchasing habits had decreased. The company created a Web site, and the combination of all of these changes produced a significant increase in the demand for information to drive these programs.

BMG's analytical systems restricted its ability to develop effective marketing campaigns to improve sales and member satisfaction. A typical request to access and read a file required six to twelve hours, much too long to meet customer requirements..

In addition, imagine if several marketing managers, each responsible for specific business areas, had free rein over customer communications. This approach created confusion, mixed messages, and an overflow of information to BMG customers.

The CRM Solution

BMG turned to SAS, a leader in E-intelligence software and services designed to transform data within an organization into information, for customer support and to aid decision making. SAS provides tools that assist companies to know their own organization, their suppliers, and their customers. Enterprise Marketing Automation (EMA), a component of CRM provided by SAS, helps coordinate huge volumes of inbound and outbound communications over multiple channels and improves the effectiveness of marketing campaigns, using measurement techniques.

EMA combines data warehousing and data mining with a campaign-management system, and empowers organizations to gain a better understanding of their customers, anticipate customer needs, identify opportunities for increased profitability, improve customer retention, and maximize revenue. It also allows organizations to integrate and analyze customer data from every customer touchpoint, including mail, fax, call centers, person-to-person, and the Web.

To manage the influx of information and increased demands of its customers, BMG invested in analytical software to manage information more effectively. BMG determined that telemarketing should be used only for the best customers, direct mail should be used for less responsive members, and e-mail should be used to reinforce direct mail for the least responsive members.

The Benefits

The benefits achieved by BMG include:

- Increased revenue and profitability, related to cross-selling and up-selling to customers
- Increased customer retention
- Decreased costs
- Better customer response and service

Industry Checklist: Lessons Learned

Organizations in the entertainment field can benefit from a CRM solution that has the following characteristics:

- A data warehousing system with data mining capability
- Campaign management using detailed customer data
- Uses every customer touchpoint to enhance understanding of customer preferences and to maximize revenue and profitability

Case Study Ent2: Harrah's Casinos

CRM Project Objectives

To reward each individual customer for every casino visit, no matter where it took place, and to analyze, predict, and maximize the value of each customer relationship.

Corporate Background

Harrah's owns 18 casinos in eight U.S. states, and is one of the largest brand names in the casino entertainment industry. Founded in 1937 in Reno, Nevada, Harrah's became the first casino to be listed on the New York Stock Exchange.

The CRM Solution

Using a sophisticated data warehousing system with an effective CRM element, Harrah's was able to gain information, retain, and reward 15 million guests. The company was also able to encourage customers to remain loyal to the Harrah's brand across the country, and over time to compile hundreds of customer attributes to help determine likelihood to visit, predicted spending, opportunities for cross-sell, customer segmentation, and event data.

The Benefits

The CRM solution enabled Harrah's to:

- Analyze each customer's preference and predict what services and rewards they will respond to in the future
- Provide access to the call center to provide customers with the same service they would get on the floor of their favorite casino

Industry Checklist: Lessons Learned

In the entertainment sector, companies with multiple operations can use CRM solutions to treat customers on a one-to-one basis by:

- Using technology to analyze large amounts of customer data
- Providing better marketing, service, support, and response to special requests
- Analyzing customer data to target customer marketing campaigns

Financial Institutions

Case Study F1: Alberta Treasury Branches (ATB)

CRM Project Objectives

To implement an E-business, customer-oriented solution that enables its contact center representatives to provide better service than its competitors.

Corporate Background

Based in Edmonton, Alberta, Canada, with 144 branches throughout the province, this U.S.$11-billion, full-service financial institution needed to be more responsive to local market conditions and provide personalized service to urban and rural agricultural areas. In order to provide that personal touch and grow its market share, ATB required a more efficient way to service customers.

ATB's cumbersome contact center system lacked the functionality to service customers quickly. Often, customers who thought they were phoning a local branch office had their calls redirected to the centralized contact center, where the customer's transaction history in the bank was unknown. To find the answers the customer needed, the contact center representative would have to bring up any one of several different screens, a laborious, time-consuming process.

ATB's field sales force (called relationship managers) were not able to service the small businesses that make up the core of the customer base, because sophisticated tools crucial to managing a sales organization — account profiles, product and service information, call-tracking or sales-management calendars — were not available. Also, no up-to-date client information was available for client meetings, and sales management did not have access to business-critical forecasting information.

The CRM Solution

ATB recognized the requirement to implement an E-business solution. The organization selected *eFinance*, from Siebel *eBusiness*, an application tailored for the financial-services industry, running on an IBM MQSeries platform. The first phase of deployment began in the contact center where communication from legacy systems provides critical back-office information to the desktops of the contact center representatives, enabling ATB representatives to engage in a continuous dialog with customers.

Whether at an ATM, an interactive voice-response unit, the Internet, or a branch office, customer interactions are captured across all touchpoints, and made available to assist representatives in the next interaction.

When a call comes into the contact center, a profile of the customer will pop up, giving the representative information about who the customer is, the customer's address, a full listing of the customer's holdings, and a description of the customer's last contact with the bank. All this information can also be used for transactional analysis. Relationship managers are able to download all the customer information they need onto a laptop, so they have current information for client visits.

The Benefits

ATB has achieved a substantial ROI (return on investment) through cost savings and new revenue opportunities, with a CRM system that:

- Tracks leads and better manages opportunities
- Provides visibility into the sales pipeline

Industry Checklist: Lessons Learned

A financial services organization can enhance customer relationships by:

- Expanding its customer knowledge base with each transaction
- Using an E-business solution to improve customer service

Case Study F2: Guaranty Bank

CRM Project Objectives

To provide a complete view of customer interaction history and individual financial services preferences.

Corporate Background

Guaranty Bank is a Boston-based financial institution providing a range of financial services to its customers, including checking and savings accounts, loans, mortgages, investments, and mutual fund portfolio services.

The bank wanted to consolidate customer contact points, deliver more personalized customer service, and develop customer loyalty and retention.

The CRM Solution

The bank contracted Nortel Networks to provide its E-business and CRM solutions to develop a customer relationship environment that will deliver more personalized and efficient services. The CRM solution brings together the services, applications, and infrastructure to create profitable, high-performance customer service environments, drive customer loyalty, and improve the return on these relationships.

Nortel Networks Clarify eFrontOffice is an application suite for routing, integrating, and consolidating customer interactions. It is part of a comprehensive portfolio of portals and E-commerce capabilities for leading service providers, high-technology manufacturing companies, and financial service companies.

The Benefits

The key customer benefits of Guaranty Bank's CRM solution include:

- Consolidation of customer touchpoints, including the Web, e-mail, phone, and face-to-face, to give agents and customers an increased ability to control relationships
- Management of e-mail communication to generate intuitive and automatic responses to inquiries
- Integrate E-commerce with existing sales and service channels to reduce costs, to collect prospect and pre-sales information, and to seamlessly complement other delivery channels
- Establish personalized self-service portals that allow sales and service professionals to update customer profiles and order status, initiate customer service cases, and manage new phone-in sales orders
- Combine services, applications, and infrastructure, which create profitable, high-performance customer service environments and improve customer relationships

Industry Checklist: Lessons Learned

A financial institution can implement a CRM solution that meets the objectives of improving customer interactions by:

- Integrating services, applications, and infrastructure
- Creating profitable customer service environments
- Adopting software tools that provide efficient, personalized, and informed customer service

Case Study F3: National Bank of Canada (NBC)

CRM Project Objectives

To enhance customer service by converting a series of disparate legacy systems and call centers into a cohesive IT structure.

Corporate Background

The National Bank of Canada (NBC), based in Montreal, Quebec, is a banking and financial services institution, as well as a brokerage and insurance organization. Over the years, NBC had established a number of call centers and customer-support offices.

NBC's systems architecture was a patchwork of equipment from a number of vendors, along with various proprietary software and legacy systems. In addition, each banking team had its own business practices, and communication among teams was difficult.

One of NBC's CRM objectives was to ensure that every front-office worker had complete customer data available, to devote more time to advising and meeting customer needs, as opposed to processing transactions. This objective required a major corporate revamping of existing technologies. On the other hand, while NBC was keen to focus on its core competencies, it neither wanted to expend capital resources nor develop the necessary expertise to build a state-of-the-art architecture.

The CRM Solution

NBC selected IBM to develop an open, seamless, and flexible architecture and to transform its legacy systems into leading-edge E-commerce platforms, which could support the best and latest CRM applications.

IBM established 12 call centers that provided NBC with access to over 1000 customer-service agents. The package features customized interactive voice applications and computer telephony integration to improve and personalize customer service and responsiveness.

A major benefit to NBC of outsourcing the complete technological infrastructure is that it simplified planning. Dealing with numerous vendors, some of them in direct competition with each other, was proving difficult and time-consuming. As with any technology project in the financial world, flexibility, scalability, and security were important factors, along with seamless integration of data and the interface.

The outsourced CRM solution provides NBC with accurate, up-to-date profiles of each customer, including information about which products and services they use and whether that customer is dealing with the bank's brokerage, insurance, or banking outlet.

An open and flexible architecture enables NBC to keep the system at the leading edge of technology, picking and choosing among the best applications on the market. New and improved solutions can be integrated into the system quickly, gaining NBC a competitive advantage in a world where building a distinctive reputation is an important corporate attribute.

The Benefits

The CRM infrastructure has provided the following benefits to NBC:

- Access to the latest technology, enabling the bank to concentrate on personalizing customer service
- Capability to develop its CRM strategy at its own pace with a focus on customer needs rather than on technology
- Customer data that enables bank employees to act as advisors on financial issues and to address individual needs
- Year-round service, day or night, for customers, and the capacity to address peak usage

Industry Checklist: Lessons Learned

A financial institution can outsource a CRM solution to convert legacy systems and call centers into a cohesive IT structure that will enable the organization to:

- Provide personalized customer service
- Enhance customer service capability among front-office staff
- Improve internal communications

Case Study F4: The Royal Bank of Canada (RBC Financial Services)

CRM Project Objectives

To be increasingly responsive and client focused in an aggressively competitive environment, combined with the leveling effect of evolutions in technology and regulatory frameworks.

Corporate Background

RBC Financial Services, formerly known as The Royal Bank of Canada, is Canada's leading provider of personal and commercial banking. The bank chose a strategy of building unique relationships with individual clients, using a product that provides insights into client information and behavior. In its ranking as Canada's premier global financial services, wealth management, and corporate and investment banking group, the bank had assets of more than U.S. $165 billion and profits of U.S. $1 billion in 1999.

The Royal Bank began collecting client data in 1978, consolidating it for use at a client/branch level. By the early 1990s, it had implemented client segmentation in its data warehouse, dividing its clients into three distinct profitability segments.

The bank identified which areas of its customer relationship strategy required greater focus. This analysis revealed that bank clients really wanted a banking relationship in which they were well-understood, their needs were anticipated, and their business was valued; they wanted a truly integrated relationship.

The CRM Solution

With a sample profitability prototype in place, the bank went on to examine the options available to support its CRM strategy. The chosen solution had to have the following characteristics:

- *Behavioral-based* — related to customer characteristics
- *Flexible* — able to aggregate profitability according to user-defined units
- *Data warehouse and rule-based* — able to house all the required data elements and avoid hard coding
- *Scalable* — able to evolve, grow, and change in line with the business direction and strategy
- *Legitimate* — based on rigorous applications of generally accepted accounting principles (GAAP)

In its vendor selection process, four major aspects were considered:

1. Availability of a straightforward solution
2. Confidence in vendor and proposed solution
3. A structured approach
4. A clear set of requirements

The bank's data warehousing system is based on NCR's Teradata platform, and an evaluation of NCR's relationship technology products led to the selection of *Value Analyzer*, a business application that leveraged the existing platform and incorporated client events in its account-level profit calculation. The data warehouse contained all the information elements — and was able to draw on marketing information files for the identification of account-to-customer relationships.

A channel-costing model was developed to assess the fulfilment costs of the various channels and to support branch sales efforts in particular. Predictive what-if modeling is another key tool that assists the bank in enhancing its CRM initiatives.

The success of the implementation was due to a range of contributing factors, including:

- *Cross-business unit support* — buy-in from business units ensured that the value solution was not the sole preserve of the finance function
- *Committed sponsor* — a highly committed internal sponsor
- *Clear project definition* — including deadlines and end state
- *Teamwork* — the project team comprised a tight-knit group of experienced individuals with diverse business and technical backgrounds
- *Current and future needs assessment* — potential for customization of the product to allow for future needs

The Benefits

The Royal Bank's CRM solution has made a significant change in the way the bank manages its customer relations, resulting in the following benefits:

- Nine million personal retail clients are now segmented into discrete segments based on attitudinal and behavioral factors — current and potential profitability, expected purchasing behavior, vulnerabilities, and channel preferences.
- Marketing strategies for hundreds of micro-segments have been developed, leading to the ultimate objective of one-to-one marketing.
- Redefined client value measures and enhanced life stage segmentation have enabled the bank to align marketing initiatives.
- Decision making and reporting for all marketing and sales initiatives have been streamlined with an accurate and concise assessment of client portfolios and their values.

Industry Checklist: Lessons Learned

Successful CRM solutions for banks and other financial institutions have the following characteristics:

- Client value metrics are applied to day-to-day operations.
- Customer service departments are empowered to provide real account management to generate greater client loyalty through product offerings relevant to specific clients.
- Enhanced channel management strategies, service and product development, and relationship pricing initiatives have been implemented.

Case Study F5: Union Bank of Norway

CRM Project Objectives

To improve margins and growing profitability by better targeting services to customers, directing business to areas that provides the best return on investment, and continuing to manage operational costs.

To develop a better way of gathering and analyzing customer transactions and individual profitability, to determine which services could be better marketed, and where.

Corporate Background

The early 1990s represented a difficult period for Norwegian banks, with many suffering substantial losses as the result of an economic downturn that saw the failure of a large number of Norwegian businesses. Despite the banking crisis, Union Bank of Norway, the country's largest savings bank group, limited its business losses while reducing operational costs.

Union Bank of Norway has over 185 branches serving 900,000 consumer and commercial customers. The bank was operating on multiple computer platforms and systems, with disparate data scattered throughout the decentralized branches, and could not easily gather and store customer-specific information, which limited its ability to understand individual profitability by customer, product, and service.

The CRM Solution

The biggest challenge was finding complete information on customers and acting on it. Most customer information was derived from various production systems that contained insufficient customer information — an information labyrinth.

Union Bank of Norway wanted a way to create, store, and access customer-specific information in a responsive, easy-to-use format. By tracking customer trends and understanding individual profitability, bank executives reasoned that they could improve revenue and margins through cross-selling and increasing customer use of its most profitable products and services.

As a first step toward a CRM solution, the bank decided to build a data warehouse to bring together its disparate data sources and create a repository for customer information from its sales districts, which have five or six branches per district. The data warehouse ensures that each branch has a complete profile of its customers.

In developing its data warehouse, the bank utilized outside services, including business and information discovery, technology solution design and integration, database design, and data transformation.

Today, Union Bank of Norway is leading the way with the implementation of relationship optimization software and practices for increased customer satisfaction, customer retention, and customer profitability.

The Benefits

The Union Bank of Norway has achieved the following benefits from its CRM solution:

- Increased its market share by reacting faster to opportunities in the marketplace
- Significantly increased response rate on directed marketing campaigns
- Created a complete profile of each customer
- Realized a better understanding of the profit and costs associated with each customer, enabling customized services to be offered to customers and generating increased profitability for the bank
- Enhanced teller performance by placing the power of the data warehouse directly at their fingertips, enabling them to instantly call up a complete customer profile to identify other services a customer may want
- Increased usage of bank's automated payment service, by promoting these services to customers who have not been using them, and calculating the amount of money each customer loses by not using the service
- Provided a strategic edge over competitors

Industry Checklist: Lessons Learned

Banking institutions can establish successful CRM solutions that enhance customer relationships, improve profitability, and customer retention by:

- Implementing a data warehousing and CRM solution that integrates all customer data and makes complete, current customer profiles available to users
- Combining and integrating customer information and providing tellers with complete, current information
- Using data handling technologies to manage and analyze customer information

Fund-Raising

Case Study Fund1: United Way of Greater Toronto

CRM Project Objectives

To ensure maximum impact from its fundraising efforts and to minimize expenditures so more funds can be allocated to social service agencies.

Corporate Background

United Way of Greater Toronto funds a network of 200 health and social-service agencies that support one in three people in Toronto, including young children, the homeless, abused women, newcomers, youths, seniors, people in crisis, and the disabled.

As the largest independent source of aid to social services in Canada, United Way depends on campaigns to drive its fundraising, encourage new contributions, and build existing donor relationships.

To meet its objectives, United Way needed to minimize expenditures so more funds could be allocated to social service agencies. Accomplishing these objectives involved a multitude of challenges.

For example, the organization wanted to personalize all its interactions with donors, yet with the high costs associated with traditional methods of communication, such as direct mail, it could not achieve the level of personalization required. Also, United Way wanted to increase its donor base; however, the high costs associated with traditional marketing campaigns prevented the organization from reaching large numbers of potential donors. United Way also had difficulty attracting and retaining the technical employees required to manage new technologies, as most E-business solutions required Java programmers to update and maintain the technology.

The CRM Solution

United Way recognized the significant impact that E-CRM, an adaptation of CRM to the electronic environment, would have on its fundraising efforts. For example, E-marketing applications would enable United Way to speed up the collection of donations and lower administration costs for campaigns, but they would also improve donor relationships through enhanced communication, interaction, and personalization. These applications would also enable United Way to increase donor outreach, while eliminating the need for highly technical internal resources to build and maintain applications.

The organization selected Delano Technology Corporation's E-business solution as the cornerstone of its E-business strategy. Comprised of an E-business platform and E-CRM application suite, Delano's solution has enabled the organization to implement interaction-based applications that ultimately drive considerable benefits for the community. These applications include:

- Automated donor campaigns
- Automated follow-up campaigns
- Programs that build strong community ties

A robust E-marketing application deployed on Delano's E-business platform manages the business processes for each campaign, including generating personalized campaign messages, processing online pledges, customizing thank-you messages, generating feedback on surveys and success stories, and processing donor feedback.

Through automation, personalization, and continued dialog with its donors, United Way improves the likelihood of continued support from contributors. As a further benefit, feedback will help the charity develop more precise profiles of its donors so future campaigns can be completely customized to fit a particular interest or donor profile.

As an initiative to follow-up with donors, United Way sends personalized thank-you letters via e-mail to its donor base. These follow-up campaigns receive excellent reviews from recipients and are very successful in eliciting feedback, additional support, and interest in the organization.

United Way plans to use an E-business platform to develop additional programs to enhance and support personal connections. By reaching more people and learning more about donors online, the organization has a better understanding of its clients in an offline setting. Future applications will enable United Way to enhance its volunteer process by managing everything from processing online volunteer applications to keeping volunteers informed of upcoming events.

United Way will also use the platform to manage the allocation of funds to the various social-service agencies in the community, as well as improve communication with these agencies.

The Benefits

United Way has achieved a number of benefits by implementing a CRM solution, including:

- Facilitating the donation process using E-marketing campaigns and the Web
- Increasing donor outreach
- Managing online interactions to sustain relationships
- Substantially reducing administration costs
- Obtaining more definitive knowledge of its donor base

Industry Checklist: Lessons Learned

Fund-raising organizations can implement E-CRM solutions to improve the application of donated funds to their charitable communities, and to communicate more effectively with donors by adopting the following processes:

- Apply E-business technology to their fund-raising activities
- Automate, personalize, and establish continued dialog with donors
- Use donor feedback to improve the likelihood of continued donations
- Develop more precise donor profiles so campaigns can be completely customized to fit particular interests or donor profiles

Healthcare

Case Study H1: Anthem Blue Cross Blue Shield

CRM Project Objectives

To provide data-driven healthcare to Anthem policyholders to help them live longer, healthier lives, while reducing their medical costs.

Corporate Background

Anthem Blue Cross Blue Shield, a multimillion dollar heathcare management company, headquartered in Indianapolis, Indiana, was established in 1997, through the mergers of Blue Cross Blue Shield (BCBS) companies in Indiana, Kentucky, Ohio, and Connecticut.

One of the largest healthcare management companies in the United States, Anthem's goal is to improve healthcare quality for its policyholders. Anthem needs information, and not just information about its policyholders, but also about the doctors and hospitals that provide that care. Healthcare cannot be managed without managing information, and the current healthcare insurance environment requires that customers and healthcare providers submit claims to be paid, and that the quality of care policyholders receive is achieved by working closely with the providers.

Anthem competes in a very dynamic, rapidly evolving industry. The fundamentals that have driven the industry for decades are changing; and to maximize the company's effectiveness as a healthcare management organization, Anthem needs to track clinical information from its doctors' offices and its hospitals, as well as from its wellness and disease-management programs.

The CRM Solution

The merger of three organizations necessitated the creation of a consistent set of data — a "system of record" — accessible to all users across the organization. The company selected NCR's data warehouse product, running on its Teradata© database, to implement a successful CRM solution.

Customer services professionals expect easy access to claims information so that they can answer specific customer questions immediately over the phone. Storing at least 36 months of information from hundreds of sources, including historical claims data, provider information, and finance and marketing research information, the data warehouse allows its users to view all four states it serves as one entity.

Using its data warehouse, Anthem conducted a study of coronary bypass surgery providers, identifying "best in class" providers who had a mortality rate of less than one percent, compared to an industry average of four percent. By routing customers to these highly skilled providers, the company demonstrated a direct correlation between the data warehouse application and better healthcare, and also saved lives.

Using data stored in its data warehouse, Anthem can locate healthcare providers who are not delivering quality healthcare, such as doctors who provide higher than average numbers of caesarean sections. By leveraging this information at both a hospital and physician level, the company has been able to reduce these numbers to within the recommended tolerance levels.

Also, the data warehouse gives Anthem the ability to monitor providers for potentially fraudulent practices. Anthem's fraud investigation staff uses the data warehouse to conduct searches for medical professionals who fall outside the norm in terms of the number of prescriptions written or procedures performed.

Anthem is also pulling information from its data warehouse to assess immunization rates of policyholders' children under age two, enabling the company to develop a targeted direct mail initiative to all parents and their primary-care physicians to encourage both parent and physician to be more proactive about immunizations.

The data warehouse and the CRM solution it provides have become the critical components in achieving Anthem's goals of bringing together the different pieces of information into one central repository — delivering one source for claims, for membership, for provider information, for billing, and for pharmacy data. Before the data warehouse was installed, Anthem estimated that business analysts spent 80 percent of their time simply collecting data, leaving little time for analysis.

Using the resources and capabilities of the data warehouse also helps control premium increases in other ways, reducing the escalation of premiums and the cost of healthcare. Complex, nonroutine searches and analyses are performed very quickly. Instead of spending most of their time gathering data, Anthem's business analysts can more easily analyze data collected from various claim systems.

The Benefits

An innovative use of a data warehousing and CRM implementation in the healthcare field, the Anthem CRM solution illustrates how healthcare programs can be managed by a CRM process, resulting in the following benefits:

- Focusing on wellness programs to help people improve their lifestyles and diets by accessing, reviewing, analyzing, testing, correlating, and sharing that data across the enterprise
- Providing easier access to information required to deliver responsive customer service, reduce administrative care costs, and enhanced quality of care
- Providing detailed reports regarding healthcare utilization and costs related to customer accounts, as well as identifying significant health risks and recommending intervention programs to reduce those risks

Industry Checklist: Lessons Learned

In the healthcare sector, the data gathering, analysis, and correlation capabilities of a CRM system can be applied to the provision of healthcare to improve services provided to clients by:

- Using data warehousing and supporting analytical technologies to store and analyze client data
- Reducing the amount of time analysts spend collecting data
- Sharing client data across the enterprise

Case Study H2: Apotex Group

CRM Project Objectives

To maintain its leadership position in the global pharmaceutical industry by improving customer relationship management processes.

Corporate Background

Apotex is a Canadian pharmaceutical company engaged in research, development, manufacturing, and distribution of high-quality generic prescription and innovative drugs. The company believes in good health and has a mission to be the industry's most successful, independent pharmaceutical company in quality, manufacturing, sales, customer service, and R&D.

In Canada, over 280 million prescriptions are filled each year, ranging from penicillin to birth control pills. With an aging population, the need for affordable medicine is critical for the Canadian public health system.

Customer service has always been of key importance for Apotex. Headquartered in Toronto, Ontario, with facilities worldwide, Apotex sells and exports to over 15 countries around the globe. The company produces more than 180 different high-quality medicines in 450 dosages and formats that are used to fill over 40 million prescriptions each year. The Apotex Group is now the largest Canadian-owned pharmaceutical company in the world, currently employing more than 3800 employees.

With the Internet economy changing communications trends and practices around the globe, meeting customer demands is a challenge that has taken on new dimensions. In the late 1990s, Apotex made an important decision for its future financial well-being: to streamline business processes and update customer relationship practices through the use of technology.

The CRM Solution

After an extensive evaluation process, Apotex chose SAP, a leading provider of E-business software solutions with a sound reputation in the pharmaceutical industry, to implement its CRM strategy. SAP established a solid IT infrastructure and assisted Apotex to develop an E-business strategy with the mySAP.com E-business platform, with end-to-end integration.

Initially, Apotex worked with disparate legacy systems that needed to be updated to implement the company's CRM solution. These systems required a consistent enterprise platform throughout Apotex global offices that allowed employees to share information seamlessly. Its CRM solution, using SAP as its backbone, enabled the company to link its legacy systems into a single enterprisewide system, dramatically increasing internal efficiency and improving customer satisfaction levels.

The Benefits

With its CRM and E-CRM solutions in place, Apotex is able to:

- Meet customer needs in an enhanced manner and improve customer satisfaction
- Improve internal efficiency through efficient sharing of internal data

Industry Checklist: Lessons Learned

Apotex has successfully applied CRM processes to its global pharmaceutical business by adopting the following practices:

- Using technology to integrate business processes and improve customer service
- Integrating legacy systems into an E-commerce platform
- Managing its business more efficiently in an E-commerce environment

Case Study H3: TLC Laser Eye Centers

CRM Project Objectives

To direct telephone calls, e-mail messages, and Web inquiries to the right call center agent.

Corporate Background

TLC Laser Eye Centers Inc. has installed a customer communication system that routes all customer communications to the customer service agents best able to handle them. TLC operates seven laser eye surgery centers in Canada, five in Ontario and one each in Moncton, New Brunswick and Halifax, Nova Scotia, and 53 in the United States. Its Canadian call center is located in Mississauga, Ontario.

The CRM Solution

To augment its customer communication facilities, TLC installed Avaya's CenterVu Internet Solutions and Definity products to handle inquiries to its internal help desk and to the customer service representatives who deal with external queries. Unlike most other CRM solutions in this Handbook, the TLC example is not built on data warehousing technology; rather, it relies on advanced communication technology.

The Avaya product has been implemented in the internal technical support center, which employs three to five people, and the customer contact center, which can have up to 25 agents.

The Benefits

The CRM solution selected by TLC has brought the following benefits:

- Customers can communicate with the call center through either text chat or e-mail.
- Customer communications are directed to the appropriate area.
- Internal and external communications have been streamlined across the organization.

Industry Checklist: Lessons Learned

TLC Laser Eye Centers has been able to implement a CRM solution using the following resources:

- Advanced communication technology
- Software products that manage and direct customer calls originating from a variety of customer touch points, no matter where they originate

Insurance

Case Study Ins1: Zurich Kemper Life Insurance

CRM Project Objectives

To integrate disparate pieces of information and disparate systems to build a customer-centric view.

Corporate Background

Marketing studies in the insurance sector have shown that companies spend five times more money on acquiring new customers than they do on retaining those they already have. Further studies demonstrate that as a customer relationship with a company lengthens, profits rise.

Typically, companies can boost profits by 100 percent by retaining just 5 percent more of their customers for one year longer. Pareto's Law applies to the insurance business as well as to others, and one insurer found that the top 20 percent of its customers made all the profit, while the other 80 percent cost it money.

Profitable growth can result from refining marketing strategies by concentrating on the most profitable opportunities and by understanding the most profitable combination of product offerings, market segment, and channel.

At Zurich Kemper Life, executives rely on a data warehouse for information that was previously delivered in stand-alone, hard-copy reports. Answers to fundamental questions are readily available from data stored in the warehousing system, and include answers to important corporate issues such as:

- Who are the customers and what are their profiles?
- What customers contribute the most to corporate profits?

This information is generally unreliable when obtained from disparate systems. For example, one prominent financial institution in the United Kingdom with a range of disparate computer systems containing customer data on different financial products and services, estimated its customer base at 25 million customers. When the institution finally cleaned up the data and used matching software to eliminate duplicates, it discovered that there were only seven million distinct customers!

To do even rudimentary customer segmentation requires basic data: names, addresses, ages, and genders. Also, it is important to know the channels through which customers have contacted the company in the past, and to identify "orphans." Traditional marketing segmentation methods that can add to this information — demographics, psychographics, geodemographics, behavioral, and clusters — are also important and can enhance an organization's capability to manage customer relationships.

Transactional information is a key to future success, and customer-specific information must be gathered continuously and from all sources. Until now, some insurers have had this depth of information to mine, but could not use it effectively. The sheer amount of data could not be turned into answers for several reasons, including duplication of inaccurate information, lack of focused database, and weakness of existing technology.

The data warehouse and CRM strategies that are enabled by technologies that have evolved to support CRM have brought some insurance companies into the 21st century. The data warehouse creates a level of reliability and consistency in enterprise information that was previously unattainable. Data warehouses with customer-focused databases, separated from traditional operational databases, are the basis upon which specific business aims can be achieved and predictive models can be built.

Companies using this technology are now able to consolidate names and addresses using matching software to clean the data. With a single version of customer data, they are now able to identify customers as individuals, to identify all the products they hold with the company, and even to recognize separate members of a single household.

The Benefits

Zurich has achieved a number of benefits from its CRM solution, including:

- A single version of customer data
- A shortened forecasting cycle
- The capability for company executives to analyze information in real-time
- Historical information on 1.5 million life insurance policies, updated daily

Industry Checklist: Lessons Learned

Insurance companies can implement effective CRM solutions by following these proven guidelines:

- Upgrading an existing data warehouse to provide better access to data
- Combining legacy systems and providing an interface with the data warehouse
- Using enhanced data warehousing capabilities to refine marketing strategies by concentrating on the most profitable opportunities
- Understanding the most profitable combination of product offering, market segment, and channel

Investment

Case Study Inv1: Yorkton Securities

CRM Project Objectives

To manage client contact by providing complete, updated client information to all investment brokers.

Corporate Background

Yorkton Securities is a Toronto-based investment firm with several hundred employees, including retail brokers and administrative staff. The company was experiencing problems in making customer data available to all of its employees in a timely, effective manner. Yorkton is a Microsoft shop, with customer data stored in 100 separate databases.

In a brokerage environment, customer data must be managed with limitations, since not all of Yorkton's departments are legally permitted to see investor capital information. For example, some departments are not permitted to have advance information on stock opportunities — information has to be delivered simultaneously to all parties.

The CRM Solution

With the assistance of the consulting firm PricewaterhouseCoopers, Yorkton selected the Finance Demand Chain Network software from Pivotal to streamline data in its sales, marketing, and customer service operations.

The Pivotal software was selected for several reasons:

- It is optimized for Windows.
- It allows for e-mail integration with handheld devices.
- It is highly customizable.
- It is delivered with a detailed security table.

The Benefits

The benefits that Yorkton achieved from its CRM solution implementation include:

- Capability to manage customer data with regard to confidentiality rules
- Providing brokers with timely customer information, based on their limits on the data they can access

Industry Checklist: Lessons Learned

CRM solutions can be implemented in a brokerage firm by adopting the following processes:

- Acquire proven software tools
- Streamline client data collection
- Make client data available to all brokers

Packaging

Case Study P1: Tipper Tie

CRM Project Objectives

To meet a competitive challenge by responding earlier and more often to clients, and changing the way its staff interfaces with customers.

Corporate Background

Tipper Tie, a $94-million-a-year division of Dover Corp., is the world's leading manufacturer of aluminum clips and wire machines for the food-processing industry. The Apex, North Carolina-based company's typical customer uses costly machines that wrap and seal its products — everything from a small summer sausage to eight-inch-diameter Italian mortadella meats. (If you check out the meat aisle in your local supermarket, those small metal clips that seal the plastic casings on chickens, hams, and sausages are likely made by Tipper Tie.)

The meat packers' machines need service, new parts, and plenty of wire and clips. Tipper Tie's field sales representatives and service technicians make in-person visits to customers, and call center representatives field questions, requests, and complaints.

Competition in this market began developing when overseas competitors entered the United States, and alternative packaging methods began making inroads into Tipper Tie's customer base. Executives sought to meet that challenge by responding earlier and more often to their clients. To do that, the company needed to change the way its customer-facing staff worked, including the eight call center operators, sixteen-member field sales force and eight repair technicians.

The company's IT department recognized that it needed to provide easy access to up-to-date customer data to its sales team, technicians, and customer call center. The former setup left sales representatives blind to customer concerns. Complaints or special needs could not be communicated to sales representatives in a timely way. They might spend three-quarters of their sales call dealing with old complaints instead of selling new products.

Tipper Tie anticipated that providing sales representatives with the same customer view as call center operators and service technicians would increase the time sales representatives could actually sell products. This system could also trim the cost of generating sales leads and produce more sales from its best customers by providing better service and better communications between its service channels.

The CRM Solution

Tipper Tie selected and implemented Siebel Systems' stand-alone call center and sales force CRM modules, anticipating that the CRM software would allow the company to understand its customers better, track customer activities better, and look more professional in front of customers.

After carefully checking consultants' backgrounds and references, the company selected two consultants to implement the system. IT teams worked closely with them for knowledge transfer.

Once the system was developed, a small group of dynamic sales representatives was selected to be the test guinea pigs. The team members actively used the software for one month and then made a presentation at Tipper Tie's annual sales meeting about their experience.

Cross-functional and pilot teams are keys to success. By employing these teams early in the planning stages of CRM projects, a significant amount of time and effort can be saved later in the project by including their insight, expertise, and gaining their support.

The Benefits

Tipper Tie has achieved the following benefits by implementing the Siebel solution:

- Trimmed the time sales representatives spend listening to customer complaints — sales representatives prep themselves prior to sales calls by reading up on technical service problems the customer had logged, machine repairs, parts sales histories, and call center complaints
- Provided each sales rep with approximately 18 more days per year in face-time selling that they would have spent generating reports or dealing with peripheral issues

- Increased its sales territory without increasing the number of sales representatives
- Improved customer responsiveness by providing better communication between the customer and the company

Industry Checklist: Lessons Learned

Tipper Tie has been able to implement an effective, successful CRM solution by adopting the following planning and implementation processes:

- Interviewing call center and sales representatives about how they did their jobs, what processes they used, and what customer data they needed
- Providing information requested by these employees — precise sales data (including dollars spent), number of units bought, parts purchased, and current and prior year sales
- Installing customer management software to handle all customer calls
- Using knowledgeable consultants to implement the system

Recruiting and Training

Case Study RT1: Eagle's Flight

CRM Project Objectives

To find a system that would keep up with the demands of Eagle's Flight's highly mobile workforce, one that would enable almost 80 users in ten different locations across Canada and the United States to access and relay vital client information.

To share client and sales data in real-time, offering users direct access to the company's database, a situation requiring a CRM solution that would give the company expanded capabilities to manage customer relationships.

Corporate Background

Eagle's Flight works with clients to help them improve their individual and company performance, and to improve their own systems to support company growth and to improve customer service. Since 1988, more than 250,000 people from leading-edge corporations and multi-nationals of all sizes have utilized the principles taught in Eagle's Flight programs. As this company grew and became more successful, it has faced a number of challenges. One of the largest has been ensuring that Eagle's Flight maintains a state-of-the-art business system to meet customer demands effectively.

Making sure everyone in the organization has the most up-to-date client information was an important priority. To accomplish this objective, the company needed to do more than just fix its data-sharing problem. A flexible product was required to improve sales cycle times and the capability of carrying promising leads through that cycle.

The CRM Solution

Identifying CRM as a mission-critical business system, Eagle's Flight needed to look closely at all CRM marketplace suppliers. After careful consideration, the company decided to implement Great Plains Siebel Front Office (GPSFO).

Introducing a new system into a business brings with it some upheaval, even with the best implementation. With the workforce spread over numerous locations, training and support was a challenge. With GPSFO, Eagle's Flight was able to introduce a single new piece of software that completely integrated with installed products, eliminating a retooling of these system components.

The first and most important step in preparing Eagle's Flight was assessing CRM readiness. As noted previously in this Handbook, successful CRM implementations must start with understanding how the business system aligns with the vision and goals of the corporation. This is a question of cultural readiness. It depends strongly on assigning ownership to the executive team, then being proactive in sponsoring and supporting the CRM solution, and finally, in Eagle Flight's case, integrating the front-office solution into corporate processes.

The key to making this integration a success is ensuring that employees are comfortable when using GPSFO, a product that has made a remarkable difference in day-to-day business dealings.

The software provides increased functionality and has enhanced the company's marketing and sales efforts by evaluating newly generated business leads and providing excellent tracking systems.

The Benefits

Eagle's Flight introduced a single new piece of software that:

- Ensures that everyone in the organization has the most up-to-date client information
- Provides a flexible CRM solution that improves sales cycle times and the capability of carrying promising leads through that cycle
- Improves customer responsiveness
- Supports company growth and impacts customer service in a positive manner

Industry Checklist: Lessons Learned

A successful CRM solution in a consulting and training organization can be implemented using the following guidelines:

- Select a suitable software product that integrates easily with in-house procedures
- Ensure that the corporate culture is prepared and committed to the new customer relationship processes

Case Study RT2: Global Interactive and Workopolis

CRM Project Objectives

To establish a system that could capture customer data and help manage complex opportunities, as well as providing a comprehensive, centralized, after-sales service application that captures both sales and service activities.

Corporate Background

Global Interactive operates the globeandmail.com Web centers, a hub of news, up-to-date business analysis, finance, and career information. Workopolis, operated by Global Interactive and Toronto Star Newspapers Ltd., is a provider of E-cruiting and job-search solutions, managing an average of 35,000 job postings daily and more than five million job searches per month. Customers of both companies are businesses on a mission. They want tools that enable them to provide their customers with the latest financial or corporate information or recruiting software that not only gets the world out to candidates but also brings candidates onto their radar screens.

The CRM Solution

CRM systems and processes in both organizations were fragmented and inefficient, resulting in staff frustration, incomplete or inaccurate customer data, increasing degrees of customer dissatisfaction and missed prospecting and up-selling opportunities. After some research, both organizations agreed to select Siebel 2000, a state-of-the-art CRM solution that provides the tools to support current and anticipated front-office work processes. For the implementation, the company selected the LGS Group, an IBM company. LGS Group's CRM practice handles Siebel implementations for businesses across a multitude of industry segments.

Consulting firm LGS implemented Siebel 2000 at Global Interactive, including up-front applications such as: requirements-gathering, fit/gap analysis, and design. Then LGS configured the application with the right screens, views, fields, and functionality for managing sales and marketing in the two organizations.

Global Interactive and Workopolis focused their effort in Phase 1 on providing functions that manage customer and contact interactions, sales pipeline and opportunities, or ad-agency partners and advertising.

The CRM project began with an examination of the processes that were not working for the two partner companies: insufficient contact data and labor-intensive management-reporting tools, among others, and this process enabled the companies to become more strategic in their thinking.

Central to a successful implementation has been the partnership between LGS and Global Interactive/Workopolis. Business owners from both organizations contributed at every stage of the project, and IT staff have been reassigned to provide ongoing support of the Siebel software and the skills transfer process from LGS to Global Interactive/Workopolis.

The Benefits

As a result of implementing a CRM solution, Global Interactive/Workopolis has achieved the following benefits:

- Acquired reporting tools that enable both companies to be strategic in their business processes
- Attained the capability to manage customer and contact interactions, sales pipeline and opportunities, advertising agency partners and advertising

Industry Checklist: Lessons Learned

A recruiting organization can implement a successful CRM solution by:

- Acquiring the right software tools
- Using the services and expertise of an outside consulting organization with experience in CRM implementations

Retail

Case Study R1: Home Depot

CRM Project Objectives

To enhance customer relationship management initiatives, particularly in call center operations.

Corporate Background

Home Depot embarked on a sweeping enterprise application integration effort and on customer relationship initiatives to meet the competitive demands of the home renovation and hardware business.

The Atlanta-based retailer of home improvement goods has implemented a wide-ranging, enterprisewide program to tie thousands of applications, stores, and systems together in real-time.

Home Depot's implementation is based on IBM's MQSeries application messaging platform and data integration software from CommerceQuest Inc. The company can convert all customer data to MQSeries messages in as close to real-time as possible, instead of in batches, which tend to clog its Frame Relay network.

The Benefits

Home Depot's CRM solution provides the following benefits:

- Allows call center agents to access information about product delivery and installation schedules
- Frees up store personnel for other activities
- Enables the company to share information with partners and individual stores

Industry Checklist: Lessons Learned

Retail organizations in the home improvement field can implement successful CRM solutions based on the following criteria:

- Select proven vendor software
- Incorporate customer service processes into call center operations

Case Study R2: M&M Meat Shops

CRM Project Objectives

To collect information and communicate with customers in the same way as the company does across the counter and accurately manage the information.

Corporate Background

In a market where M&M has virtually no competition operating in the frozen food retail space, the company recognizes that gathering data on its customers will only strengthen its operation. The company is built around customer service, therefore, understanding the customer is crucial to the company's success.

After a lengthy search, the company decided on a software product from Triversity to implement its CRM solution. Triversity's Allegiance Intelligent CRM was chosen because of the flexibility it allowed and because it did not require further programming.

A series of standard reports is provided to individual franchisees, who e-mail them back to the company's head office. Data is collected from individual stores where it is then transferred to the head office in Kitchener, Ontario, and fed into the CRM solution. Triversity is supplying all IT requirements, programming the systems, and training marketing and management people at M&M.

The company views transaction sets and all the data collected at the point-of-sale, and the CRM solution provides both a micro and macro analysis. The macro analysis provides information for the head office on what products move best in cross-promotional purposes. It allows them to better understand product affinity relationships. On the micro side, it can break down specific purchases on an individual-to-individual basis, aiding in personalizing certain types of promotions.

The Benefits

The benefits to implementing a CRM solution in a food-oriented franchise are:

- Better understanding of customer requirements
- The opportunity to build detailed background history to meet future customer needs

Industry Checklist: Lessons Learned

A retail company with franchise operations and no internal IT staff can implement a CRM solution using the following guidelines:

- Acquire proven vendor software and services
- Apply business software to analyze customer data

Case Study R3: Migros Cooperatives

CRM Project Objectives

To develop new methods to regulate product range and marketing to strengthen client relationships and profitability.

Corporate Background

The Federation of Migros Cooperatives (FMC), a Swiss retailer located in Zurich, is a cooperative of retail outlets, founded in 1925, employing over 50,000 people, with revenues in excess of U.S.$10 billion.

A conservative sales climate, aggressive competition, the expansion of new forms of marketing, and the resulting pressure on prices and margins are typical features of the commercial landscape in Switzerland.

The CRM Solution

To initiate its CRM strategy, Migros decided to use article-specific, final-sales dates, which could be recorded by their checkout scanners. To incorporate this idea, they decided on a comprehensive program to equip more than 500 subsidiaries with checkout scanners. These subsidiaries represent about 90 percent of the total sales for the Migros cooperative associations.

Technical project leaders and departmental representatives agreed from the beginning of the project that considerable efforts would have to be made in parallel to these new point-of-sale (POS) equipment investments, in order to ensure a beneficial evaluation of the scanner data.

The first rough calculations rapidly showed that several hundred gigabytes of data would be generated with a product range of up to 150,000 articles per distribution warehouse, along with the storage of daily sales and deliveries with a history of at least 25 months.

At Migros, the process began by using a data discovery activity with authentic data from Migros on a parallel processing server. Actual Migros scanner and delivery data were used to demonstrate the importance of detailed data per day and article and per subsidiary.

Following a comprehensive benefit calculation, three Migros cooperative associations decided to build the Migros data discovery data warehouse. With the data warehouse expanding tremendously in its first two years, the group then added a second massively parallel server using a parallel relational database management system to accommodate growth.

There were several project objectives:

- Increase the trading margin
- Reduce the depreciation ratio
- Optimize sales campaigns
- Optimize the selling off of seasonal articles
- Reduce inventory levels
- Use the advertising media more efficiently

Buyers at the cooperative associations in Aargau/Solothurn, Berne, and Lucerne, after having access for almost two years to product ranges to give day-specific sales, delivery, and inventory data, created a new vision for the data warehouse and the use of their data resources. Various changes in sales and inventory levels were implemented over a period of 110 weeks. If, on a particular day, the same article is sold at different prices (this is possible as a result of the pricing policy of Migros), then the sales figures are also stored separately in accordance with prices. A separate examination per weekday of weekly, monthly, quarterly, or seasonal values is also now commonly and readily available.

Migros employees usually work from the totals over the groups of products for their areas of responsibility down to the individual article. In this way, depending on the task, they can optionally select a purchase-based hierarchy or sales (demand)-oriented viewpoint. In the geographic dimensions, they can analyze the results of the entire cooperative society, individual regions and districts, particular types of location, and each individual subsidiary.

As a result of additional filter adjustments, they can concentrate on defined criteria, such as suppliers' brands or their own brands, models, colors, sizes, or import goods. In addition, differentiation of sales in accordance with normal selling and various sales campaigns for articles that are to be sold can be specified in the query. The average time to respond to such a combined polling query is in the range from ten seconds to approximately one minute.

Sales changes and inventory changes can be illustrated graphically on the screen of the monitor in a matter of seconds by pressing a button. Without the help of the data warehouse, sales data and delivery data would have to be called up separately from different computers and manually compiled by the technical department.

The most important control programs monitor and manage the following aspects of Migros' business:

- Degree of sales by the latest selling data
- Zero inventory levels
- Inventory level
- Special sales or exceptional pricing

For support, Migros developed additional queries that can be initiated by the users, but which also run automatically on specified occasions, usually overnight. Migros has also developed very complex queries and models to assist in predicting inventory requirements.

Depending upon the product range, a comparison takes place with parameters that were previously set. Each responsible buyer or managing clerk receives clear instructions for action on steps he or she needs to take for which ranges of product or individual articles in order to prevent zero sales or to reduce excessive inventories. Lists of winners and losers and activity-based costing analyses also help employees focus on the assignments to yield a high leverage effect.

The control of sales campaign articles and a comparison with the "before and after" periods give clear information not only for successful pricing but also for the correct announcement policy. Sales rebates that are announced too early on high-value non-food product ranges (for example, TV sets) led to a strong sales decline prior to the sales period and led to a worse overall result. In the future, sales campaigns will be announced with a shorter lead-time and gross profits will be monitored more closely.

The regular optimization of sales ratios and inventory levels is a challenge in each product line. This applies to both seasonal products and standard articles. With the help of automatic functions, Migros can determine where zero inventory levels or excess inventory levels threaten to take place, and take action on timely price reductions, rearranging the selling location of the article or changing the ordering cycles.

The current integrated data system, which gives a high level of integration with its production plants, makes it easy to link sales data and inventory data for optimizing the future supply of goods. This occurs using the improved basis for short-term supply of goods and for medium-term sales planning.

The data warehouse and the decision-making capability it provides have assisted with internal sales, such as the automatic charging of a subsidiary with the actual selling in sales campaigns (without control stock-keeping) and the implementation of a rolling inventory level. In other applications, sales campaigns can be researched even more accurately and new marketing procedures can be planned better, if a sales receipt analysis is compiled alongside a general analysis of the scanner data.

The previously utilized and additionally recognized benefit potential convinced the Migros society of cooperative associations to extend the investment decision for the data warehouse to all cooperative associations in Switzerland. Migros has grown its NCR Teradata database to 420 gigabytes of storage capacity while connecting approximately 500 users in the various cooperative association head offices and also in the subsidiaries.

In Turkey, the local country licenses of Migros stores have created a separate and distinct data warehouse environment to manage the inventory and financial processes. This new data warehouse is a partnership of Migros Turkey.

The Benefits

The data warehouse and CRM solution have provided several significant benefits to Migros, including:

- The capability to make more uniform ordering decisions over all subsidiaries
- The integrated data system, which gives a high level of integration with the production plants, making it easy to link sales data and inventory data for optimizing the future supply of goods
- An improved short-term supply of goods and medium-term sales planning
- Sales changes and inventory changes, which are illustrated graphically on a computer monitor in a matter of seconds by pressing a button

Industry Checklist: Lessons Learned

A major global retail organization can successfully implement a CRM solution by adopting the following guidelines:

- Establish a corporatewide data warehouse and gather customer data for all touchpoints.
- Implement an integrated data system, with a high level of integration with production plants, linking sales data and inventory data for optimizing the future supply of goods.
- Use the new system to provide regular optimization of sales ratios and inventory levels in each product category.

Case Study R4: RadioShack Canada

CRM Project Objectives

To improve reach, offerings, and service by using the Internet to interact with customers 24 hours a day, seven days a week, and to fulfill its mandate to provide answers to customer questions, offline and online.

Corporate Background

RadioShack Canada, Canada's largest consumer electronics retailer, recognized that beyond sales and support, customer service and satisfaction are paramount goals that cannot be ignored in today's business world.

In-store and catalog sales have been the mainstay of RadioShack Canada's business since 1970. With the proliferation of the Internet in all aspects of daily life, RadioShack Canada realized it could enhance its business operation by using the Internet to interact with customers and to respond to customer queries, 24 hours a day, seven days a week, online or offline.

RadioShack Canada's executives also understood that the customer is in control in today's digital economy, because the competition is literally a click away. Products and services are commodities in today's economy; the differentiator is the customer's experience with the supplier. Customer-centric companies are always searching for ways to achieve higher customer satisfaction and retention, higher revenues per customer, and lower costs for acquiring and servicing customers. They also understand that their competitors are going to great lengths to lure customers away.

In trying to find that competitive advantage, RadioShack Canada wanted a solution that would provide its customers with a comprehensive and enjoyable online shopping experience and also provide the organization with a detailed view of its customers. RadioShack Canada's goal was to get to know its customers better wherever they were located, at home or at a RadioShack Canada store. By developing deeper relationships with its customers, RadioShack Canada knew it could create a custom-tailored experience that delivers relevant information on products and services.

However, to compete in a fast-moving marketplace, RadioShack Canada needed to implement a full online store in a very short time period. Instead of adding pieces bit by bit, it was important that the company place its entire product offering online, so the site would be a true extension of the store.

The CRM Solution

To create this extension of the company's bricks-and-mortar presence in the shortest possible time, careful planning was required to ensure that customers received prompt service. RadioShack Canada knew the technology it chose to support its online presence had to be both reliable and available, so there would be little or no downtime. It also had to be scalable, so it could handle increased customer-user demands.

From the very beginning, the company's objectives were to have the two sales channels — direct and Internet — work together, and the online presence would complement store presence. Technology makes its possible to integrate product and service offerings and to make the Web site a true extension of the physical stores.

A critical component of each store is its database, which collects product and customer information, interacting quickly, efficiently, and securely not only with RadioShack Canada's wired customers but also with the company's existing business applications. This database enabled RadioShack Canada to get its Web store up and running quickly, so online shoppers could browse and purchase a complete range of products as soon as the site launched.

The site offers visitors access to thousands of products, most major brands, and a huge selection of electronic equipment and accessories, including the addition of digital entertainment hardware, software, books, games, movies, and music. Items ordered online can be delivered directly to customers' homes or the closest retail outlet, even if it is an item the store does not usually stock.

To complement its Web strategy, the company chose to offer Internet-enabled, in-store kiosks in all of its RadioShack Canada corporate locations. This strategy weds the online and offline marketplaces by giving consumers the choice of shopping from home and having their products shipped directly there or visiting their local store for order fulfillment.

The company is able to meet its goal of 24/7 response to customer queries, with Microsoft technology supporting a customer-centric vision.

The Benefits

RadioShack Canada has achieved the following benefits from its CRM solution:

- Better in-store customer service on a national scale
- A range of customer-centric ordering and pickup choices

Industry Checklist: Lessons Learned

A national retail electronics firm can implement a successful E-CRM solution, using carefully selected vendor software with the following characteristics:

- Capability of integrating online and offline marketplaces
- Capability of responding to customer queries on a 24/7 basis

Case Study R5: Wal-Mart

CRM Project Objectives

To enhance sales analysis, inventory management and item replenishment, forecasting applications, and improve vendor relationships.

Corporate Background

There are many customer examples of growth within a data warehouse, and Atlanta-based Wal-Mart, with its large NCR Teradata database — one of the early retail data warehousing pioneers, and now perhaps the largest in the world — is one of the most interesting retail case studies. The company's initial NCR Teradata system was less than 30 gigabytes and consisted solely of summarized data taken off a database system. By extracting the data and putting it into a relational format, users were able to ask questions that had previously eluded them. This power and flexibility demonstrated the capability of parallel processing and true relational database design.

The CRM Solution

From its initial concept, Wal-Mart established what data was really necessary to solve problems and what level of detail was required. In order to give users access to the necessary data, the company had to provide daily sales of every item at every store in its vast chain of outlets.

To provide maximum benefit, all users were required to directly query the detail data rather than provide summary tables. This allowed end users to quickly become accustomed to asking in-depth, complex, ad hoc queries. Only as the usage of the system grew and queries were tracked did the account look toward summary tables to improve performance on those often-asked, low-value queries.

The other business applications — inventory management and item replenishment, forecasting, and vendor relationships — required an increase in the database by a factor of three, to over one terabyte of data space.

The company has expanded its data warehousing complex many times. There has been an increase in the number of queries from 200 a day to over 25,000 per week, the majority of which run against detailed data in one way or another. Also, there has been an increase of 200 times in data volume, approximately 100 times in user base, 20 times in queries, and a significant increase in complexity since the original installation.

The Benefits

In the marketplace of the 21st century, Wal-Mart has developed a commanding lead in the retail sector, with operations in several countries. Specifically, the data warehouse and the subsequent CRM solution enable the company to:

- Ask questions that predict trends and outages
- Allow for stronger vendor negotiation
- Increase profits
- Foster customer loyalty

Industry Checklist: Lessons Learned

A major, global retail operation with a customer database in the millions can successfully implement a CRM solution to meet its business needs by using the following guidelines:

- Focus on detail customer transaction data
- Train users to use this data to develop marketing programs
- Install a large data warehouse to manage the customer data volume

Technology

Case Study Tech1: Canon Canada

CRM Project Objectives

To provide a single customer relationship management solution to internal customer support groups.

Corporate Background

Keeping a finger on the pulse of consumer inclinations is invaluable to any company striving to be differentiated by its products and customer service support. Canon Canada's customer-focused mandate prompted the company to move its disparate support groups to a singular customer relationship management solution. With potential inquiries for over 650 different office and general consumer products, Canon Canada needed to centralize its customer-contact processes.

The CRM Solution

The company decided a scalable and customizable system would help manage customer relationships and generate valuable consumer data.

Canon customers depend on the company for everything from printers to cameras. The goal is to deliver Canon know-how to customers and to become the bridge between Canon technology and the people who use it. Canon felt that a flexible CRM application would allow the company to better understand its customers, reduce redundant processes, and provide customer feedback to both sales and product planning and development groups. The product chosen to accomplish this goal was PeopleSoft's Vantive Support CRM application.

After establishing some best-of-class CRM business processes, Canon successfully integrated all its major customer-contact centers into the central Vantive systems, allowing customers to request support through any number of channels, including voice, Internet, fax, or mail.

The data that Canon's CRM solution generates from these inquiries is instrumental to the company's ongoing customer-service efforts. In addition to 24-hour live telephone support, Canon Canada is now able to offer self-help over the Web through frequently asked questions, based directly on customer feedback. To get further assistance, the customer simply fills out an e-mail form and gets a response within 24 hours. With every contact, customer profiles are created and traced, so customer history is readily available.

The primary function of Canon Canada's customer-contact center is providing technical support to end users of its consumer products. But it is the information about the consumer captured by the CRM system that is critical to the company's continued commitment to customer service.

Customer data is mined to produce reports for the sales and marketing team, which assists in more effectively managing promotions and product launches.

The Benefits

Canon Canada's CRM initiative has achieved some significant benefits, including:

- Significant and measurable return on investment
- Functionality with other enterprise applications — capability to transfer information directly to business partners to facilitate warranty exchanges
- Reduced cost per transaction by 10 to 15 percent

Industry Checklist: Lessons Learned

An office product vendor can implement a CRM solution by:

- Installing vendor software that provides a scalable and customizable solution
- Mining customer data to provide better customer knowledge to sales and support personnel

Case Study Tech2: Hewlett-Packard (HP)

CRM Project Objectives

CRM Project #1: To collaborate and share real-time information globally, over the Internet.

CRM Project #2: To use its Web presence more effectively and to develop a central strategy for e-mail marketing.

Corporate Background

In today's global economy, customers have come to expect the best products, the best services, and the best solutions for the lowest possible cost. If a business cannot meet — and, wherever possible, exceed — these expectations, chances are customers will find someone who can.

Hewlett-Packard (HP) is one of the world's leading providers of computing and imaging solutions and services for business and home.

Managing customer relationships means applying the strengths and skills of the entire organization behind every customer interaction — from the time the organization begins to market its products and services to the customization of each deliverable. To ensure that this level of service is never compromised, HP needed to have the capability to provide its internal staff with a complete customer history on a global basis, at the click of a button.

The company had established two major distinct but related requirements for a CRM solution. One requirement was to be able to share customer information on a global basis and the other was to take control of e-mail campaigns from nine different marketing groups.

CRM Solution #1

To meet the objectives of CRM Project #1, HP turned to Oracle Corporation to develop the sales force automation (SFA) portion of a complete CRM solution. Both HP and Oracle have a common vision of the future of the Internet and the need to provide customer-centric solutions.

The company's typical customers include IT managers whose business division has purchased servers, printers, and services from Hewlett-Packard. These customers also include managers in other parts of the business, and those managers request e-mail updates and newsletters that tell them when new printer drivers are available, when security updates are posted, and when product updates come to market.

Occasionally, customers call a help line, but they are much more likely to get most of their answers from online sources. These customers prefer to get news and updates by e-mail and are quite responsive to online marketing offers.

Forward-thinking companies and organizations like HP realize that the key to creating, maintaining, and extending competitive advantage is to move their products and services to market faster, better, and cheaper. Increasingly, the power of the Internet is revolutionizing the policies, procedures, and go-to-market strategies for companies of all sizes, across all industry sectors, the world over.

The CRM platform, provided by Oracle to meet HP CRM Project #1 objectives, enabled the company to perform real-time forecasting and efficient allocation of resources to meet customer requirements.

CRM Solution #2

Recognizing a changing marketplace, HP realized that it needed to use its Web presence more effectively, and had been steadily collecting business customer data and e-mail addresses from all of its sales channels, but did not have a central program or strategy for e-mail marketing. At times, as many as nine different marketing groups would send out e-mail marketing campaigns to segments of the list, but each one was a single-shot effort.

These programs were not coordinated or leveraged in any way, and did not promote loyalty among its business customers. In fact, they were more likely to promote irritation by inundating people with information they did not want or ask for.

To meet the objectives of CRM Project #2, HP recognized that it needed to take control of e-mail campaigns from those nine different marketing groups. It also had to champion the customer-centric idea that marketing should be a long-term process that focuses on the life cycle of customers instead of looking at a sale as a singular occurrence.

The project team worked with HP's corporate CRM strategy groups to develop an e-mail marketing strategy that would fit into the larger CRM framework. The e-mail project focused on e-mail marketing while coordinating its efforts with the larger corporate strategy that included other customer-facing groups like call centers and customer service teams.

To meet the requirements of both groups, the team developed a comparison program to find out which type of marketing campaign best suited each customer's individual preferences. A carefully controlled pilot project was initiated to compare e-mail campaigns with direct-mail offers. Cost savings and revenues generated from both campaigns were analyzed, as well as the effect of the e-mail marketing on the customer experience.

The results showed that more customers responded to the low-cost e-mail offer, making it over 20 times more cost-effective. (It costs $1 per direct mailing per customer but only between 10 and 15 cents per customer to create and send monthly e-mail, to more than a million customers per month). Customers responded positively to the e-mail alerts and updates, and new sales revenues were generated.

The E-marketing division also estimates that significant cost savings were achieved by combining and reducing multiple e-mail campaigns. Sending out product support alerts and e-mails also resulted in reduced calls made to support lines.

The Benefits

For CRM Project #1, Oracle has provided HP with a CRM platform that:

- Performs real-time forecasting to develop more efficient business and sales processes
- Prioritizes opportunities and applies the requisite resources to the market
- Improves the total customer experience

The CRM solution for Project #2 provided the following benefits to HP:

- The company developed a low-cost e-mail strategy that was over 20 times more cost-effective than a direct-mail campaign.
- Customer response to the e-mail alerts and updates was positive — more than 85 percent were quite satisfied with the content they received.
- E-mail campaigns generated an estimated $15 million in new sales revenues per month.
- Cost savings of a half million dollars per month resulted from combining and reducing multiple e-mail campaigns.
- A reduction in calls made to support lines saved close to $150,000 per month.

Industry Checklist: Lessons Learned

A major international manufacturer of high-technology products can implement CRM strategies that:

- Use selected software tools and business applications effectively
- Use its Web presence more effectively to consolidate customer data from all sales channels and develop a corporate strategy for e-mail marketing
- Develop and leverage a partner relationship with a major database vendor with extensive experience in CRM solutions

Case Study Tech3: Western Digital

CRM Project Objectives

To effectively use stored product information to detect problems and improve product quality.

Corporate Background

Western Digital is a manufacturer of hard disk drives for PC manufacturers, as well as providing replacement and add-on data storage to the consumer market. Western was established in 1970, and is the first U.S.-headquartered, multinational company to achieve ISO 9001 registration.

In an industry with extremely short and rapidly decreasing product life cycles and a short time to bring products to market, the company's focus on quality and continuous product improvement has enabled it to stay ahead of the competition. Market share is a volatile number that can vary significantly from quarter to quarter, and past performance is no predictor of the future.

A typical Western hard drive product has up to 250 parts, 2000 product attributes, and hundreds of suppliers providing parts, a factor that makes detecting and correcting errors a very difficult task. The data was available; however, it was difficult to access because it resided in a variety of data sources.

Western stores detailed product information for the entire product warranty period, for each of the 100,000 hard drives it produces daily. With information on these products located in disparate information systems, the company lacked the tools to effectively use the stored information to improve product quality.

A few defective components could wind up in the end product and be shipped to the customer; however, these defects would escape the summary assessment of the product. The company needed the capability to drill-down into detail data to improve its products and manufacturing process, a characteristic that could be met by implementing a data warehouse project.

The CRM Solution

The company evaluated several vendor sources and selected NCR Corporation's Teradata warehouse to store and track the many processes and component variables involved in the production of its products. Western Digital uses the data warehouse to track all of the process and component variables involved in the manufacture of its hard drives, to improve product quality, reduce costs, and improve revenue. The data warehouse provides the company with a single, detailed view of each product as it moves through the production and distribution processes.

This single, detailed view gives Western Digital the tools to find defective drives before being shipped to the customer. In the event that defects are discovered during the production or distribution process, users of the data warehouse can quickly determine which serial numbers have the defective components and identify exactly where each drive is in the process. Prior to building the data warehouse, defective components caused production to grind to a halt as pallets and boxes were hand-sorted to find the faulty drives.

The company can quickly identify where the affected product is, down to the slot in the box on an individual pallet, and then replace those drives without shutting down the manufacturing process. The Teradata data warehouse is having a dramatic effect on quality because it can find 100 percent of the drives before they get to the customer.

The capability to quickly find defective drives is essential to improving overall quality, but it is still an expensive process at $70 per drive to retrieve, rework, and relaunch the product. That is why Western Digital uses the power of the data warehouse to engineer better products so costly defects can be avoided prior to production. Through data mining, users can identify the correlation of drive failures to particular testing parameters. By performing sophisticated "what-if" analysis, they can determine where failed drives are likely to appear in the process and determine how to eliminate the failures by tweaking the process.

In the event that drives do fail once in the field, Western Digital retrieves such data as starts and stops, power-on hours, and error correction history from returned drives. The data is then stored in the data warehouse and used to enhance future designs. The company needed a solution that would grow if production volumes expanded, if warranty periods were extended, or any other number of factors occurred.

Performance and flexibility were two other key factors in Western Digital's decision. It is impossible to anticipate the types of complex queries that company engineers will place on the system. The CRM solution had to have the power and flexibility to drill-down to the atomic detail very efficiently while supporting an ad hoc environment.

The Benefits

The data warehouse and subsequent CRM strategy have benefited Western Digital in several ways, including:

- Reduction in manufacturing and support costs
- Increased performance
- Revealing vast new arenas of business forecasting, prediction, complex analysis, and uncovering unknown opportunities

Industry Checklist: Lessons Learned

A high-tech manufacturing company can use a data warehousing implementation to develop a CRM strategy that dramatically improves product quality and customer satisfaction by:

- Selecting an experienced data warehousing vendor as a partner
- Using the data warehouse to drill-down into detailed product data to track and correct product defects

Transportation and Travel

Case Study TT1: AeroXchange

CRM Project Objectives

To develop a customer-oriented E-commerce platform for airline companies to consolidate purchasing activities.

Corporate Background

One of the hottest phenomena in business-to-business E-commerce is the advent of online exchanges — effective E-marketplaces that enable participating enterprises to streamline processes, time variances in supply and demand, and reduce inventories by collaborating on a single, integrated, Web-based platform.

AeroXchange is the airline industry's largest, buyer-driven, business-to-business E-commerce exchange. Star Alliance members had been pooling resources in the area of procurement for several years, and the Alliance wanted to take this business online to enhance collaboration among member organizations.

After reviewing several possibilities, the Star Alliance purchasing executives concluded that a dedicated, global E-marketplace for the airline industry was needed and AeroXchange was formed. The company is owned by 13 international airlines, including six non-Star Alliance carriers.

The CRM Solution

Oracle's suite of fully integrated applications was selected as the E-commerce platform for AeroXchange's E-commerce applications. Oracle Exchange Marketplace enables various classes of products and services to be traded on AeroXchange. It enables direct procurement of technological parts and services used in the manufacture of aircraft, as well as nonstrategic procurement of such commodities as food, cabin supplies, and ground equipment. It also allows AeroXchange participants to source and purchase products and services using an array of E-commerce transactions, including electronic catalog-based orders, auctions, reverse auctions, and spot purchasing.

The 30 airlines that are now participating in AeroXchange will leverage these applications to move from manual procurement processes to E-sourcing. This tremendously enhances the efficiency of the procurement process. Conventional sourcing involved reviewing paper catalogs or telephoning suppliers to determine who had what. At AeroXchange, however, electronic catalogs — hosted by Oracle — have grounded these tedious procedures.

Users simply log on to AeroXchange, specify the product required, and the system will execute a search and display the names of suppliers or airlines that have the item, along with the list price. An order can then immediately be placed via the Internet.

Oracle's Order Management application permits most procurement activity to be conducted by end users. Instead of calling the purchasing department, they can log onto the exchange and order the items themselves, a capability that can save airlines a great deal of money and effort.

Few things inflate an airline's costs as much as surplus parts, Oracle's Advanced Planning and Scheduling (APS) harnesses the power of the Internet for real-time exchange of demand information, forecasts, manufacturing schedules, availability, capacity, and other data among AeroXchange participants. Furthermore, it enables AeroXchange members to share inventory levels. This process optimizes inventory requirements among the airlines.

The most efficient way to deal with the surplus inventory is to prevent the buildup in the first place. In the airline business, one needs a lot of safety stock. The tendency is to buy far in excess of what is actually required, because of individual airline planning.

This is where strength in numbers can result in huge savings. Air Canada, Northwest Airlines, and Federal Express use spare computers for cockpit protection that cost $250,000 apiece. If each of these airlines has five such computers, fifteen machines support three different fleets. For demand-planning purposes, consider the case where three fleets are treated as one; the three organizations could manage with 30 percent fewer machines. Repeating the same process for 250 to 300 major components can generate very significant savings in both procurement and inventory costs.

By acting as a central hub that allows airlines and suppliers to link seamlessly to one another's systems, AeroXchange will pilot huge savings for the participants. Today, it is possible to link electronically to vendor or partner systems, although each vendor requires separate or different software.

The Benefits

The key benefits that AeroXchange has realized for its airline partners, as a result of implementing a successful CRM strategy, include:

- Bulk buying discounts airlines can realize through collaborative planning
- Preventing inventory buildup of individual airline inventories by pooling inventories of selected major items

Industry Checklist: Lessons Learned

An airline E-commerce exchange organization can implement a successful CRM strategy by acquiring database software that:

- Harnesses the power of the Internet for real-time exchange of demand information, forecasts, manufacturing schedules, availability, capacity, and other data between exchange participants
- Uses a single common database that enables members to share inventory levels and optimize inventory requirements among airline partners

Case Study TT2: Burlington Northern Santa Fe Railway (BNSF)

CRM Project Objectives

To integrate information from two merged companies, understand revenues and profitability, as well as improve operations through better understanding of customer requirements.

Corporate Background

Based in Fort Worth, Texas, the Burlington Northern Santa Fe Railway (BNSF) operates one of the largest railroad networks in North America with more than 35,000 route miles, covering 29 states and two Canadian provinces. BNSF was created in 1995 by the merger of Burlington Northern and Santa Fe Pacific corporations, and has more than 43,000 employees.

The CRM Solution

To accomplish the CRM project objectives, BNSF needed to merge the two companies' separate and distinctly different data warehouses into an integrated system that would accurately report on and support the newly combined company. BNSF faced a unique challenge because it had to meld information from two different transaction systems in different formats, locations, and states.

The railway company recognized early on that the analytical requirements of its business users would play a key role in the selection of the right computing platform. Users needed to perform ad hoc queries and access both detail and summary data.

BNSF's data warehouse runs on a massively parallel processing (MPP) server. During the first two years of operation, the data warehouse grew from 200 gigabytes to more than 900. It is stocked with very granular data, exacted from numerous computers running operational applications, as well as financial and human resource data.

In addition, BNSF built a custom graphical point-and-click interface tool for users in the field who have limited experience using computers and little time for training. To ensure data quality for all of its users, BNSF updates and refreshes its data nightly with ultra-high-speed warehouse load utilities through direct channel connections into two mainframes, which are fed from 20 different source systems.

The Benefits

The benefits that BNSF has derived from its CRM solution include:

- The capability of reviewing detailed crew expenses on a daily basis — better crew utilization and control of overtime
- Better analysis of cycle times for loading and reloading cargo to improve customer service and asset utilization
- Better analysis by field operations managers, such as train masters, on how their terminals, trains, and traffic lanes are performing
- More effective reporting and compliance with regulatory requirements, such as Equal Employment Opportunity (EEO), by analyzing breakdowns of its workforce by age, race, sex, and other demographics
- More consistent, nonredundant information from various systems, leading to accurate analysis and reporting, efficient equipment utilization, and efficient crew management
- Better understanding of revenue and profitability by customer, product, route, and business unit, enabling the company to price its services more accurately and ensure positive margins
- Significant savings by improving expense management of everything from accounts payable to labor and materials

Industry Checklist: Lessons Learned

A railway can implement a successful CRM solution to achieve significant business benefits, financial as well as operational, by adopting the following processes:

- Using data warehousing technology and customer-centric information for managing future resource allocations and planning equipment acquisitions
- Gathering and integrating information from disparate sources for analysis to improve business results

Case Study TT3: Canadian Pacific Railway (CPR)

CRM Project Objectives

To provide end-to-end management of customer shipments, and to reduce costs through improved service.

Corporate Background

Canadian Pacific Railway (CPR) is one of Canada's two major rail systems, providing freight services to Canadian and international companies, transporting a broad variety of goods across Canada. Customer requirements have changed over the years, and they now expect CPR to keep daily track of shipments, monitoring them on an end-to-end basis, whether or not CPR is handling the goods from pickup to delivery. The railway industry is changing, as railways become larger and their biggest competitors, trucks, become more powerful and capable of moving bigger loads.

The CRM Solution

For CPR, a CRM solution offered an integrated enterprisewide approach to customer relationships, the sum of processes and principles to place customers at the center. The company was seeking a solution that recognized its business focus and normal daily occurrences as the mainline of the business.

CPR selected PeopleSoft to implement an upgraded version of Vantive, a software product the company had previously implemented as a CRM tool.

For any business, a CRM solution needs to incorporate normal daily occurrences, not the odd situation that may occur infrequently. This is the approach CPR took when it first implemented a CRM tool from Vantive in 1996. When it was time to upgrade, CPR again went with the Vantive product because it had proven itself in the initial installation. Every CRM product needs to go through a critical change, to transform itself to become part of the complete E-business solution.

The Benefits

The software tool acquired and upgraded by CPR enabled the company to meet changing customer requirements for information and provide the following benefits:

- Daily tracking of shipments
- Capability to monitor shipments on an end-to-end basis
- Reduced costs through improved service

Industry Checklist: Lessons Learned

A major railway company can implement a CRM strategy that enhances customer relationships and reduces internal costs by:

- Implementing proven CRM software tools
- Adopting an enterprisewide approach to customer relations

Case Study TT4: Delta Airlines

CRM Project Objectives

To develop an enterprisewide data warehousing strategy that would provide users easy access to a central view of near real-time business information.

Corporate Background

Delta Airlines carries more than 100 million passengers annually on more than 2600 daily flights. In the extremely competitive airline industry, Delta strives to reduce costs, develop better customer relationships, and differentiate itself in the air travel marketplace.

Delta had created numerous decision-support and customer-information systems throughout many parts of the company. The airline found that it was difficult to correlate information across the company, because various organizations had over 25 data marts — smaller segments of customer data referred to and described in Chapter 3.

The CRM Solution

The installation of an active data warehousing system brought together information from various operational systems into one, resulting in several major improvements in the airline's capability to manage its customer relationships and in cost savings: business and management users now get most answers within minutes, where previously it took three to eight weeks to get a response to a typical information request. More than 1300 users make fact-based business decisions with positive, daily impacts on customers and operations.

The Benefits

Delta has achieved a number of benefits with its CRM solution, including:

- The capability to measure customer value by focusing marketing efforts on high-revenue customers
- Improved understanding of sales and distribution channels — how passengers buy tickets
- An accurate assessment of customer purchasing channels through a 100 percent tracking of ticket sales
- The capability to tie in all customer touchpoints
- The integration of real-time analytical decision-support activities directly with customer interactions
- An ROI of seven to eight times the company's investment in the first 18 months of its operation

Industry Checklist: Lessons Learned

A major airline can implement a successful CRM solution using an active data warehouse with a fast analysis capability, where there are a large number of users and vast amounts of data. Success of the implementation depended on the following factors:

- Correlation of customer data from all sources in a single data warehouse
- Easy access to users
- Opportunities for user input to effect changes in the system

Case Study TT5: Travel Unie

CRM Project Objectives

To offer the highest quality "on-demand" travel service for the best price, with superior customer service.

Corporate Background

Travel Unie is one of Europe's fastest-growing tour operators and specialized travel agencies. Based in the Netherlands, the company was one of the first travel agencies to use computers to track reservations and also the first to install a parallel processing computer system and provide 24/7 online access to its services.

The company offers tour packages directly to travelers through 400 branch offices, as well as providing travel package services to more than 1400 independent travel agents.

The CRM Solution

Travel Unie had a solid base of IT strategies, based on its existing computer installation and its collaborative effort with NCR Corporation's Teradata Division, that enabled the company to leverage this technology to deliver high-availability transaction processing and data warehousing solutions.

The parallel processing computer installation enables a large number of users to run applications on multiple nodes to access a single source. Other nodes on the same system provide additional processing for extra reservations capacity to replace overloaded systems, as well as a flexible online system with application management services and a single overall graphic view of the business enterprise.

Travel Unie has also implemented a multimedia capability to store, retrieve, and manipulate a range of complex objects such as video, audio, graphics, animation, and images. This capability enables the company to provide virtual tours of selected destinations so agents and customers can "see" and analyze these destinations for suitability.

The Benefits

Using a data warehousing system and focusing on CRM has enabled Travel Unie to derive the following benefits:

- In-depth customer profiling and trend and marketing analysis
- Customer service response time of less than one second
- More efficient interaction, more satisfied customers, and a higher tour-booking capability

- Immediate access to current detail from all transportation, hotel, and tour data sources
- The capability to analyze customer data to uncover trends and to create customized tour packages

Industry Checklist: Lessons Learned

A major travel organization with a commitment to advanced technology can implement a successful CRM solution using:

- Data warehousing, a customer database, graphic interfaces, and other related technologies
- Consultants knowledgeable in CRM implementation

Wholesale

Case Study W1: Clearwater Fine Foods

CRM Project Objectives

To correctly target, acquire, grow, and retain the best customers to generate profitable revenue growth.

Corporate Background

Clearwater Fine Foods was established in 1976 with nothing more than a pickup truck and an optimistic vision. Since then the company has been harvesting, producing, and exporting Canada's best shellfish. Clearwater products are prized throughout Canada, the United States, Japan, China, Europe and the United Kingdom.

The company has capitalized on technology and economies of scale, while keeping a firm hold on its homegrown, Maritime traditions of providing excellent service and value to each and every customer.

As a progressive, $300-million-a-year company, Clearwater annually ships tens of millions of pounds of scallops, crabs, shrimp, and lobsters to its customer-distributors, restaurants, and individual consumers. However, despite its 21st-century harvesting and production techniques, Clearwater's business processes depended to a great extent on faxes, telephones, and paper reports.

In an increasingly globalized market, the business challenge was to provide more efficient and effective service for customers and sales staff. Improvements in account and contact management were required, along with a knowledge management system for the sales force and automated order-entry and tracking for customers, to help reduce their costs.

The CRM Solution

Clearwater had four specific goals for its CRM strategy:

1. Increase sales productivity through automated, integrated processes
2. Develop a growth strategy to increase current and new business
3. Enhance business-to-business (B2B) through E-commerce initiatives
4. Create a customer-centric philosophy

IBM Global Services' customer relationship management team was contracted to work with Clearwater to understand their vision, current business and technological environment, and the company's options and priorities. As a result of IBM's analysis, Clearwater selected Siebel 2000, a software product that would deliver a fully integrated, multichannel CRM solution.

A three-phase implementation approach was recommended that included the provision of integrated capabilities, allowing Clearwater's customer base to interact with the company through its traditional channels or through a B2B Internet channel.

In phase one, the following features were delivered: account and contact management services, simplified order entry, automated processes (credit checks and sales and satisfaction reporting), support for manual tracking of delivery, automated inventory tracking, and a knowledge management system for the sales force and B2B customers.

Phase two integrated Clearwater's processes with suppliers' systems for automated delivery tracking, and offers individual, Web-based customer marketing information such as order history, improves communication for sales representatives, automates opportunity and campaign management, and provides certain analytical tools.

In phase three, Clearwater's existing processes were integrated with inventory management and billing systems and B2B order processing, with facilitation by its sales staff until its enterprise resource planning (ERP) system was fully operational.

The Benefits

The implementation of an enterprisewide CRM solution has provided the following benefits to Clearwater:

- The capability to capture customer account and prospect information and better respond to customer situations
- Plants that can receive, approve, and track orders electronically
- Sales administration that can enter, track, and edit orders, produce shipping documentation, and prepare knowledge-based customer mailings and reporting
- Elimination of manual order writing, faxing, and paper-based inventory and sales reporting files

- Customers that can place and track orders more easily
- Employees that can have internal access to timely, consistent, and accurate information

Industry Checklist: Lessons Learned

A food wholesaler with global markets can develop a successful CRM strategy, based on the following parameters:

- Selecting a CRM-knowledgeable partner to analyze requirements and recommend solutions
- Implementing a fully integrated, multichannel delivery solution
- Dividing the project into several phases to introduce the processes gradually

Case Study W2: Fujifilm France

CRM Project Objectives

To provide a single, dynamic view of all customer activities and develop an effective relationship with distributors and retailers.

Corporate Background

Consolidation, advanced technologies, and evolving channels of distribution are having a dramatic impact on the way companies interact with their customers. To remain competitive, Fujifilm France must not only be more skilled in its use of information, but must also maintain the highest levels of customer service, as well as an effective relationship with its many distributors and retailers.

Fujifilm relied on a paper-based system to manage its sales and distribution strategy. The company was unable to exploit market opportunities quickly enough, increase its market position, or deliver first-class service. Customer data was static and unresponsive, and the company did not have a single, dynamic view of all customer activities.

The CRM Solution

To address these and other corporate customer-oriented problems, Fujifilm acquired Siebel eBusiness Applications, including eConsumer Goods software, to manage and coordinate customer interactions across all touchpoints through the entire customer-relationship life cycle. The Siebel products ensure that the right mix of products is in the right retail outlets and in the right position on the shelves.

This E-business solution enables sales representatives to generate a single view of the customer, which means they can more successfully manage and coordinate interaction with distributors, the 5000 retail outlets served by the company, and end customers. It was important for the company to ensure a quicker, more accurate, and easier flow of customer and product information throughout the company, and to act on this information for competitive advantage.

The Siebel software is rapidly transforming the company's approach to team selling and the entire customer relationship. It has dramatically improved Fujifilm's capability to react and to identify and act on opportunities proactively.

Fujifilm uses Siebel eConsumer Goods to integrate and manage its sales, service, and marketing processes across multiple distribution channels. This software also increases the effectiveness of trade promotions and improves retail sales execution. Sales representatives access key account and company information over the Web.

The emphasis is on maximizing product visibility and retail point-of-sale presentation. The eConsumer Goods software provides valuable information about individual retail sales environments, identifying emerging customer buying behavior patterns at the point of sale and enabling sales personnel to translate this information into new trade promotions and targeted product offerings.

The application is also helping Fujifilm's sales representatives operate more effectively, route their account calls more efficiently, and execute and report on assigned retail objectives. The sales management team has the knowledge to develop comprehensive account plans and effectively evaluate the costs associated with different trade campaigns. Sales teams also have access to an online catalog containing all 8000 Fujifilm products on their laptops — giving them the flexibility to sell film one minute and cross-sell digital cameras the next.

Fujifilm sales teams are using this new, single source of customer and product information to actively work together and communicate with each other about account-specific issues.

The Benefits

The fundamental benefits of the Fujifilm CRM and E-business solution are:

- The sales team has access to the most up-to-date information, so they are effective on every call they make to our distributors.
- Sales representatives can precisely identify the location of the products in the supply chain and when delivery can be expected.
- The software provides a complete solution for identifying product-distribution opportunities, improving trade-promotion effectiveness, and delivering world-class customer service.
- The capability now exists to continue to improve market share and profitability in the face of increasing competition.

Industry Checklist: Lessons Learned

Organizations in a multi-product retail business can implement a successful CRM solution using the following processes:

- Select proven, evaluated vendor software with the capability of handling the product volume and range.
- Identify sales opportunities and manage marketing campaigns.

Analyzing Case Studies for Maximum Benefit

The foregoing selected 38 case studies in CRM represent only a few of the many CRM success stories. However, they reflect the range of customer-oriented issues that must be addressed by CRM. They also provide some excellent examples of how both large and small organizations, with existing data warehouses, or just getting started, from virtually every major business sector, have successfully addressed the evolution of customer relations to CRM in their own sectors.

IS professionals and senior managers involved in data warehousing and CRM projects can use these examples to assist in analyzing corporate requirements, developing business objectives, and designing the ultimate CRM solution that will meet their organization's CRM objectives, based on customer buying patterns and other characteristics in their own market sector.

Chapter 5

Privacy in CRM

Unless the public's very real and growing privacy concerns are addressed, electronic commerce will not reach its full potential; consumer confidence and trust are necessary for E-commerce to flourish.

— Dr. Ann Cavoukian, Ontario's Information and Privacy Commissioner

The rapid growth of data warehousing as a business tool in a variety of business sectors — financial, retailing, healthcare, travel — has placed new emphasis on the issue of individual privacy, vastly increasing the opportunity and ease with which personal information is collected, stored, and manipulated (see Exhibit 1).

Advances in technology have dramatically altered the global marketplace, offering significant benefits to consumers in terms of greater choice and convenience, and providing companies with availability and access to personal information on a global scale. This ready access has increased the opportunity and ease with which personal information can be obtained and compromised.

Personal privacy is also becoming an increasingly important issue for consumers as they become more aware of how organizations with data warehousing systems are gathering, storing, and using personal data to develop customer profiles. This is an issue that must be addressed by organizations, and consumers must know that the organizations they do business with have policies and practices to protect personal information.

Until recently, the concept of privacy of personal information was clear-cut and its dictionary definition could be summed up in eight simple words: "The state of being free from unsanctioned intrusion." However, changing times bring changes to the common lexicon, and in the new wired world, where personal information can be obtained at the click of a mouse or the

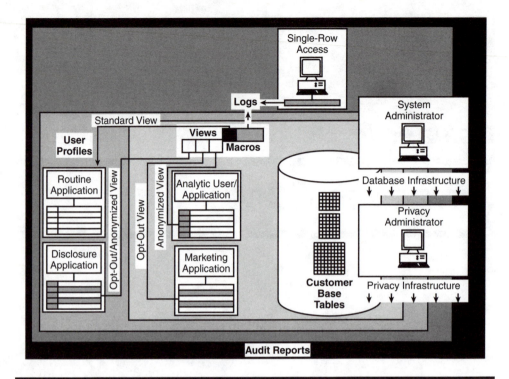

Exhibit 1. Privacy Processes in CRM

punch of a button, the commonly accepted principles of privacy have been turned upside down.

While information harvesting is neither good nor bad in itself, the way in which the data is used determines positive or negative value of the harvesting process. One of the key consumer concerns is that they have little or no control over how their personal information is used. However, this situation is changing, and there has been evolving concern, interest, and action on privacy issues, by industry, consumer groups, and governments around the world.

Data Privacy

The availability and proliferation of previously confidential personal information is illustrated by the personal knowledge about individuals revealed by telemarketers. On telephone campaigns, these individuals often use and refer to information provided by their contracting firms through mailing lists, surveys, the Internet, financial applications, credit bureaus, and other sources.

The source of this information is frequently a mystery to the consumer, and for many individuals it is disturbing to realize that this information seems to be freely available, exchanged among organizations, without consideration for its impact on personal privacy.

Corporate Privacy Policies

There is a requirement for a clear set of corporate privacy policies in the creation and administration of databases that gather and store personal information about customers — transaction data, demographic data, and in particular, more sensitive and personal information such as marital status, race, religion, etc. These policies should control all aspects of this process, including:

- Collection
- Usage
- Dissemination
- Administration
- Customer direction on handling data

Customers Demand Privacy

While privacy has been a background issue for database administration, consumers are becoming more knowledgeable about how many organizations are gathering data and what they are doing with it. As a result of this increased awareness, privacy of personal data has become a major focus of government, media, and consumer advocate organizations. The Internet has become a major collector of personal data as more and more E-business is conducted on the Web, and has contributed significantly to the increased concern over privacy issues. However, the issue of privacy is an important consideration in any form of commerce, no matter how personal information is gathered.

The retail sector offers some excellent examples of data gathering without much control over the ultimate use of the data, because customer data is routinely collected and used in loyalty programs, or in point-award membership programs, where consumers are encouraged to shop and collect points to exchange for awards. The benefit to consumers for participating in these programs is that they are offered price discounts and have the opportunity to collect awards in exchange for points. These programs provide a method for retailers to gather information on customer purchasing habits and other behavioral information.

If the retailer has a data warehouse and has not developed and provided customer notice of a privacy policy, this customer information can be stored in it, processed, and used without customer approval or knowledge for the company's own business purposes. This information can be collected from a variety of sources — debit or credit cards, smart cards, telephone cards, direct purchases from a company store, as well as Web site purchases.

With the technology available today, organizations that recognize the right of customers to provide direction as to how their personal data will be used, or even if it will be used, can incorporate privacy systems into their CRM solutions.

Defining Privacy of Personal Data

Privacy, in a CRM environment, means individual control and protection over the use of personal information. Personal information is any information of a private, confidential nature about an individual, such as the following:

- Age
- Race
- Religion
- Gender
- Income

When personal information is stored in databases, mailing lists, or data warehouses, the new paradigm for protecting the privacy of personal information requires that organizations with data warehouses take responsibility for the protection of this data from abuses. Protection and privacy of personal information is an ongoing, dynamic process.

There are several areas of impact on the privacy of personal information in a CRM system, as defined below:

- *Notice* — providing notice to customers of an organization's policies and practices regarding personal information
- *Limits on collection and use* — determining how information is collected and how it is used
- *Choice/consent* — allowing customers to choose which personal information can be used and for what purpose(s)
- *Data quality, access, and correction* — determining who can access what level of personal information and who can update
- *Data security* — taking measures to protect unlawful or unauthorized use of personal information
- *Accountability* — accepting responsibility for protection of personal privacy

In a privacy system, there are typically three defined layers of identification data, with the highest level of personal data content defining the highest layer in a subsystem called the "logical data model." Each layer has specifically defined content that determines how it is handled in a data warehouse (see Exhibit 2):

- *Layer 1* — contains basic information on the individual's identity — name, address, and phone number
- *Layer 2* — more restrictive, and contains personal information — age, sex, and marital status
- *Layer 3* — contains the most sensitive data, for example, race, religion, and credit status

Privacy systems in the most advanced data warehouses and CRM solutions provide specific opt-in/opt-out features for customers to specify what personal data may be accessed and how it may be used.

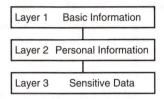

Exhibit 2. The Logical Data Model

Control of access is a primary feature of a well-conceived privacy system that is designed to protect the unwarranted and unauthorized use of personal information. This process involves the restriction of user access to private data, by using database views with their associated security. Views are database mechanisms that restrict access to data and return appropriate subsets of data to authorized users or applications. These views protect personal data in several ways:

- By restricting access to personal data fields by routine users or applications
- By making personal data more anonymous for analytical applications
- By preventing access to records on opted-out customers to any user or application involved in direct marketing
- By preventing disclosure of data to third parties

Government Initiatives

The U.S. Federal Trade Commission sampled more than 1400 Web sites and determined that more than 85 percent collect personal information from consumers. As noted above, privacy is growing as a legal, political, and social issue throughout the world. With these statistics in mind, governments have not been hesitant to regulate and legislate, where citizen concerns about the privacy of personal information and what corporations were doing to protect it have come to the fore.

Government initiatives that centered on privacy issues have typically established legal systems which represent a compromise between the absolute principle of personal privacy and complete freedom to collect and use all information for any purpose.

Europe and the EU Directive

In Europe, beginning with the initial Privacy Guidelines adopted in 1980 by the Organization for Economic Cooperation and Development (OECD), there has been a steady progression of both legal and nonlegal initiatives. These initiatives have ranged from guidance for collectors of information to national and subnational legislation that places legal restrictions, with penalties for noncompliance, on the collection and use of personal data.

In 1995, the European Union (EU) further advanced the privacy issue by adopting the *European Directive on Personal Data Protection*, which came into effect on October 25, 1998. The Directive applies restrictions to all forms of personal data processing, in both electronic and nonelectronic environments, and will affect all companies either operating in Europe or collecting or using European personal data. In recognition of the fact that privacy is a global issue, the Directive's Article 25 restricts the transfer of personal data on European citizens to third countries unless those countries have adequate personal data protection. This provision has resulted in a number of other privacy initiatives among countries of the world that do not wish to be caught short on privacy protection when doing business with EU member countries.

In the United States, privacy issues have been legislated in several business sectors where customer data has traditionally been gathered and stored, including the financial, healthcare, and communications sectors. Further legislation is pending at the federal and state levels to ensure that companies address privacy/data protection concerns of the consumer.

In addition to collaborating with the EU, there has been other government activity in the United States, supplementing and combining existing laws governing specific and more sensitive personal information and enforcement of protective legislation.

The EU Directive has some additional privacy requirements as guidelines for organizations that want to use a recognized framework for their privacy systems, including:

- The right not to be party to an automated decision with legal or other significant effects (e.g., creditworthiness) to an individual, unless there are suitable measures to safeguard the individuals legitimate interests
- Notice of the logic involved in any automatic processing
- Explicit opt-in for special categories of data
- The right to rectification, erasure, or blocking of certain data

The implications of these requirements on activities engaged in by many organizations' data mining, data warehousing, and CRM systems are significant, and need to be addressed by these organizations in the implementation of a new CRM solution or in upgrading an existing CRM system.

Canada

In Canada, two federal acts have been in place since 1983: (1) the Access to Information Act and (2) the Privacy Act. These acts provide individuals with right of access to both nonpersonal and personal information held by the federal public sector, and regulate the confidentiality, collection, correction, disclosure, retention, and use of personal information. Bill C-6, The Personal Information Protection and Electronic Privacy Act, was passed in 2000, and this legislation will make it easier for firms in the private sector to conduct business online. It also sets limits on how businesses can use the information they gather about their clients and customers.

The Canadian federal government has also adopted a set of general principles regarding privacy of information, under the National Standard of Canada (see Exhibit 3).

Another privacy tool that has been developed in Canada is the Privacy Diagnostic Tool (PDT), a self-administered diagnostic tool that provides a snapshot of an organization's privacy posture and creates a roadmap of what it needs to do to meet international privacy standards. The PDT was jointly developed by the Information and Privacy Commission of Ontario and security and privacy consultants from PricewaterhouseCoopers and Guardent.

The PDT enables businesses to develop and strengthen privacy policies, because it addresses customer concerns while still allowing businesses to grow. The PDT addresses ten principles based on internationally recognized fair information practices, and defined in the National Standard of Canada, including these four key privacy concepts:

1. Accountability
2. Consent
3. Security safeguards
4. Individual access

Each principle relates to a series of questions to which users (based on current practices) answer yes or no. The self-assessment guide then notes the risks involved with noncompliance and alerts users to the best practices associated with each principle.

The PDT is not compliant with current or pending privacy legislation and is not designed to provide a detailed privacy audit. It should be used as a measure of privacy readiness to complement current business privacy policies. Completing the PDT can be a first step for compliance with most privacy statutes.

CRM: Opportunities to Address Privacy Concerns

There are opportunities in a corporate CRM solution for developing privacy policies and for implementing privacy practices. In addition to incorporating an internal systems infrastructure to manage customer data, an effective, customer-centric CRM system must be designed with opt-in/opt-out features on the collection of customer data. As noted above, this feature enables the customer to know what data is being collected, who has access to it, and how it will be used (see Exhibit 4).

Establishing the Privacy Infrastructure

The first step in establishing a privacy policy is to define an approach to support the handling of personal information, first by formalizing a consolidated set of general privacy requirements, then by examining their impact on

Exhibit 3.   General Principles of Fair Information Practices

Summary of Main Principles set out in the National Standard of Canada, entitled: Model Code for the Protection of Personal Information, CAN/CSA-Q830–96

Principle 1. Accountability
An organization is responsible for personal information under its control and shall designate an individual or individuals who are accountable for the organization's compliance with the following principles.

Principle 2. Identifying Purposes
The purposes for which personal information is collected shall be identified by the organization at or before the time the information is collected.

Principle 3. Consent
The knowledge and consent of the individual are required for the collection, use, or disclosure of personal information, except where inappropriate.

Principle 4. Limiting Collection
The collection of personal information shall be limited to that which is necessary for the purposes identified by the organization. Information shall be collected by fair and lawful means.

Principle 5. Limiting Use, Disclosure, and Retention
Personal information shall not be used or disclosed for purposes other than those for which it was collected, except with the consent of the individual or as required by law. Personal information shall be retained only as long as necessary for the fulfillment of those purposes.

Principle 6. Accuracy
Personal information shall be as accurate, complete, and up-to-date as is necessary for the purposes for which it is to be used.

Principle 7. Safeguards
Personal information shall be protected by security safeguards appropriate to the sensitivity of the information.

Principle 8. Openness
An organization shall make readily available to individuals specific information about its policies and practices relating to the management of personal information.

Principle 9. Individual Access
Upon request, an individual shall be informed of the existence, use, and disclosure of his or her personal information and shall be given access to that information. An individual shall be able to challenge the accuracy and completeness of the information and have it amended as appropriate.

Principle 10. Challenging Compliance
An individual shall be able to address a challenge concerning compliance with the above principles to the designated individual or individuals accountable for the organization's compliance.

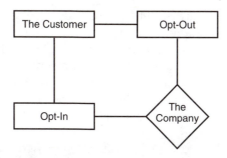

Exhibit 4. Customer Opt-In/Opt-Out Provisions

information system's info-structures, data warehousing, data mining, and database marketing.

To establish privacy as a means of expanding and enhancing the customer relationship within a CRM solution, an organization must begin by adopting a methodology for incorporating privacy mechanisms into its data warehouse environment. The *OECD Principles*, as described below, provide a recognized set of protocols that organizations can follow to ensure that the privacy of personal data is protected.

Privacy Guidelines — Applying the OECD Principles

The *Guidelines Governing the Protection of Privacy*, adopted in 1980 by the Organization for Economic Cooperation and Development (OECD) established a foundation for the protection of personal data in a series of well-defined, voluntary principles, which encouraged member nations to adopt laws and practices to recognize the rights of individual citizens with regard to the collection and use of personal data. These principles are:

- *Purpose specification* — At the time of collection of personal data, consumers should be provided with an easily understood notice of the data collector's intent with regard to the collection and processing of the personal data.
- *Collection limitation* — The collection of personal data should be limited to that which is needed for valid business purposes, and any personal data should be obtained only by lawful and fair means.
- *Data quality* — Personal data should be relevant to the purposes for which it is to be used, and should be accurate, complete, and kept up-to-date.
- *Use limitation* — Personal data should not be disclosed, sold, made available, or otherwise used for purposes other than those specified during the time of collection, except with the consent of the consumer (via an opt-out or an opt-in), or by the authority of law.
- *Openness* — Consumers should be able to receive information about developments, practices, and policies with respect to personal data. Means should be available to establish the existence and nature of personal data and the main purposes of its use, as well as the identity and the usual residence of the data controller.

- *Access* — Opportunity should be provided to consumers to have their personal data communicated to them in a readable form and to challenge data relating to them and, if the challenge is successful, to have the data erased, rectified, completed, or amended.
- *Data security* — Personal data should be protected by reasonable security safeguards against such risks as loss or unauthorized access, destruction, use, modification, or disclosure.
- *Accountability* — Managers of data should be accountable for complying with measures that give effect to these principles.

Advising Customers

These OECD Principles require that before collecting or making use of personal information, companies should notify their customers about the data they are collecting, why, and how it is to be used. Most financial institutions in Canada now provide this information to customers

Customers need to be advised that they can opt-out of collection and uses of their personal data, except where it is required by law, or to complete a contract with the individual, or to protect individual rights.

Consumers may wish to exercise this opt-out right to deny use of their personal data for specific purposes, for example:

- To use it for purposes such as direct marketing
- To disclose or sell personal data to third parties

Regulating and applying these opt-out rights mean that the managers and administrators of data handling within an organization need to implement mechanisms that control the collection, use, access, and other similar data processing functions. In some countries of the world, these requirements are legislated by law and are mandatory.

Indirectly, all these principles raise the further issue of anonymity, which is defined as "maintaining personal data in an anonymous form." Generally, most consumers do not object to collection of personal information if it is done anonymously. As well, data protection legislation usually does not preclude the use of this data for statistical purposes.

Privacy and E-Commerce

Businesses consider the Internet to be the ultimate channel for achieving one-on-one relationships with individual customers, because of its all-pervading, global cyber-presence. Internet sales, marketing, and advertising activities have dramatically increased the opportunities to invade personal privacy by gathering information from those who access Web sites for shopping or just for seeking information.

Internet businesses solicit personal background data, areas of personal interest, credit card information, and other forms of individual identification, for each commercial site accessed, while "cookies" are stored in an individual's computer, enabling that computer to remember the site.

Public concern over privacy is a deterrent to Internet commerce. This concern relates to issues of revealing financial information and security of business transacted on the Internet, as well as to a reluctance to provide personal information without knowing how that personal data will be used. Most Web sites have a "Privacy Policy" section, which visitors to the site can access to determine how their personal data will be used.

Loyalty and membership award programs, referenced previously in this chapter and in Chapter 2, require the collection and use of personal data. Many consumers are reluctant to conduct business on the Internet for several reasons, not the least of which, as stated previously, is the perceived lack of protection of personal privacy. Sites that have established and posted their privacy policy statements provide some assurance to site visitors that a privacy policy is in place to protect the use of their personal data. The absence of a privacy policy is certain to discourage the use of emerging technologies, such as cash cards, and foster continuation of more traditional payment methods that do not compromise personal data.

P3P Standard and Definitions

The primary technology mechanism that has emerged in the United States to support privacy self-regulation is the *Platform for Privacy Preferences (P3P)*, a privacy standard under development by the World Wide Web Consortium (W3C).

P3P Privacy Platform

The first draft of this standard was issued in 1998, and its protocol will be introduced into browsers by major software vendors. The objective of the P3P standard is to provide a methodology for implementing privacy policies and procedures for electronic commerce and for any other form of business that gathers and stores customer data. For the E-business market, P3P would enable consumers to provide personal information to Web sites, accompanied by privacy rules explicitly stating how it will be used. This privacy platform consists of three major elements: (1) personal profile, (2) profile of Web site privacy practices, and (3) a protocol for negotiation between user system and Web site. These elements are defined as follows:

- *Personal profile* — details personal information (identification, contact information, demographic and lifestyle data, transaction data, clickstream data, personal preference data) and privacy rules regarding usage of the data
- *Profile of Web site privacy practices* — developed by each Web site to describe the personal information requested by the site as well as the site's usage practices

■ *Protocol for negotiation between the user system and Web site* — to reach automated agreement concerning what personal information will be provided and how it will be used. This protocol will automatically enable access by a user to a Web site, as well as providing the capability for a user to access a site using a manual negotiating procedure.

P3P and Customer Databases

While P3P is clearly designed for electronic commerce, it is a major advance in the field of privacy technology and incorporates features that can be applied equally well to a data warehousing environment. The P3P definitions for personal profile, to the level of specific data fields, and in general, provide a basis for the collection, storage, and usage of personal information in any customer-centric database.

The P3P standard has been designed to allow extension to include customer-specific information from any source, and this standard offers opportunities for enhancing future customer relationships.

Companies with data warehouses and CRM solutions in place that lead the way in adopting P3P standards will demonstrate their response to customer demands for protection of personal data, a practice that will result in significant competitive advantage through improved customer relationships. In addition, these organizations will avoid the possibility of legal action in jurisdictions where civil or criminal actions may be taken for noncompliance with laws regulating the protection of personal data.

As the foregoing analysis of privacy concerns indicates, the protection of personal customer data represents an opportunity to enhance customer relationships. Abuses of privacy have a negative impact on corporations and reflect badly on the collection and storage of customer data in data warehouses. Customers have both a moral and often a legal right, as the previous review of legislation regarding privacy indicates.

In Europe, Hong Kong, New Zealand, and Canada, inappropriate use of consumer data carries judicial sanctions that may be levied against companies that do not comply with local data protection legislation. In other jurisdictions, there may be no legal penalties; however, the damage to a company's reputation may be a sufficient deterrent.

As referenced in other sections of this Handbook, organizations that promote and implement good privacy policies will benefit in terms of enhanced customer relationships. Protection of personal privacy is an ongoing and dynamic process and is good for business, because it fosters consumer confidence, brand recognition, and customer loyalty.

Privacy of personal information is also a requirement to ensure the growth of E-commerce — restrictions must be placed on the capability to share consumer information without consent, in this new business environment.

Industry Support for Privacy Initiatives

In the global marketplace, a number of companies and trade associations have developed their own information privacy guidelines and self-regulatory codes to address consumer concerns, as the application of data warehousing in business proliferates. These privacy processes are based on restriction of access to information and control of both its availability and use.

Support for privacy initiatives has been adopted by a number of vendor organizations and associations. These initiatives involve specific privacy services, views, frameworks, architectures, and the use of software products. Developing a privacy blueprint requires a legal review and evaluation of the proposed blueprint to ensure that it will meet the legal requirements of the jurisdiction in which the company operates.

Among the trade associations and industry groups that have endorsed privacy principles, the Online Privacy Alliance, located at www.privacyalliance.org on the World Wide Web, has established a set of privacy principles for online activities and electronic commerce. These privacy principles involve a combination of technology and operating procedures that address the privacy issues arising from the growth of data warehousing.

The basic tenets of the Online Privacy Alliance are to encourage the adoption by organizations of a "customer choice" policy; that is, to offer customers the choice of opting out of the authorization to collect and use personal data at three levels:

1. Opt-out of identifiable personal data being used to target an individual for direct marketing
2. Opt-out of disclosure of identifiable personal data to third parties
3. Opt-out of disclosure of identifiable personal data to affiliate organizations

The opt-in/opt-out features developed by this organization are described in detail in the following paragraphs.

The Direct Marketing Opt-Out

Direct marketing campaigns, unlike mass marketing, target specific customers or prospective customers who may be interested in a product or service. Mass marketing usually involves a broadcast technique — mail, phone, or e-mail — to a large number of untargeted prospects. Customers who opt-out of direct marketing are informing the supplier organization of their wishes, which need to be respected. Moreover, and this is an important factor often ignored by some organizations, these customers would not be good prospects for direct marketing campaigns, and removing them from direct marketing campaigns is a cost-saving benefit to the marketing organization.

In the long term, this opt-out will improve customer relationships as well as decrease marketing costs. It can also be augmented by implementing higher levels of marketing opt-outs based on individual customer preferences — contact preference, type of product or service, or other customer trait — further improving sales opportunities.

This opt-out customer preference does allow for the use of personal data in an anonymous format to develop marketing campaigns based on customer data. Business analysis can be used to perform statistical analysis of customer information such as personal characteristics, which may then be used to identify and categorize customers who may be good prospects for specific products or services.

Opt-Out of Disclosure of Personal Data to Third Parties or Affiliated Organizations

These opt-out provisions enable the customer to specify that personal data will not be provided to third parties or other organizations affiliated with the supplier, for any reason.

The application of these two opt-out provisions in an organization's privacy policies will further demonstrate the acknowledgment that customers have the right to direct supplier organizations on the use of their personal data.

Protecting Personal Privacy in CRM

As demonstrated above, the need to communicate with customers on the subject of privacy and the establishment of privacy practices open up the opportunity to seek more detailed personal background and personal preference information from them, along with their wishes regarding the use and protection of such information. For example, companies could find out more details on current demographics, lifestyle, life-cycle position, and financial profile of their customers if these customers are able to provide direction as to how the information will be used and who will have access to it.

There have been several privacy frameworks proposed for data warehouses to meet customer demands for protection of personal information. The common elements of these proposals involve the following aspects in the management of customer data:

- Providing an interactive customer service interface for administration of personal data
- Using privacy views to respond to requests for restricted access, opt-outs, and anonymity
- Verifying privacy adherence in the data warehouse
- Enhancing the logical data model

Examining the Logical Data Model

The logical data model, referred to previously in this chapter, defines customer profiles and is a significant design component of a data warehouse, directly related to customer data that is collected, stored, and used by an organization. To address privacy issues, the logical data model must be examined to identify all data entities related to customers, for example:

- *Identify* — account number, name, address, phone number
- *Personal information* — age, marital status, number of children, estimated income, shoe size, purchase habits
- *Sensitive personal information* — race, religion, credit status

Opt-out tables or columns are added to the logical data model to support individual customer opt-out of certain uses of personal data. Ideally, there should be no fewer than five customer opt-outs:

1. Direct marketing
2. Third-party disclosure
3. Automated decisions
4. Use of sensitive data
5. Affiliate disclosure

The customer profile represents the current dataset related to a customer, and needs to be reviewed with these two objectives:

1. Identification of additional data entities that would assist in developing more detailed and more useful customer profiles to gain useful knowledge about individual customer preferences
2. Analysis of stored customer data to determine how it can be modified to meet customer preferences on protection of personal information

In a direct marketing context, such information will result in a richer, more individual profile of each customer, together with a more detailed set of marketing opt-outs, based on individual customer preferences, by product category, or by customer touchpoint.

Addressing Privacy Issues: Benefits

Examples of the effectiveness and benefits of protecting personal privacy can be drawn from several business sectors. In the financial sector, for example, banks can determine financial product or service interests of their customers (including use of competitor offerings). Retailers can develop detailed profiles on the specific interests and preferences of their customers by product category, packaging, and brand. Telecommunications companies can analyze the near-term communications needs of their customers and conduct research into the aspects of products or service these customers value most in a long-term relationship.

Summing Up: Personal Privacy Is a Key Component of CRM

The information presented in this chapter describes how the protection of personal information affects a variety of business activities, from the design and infrastructure of a data warehouse to the collection, access, and use of customer data.

The recommended approach to responding to customer requirements to know what data organizations are collecting on them, what the data is used for, and to enable them to opt-out of selected programs, is to keep the data in the database, develop privacy protocol and practices around the data, adhere strictly to these practices, and inform customers about these practices.

The protection of this data can then be accomplished through views that restrict access, by providing anonymity, and by respecting customer-stated opt-outs.

The availability of the PDT analysis tool, P3P Guidelines, and other privacy tools are a valuable aid to project teams responsible for the development of data warehousing systems and CRM strategies. Applying these tools and guidelines to managing customer data in accordance with individual customer preferences will enable organizations to develop a better association with customers, and will be an important element in the long-term success of a corporate CRM strategy.

Chapter 6

Benefits of CRM

Businessmen tend to grow old early. They are committed to security and stability. They won't rock the boat and won't gamble, denying the future for a near-sighted present. They forget what made them successful in the first place.

— Peter C. Goldmark, CBS Chief Scientist, May 1972

The benefits of an effective CRM strategy are numerous, and in each industry or business sector these benefits are reflected in the way companies do business with their customers. However, as noted previously in this Handbook, a customer is a customer, no matter what business a company is in. The variations in CRM strategies from one business sector to another are often a simple differentiation of customer relationship strategies as they relate to products and services.

These benefits begin with the development and implementation of a data warehouse, the first technology step in the evolution to a CRM strategy. Some of the benefits described below are available to organizations once the data warehouse has been implemented and data has been stored and organized for analysis, while others will follow with a full CRM implementation.

Benefits of CRM in Four Major Business Sectors

The following subsections are a summation of the benefits of CRM in four major industry sectors, with examples, to further reinforce the specific benefits presented in the case studies described in detail in Chapter 4.

Communications

The communications sector is an industry sector where customer numbers are very large, often in the millions. Some of the benefits of data warehousing and CRM solutions are described below in detail.

- *Identify customers at risk:* Based on usage trends, customers who may be moving to other services, or who have already defected, can be identified by analyzing the profile and call patterns and determining which call detail variables have a high correlation to attrition. Companies that incorporate call detail into analytical models of propensity to customer churn, can then target those high-risk customers with loyalty programs and marketing campaigns.
- *Identify new revenue opportunities:* By identifying factors such as: which customers have a certain number of blocked incoming calls in a month, which customers placed calls to two different numbers within 30 seconds, which customer placed multiple calls to the same number within 60 seconds, etc., companies can build marketing campaigns and product packages. These packages enable the company to upgrade selling based on usage patterns for features such as conferencing, messaging, automatic callback, and other communication services.
- *Reduce marketing expenses:* This analysis can assist in increasing profits and loyalty through customer profiling. One major long distance carrier analyzed usage levels and communication habits to divide its customer base into several customer segments. This analysis revealed that the customer base included millions of unprofitable customers.

In one communications company, the elimination of unprofitable customers from targeting programs saved over $100 million in marketing and advertising costs in the second half of the year. At the same time, marketing to high-value segments intensified. Customers with high usage were proactively moved to the most favorable rate plan, and selling of bundled offers accelerated. The plan was to support highly profitable customers with good rates — which further stimulates usage — and packages of services that change the way they communicate.

Increasing Network Utilization and Profitability

By combining marketing network data, an organization can analyze cross-functional data from marketing and network areas. This allows marketing programs to be established that specifically target products and services to those areas where capacity already exists.

A pilot program at one firm compared the results of a typical mass marketing campaign to a campaign based upon targeted marketing through the use of data-warehoused, cross-functional data and modeling techniques. By marketing only to those customers identified with a high propensity to purchase this product, and only in areas where existing network capacity existed, the company realized a positive impact to the company of $10.8 million dollars on a single campaign in a single city, as compared to the traditional marketing approach!

Improving Operating Results

In today's environment, the time and effort required for performing analysis and reporting functions is costly. A data warehouse can make all the relevant source data available in a single integrated platform and database, enabling more efficient use of the data leading to lower operating costs.

Communications service providers have, in a number of cases, deployed many function-oriented analysis and reporting systems. The high cost of maintaining these systems can be displaced through the implementation of a single network-oriented warehouse. With this approach, decision makers have direct access to the information they need to efficiently support decision-making processes. They can undertake analyses which are not practical from a time or cost perspective in existing non-data warehouse environments, consequently capturing the value in the enterprise's data.

Analyzing Effects of Competitive Offerings

In the competitive communications environment, companies deal with new and innovative offerings by their competitors on a regular basis. By having a data warehouse with detailed customer data, these companies can quickly analyze the impact to their business on matching, beating, or ignoring the latest competitive offer.

Insurance

The insurance industry is one that has a special relationship with its customers, and data warehousing and CRM solutions offer significant benefits to those organizations that adopt effective strategies.

- *Product pricing:* This enables companies to establish the most significant factors to be considered for setting the price of an insurance product to cover losses, including underwriting factors — deciding who to insure at what cost.
- *Impact of pricing changes:* Assessing the impact of proposed pricing changes on each customer for use in the filing of rates with insurance regulatory commissions and communicating proactively with customers can improve retention after rate increases.
- *Reserves:* Deciding on the reserves to be maintained in liquid investments can cover potential losses. One company reduced its reserves to cover worker compensation by 23 percent, using an eight-way segmentation criterion, while increasing confidence that the reserves would cover potential losses.

- *Reducing fraud:* Identifying patterns of fraud can reduce the cost of false insurance claims.

- *Identification of providers:* To control costs, improve customer satisfaction, and reduce recurrence of injury, the data warehouse can identify low cost, high quality providers.

- *Analysis of geographic clustering of risk:* Natural disasters — hurricanes, earthquakes, tornados, etc. — can be analyzed to more effectively sell off risk through re-insurance and to prevent catastrophic losses from single events.

- *Analysis of agent sales:* Based on product profitability, a company can track good agents who improve the bottom line.

Manufacturing

Manufacturing industries with successful data warehousing installations and the first stages of a CRM solution achieve a number of specific benefits in their day-to-day operation and in conducting their businesses in general. Here are brief descriptions of each of these operational areas.

- *Analysis of supplier quality:* By tying finished product quality back to the supplier, problems can be corrected at the source. In a number of cases, suppliers are expected to access the manufacturer's data warehouse to improve delivered quality.

- *Analysis of raw material costs to determine alternative sourcing strategies:* Enabling global purchasing managers to leverage global prices against local suppliers can result in significant cost savings.

- *Product forecasting:* These formal systems for managing this function on a day-to-day basis can be supported by the data warehouse, which provides information needed to react to unusual shortages, strikes or demands.

- *Product recall:* Single instances, such as the *E. coli* bacterial dumping of millions of pounds of meat, can pay for the data warehouse with a single use. One manufacturer identified a problem with a valve and fixed the majority of products that were still in inventory, avoiding damage to consumer's homes.

- *Distribution logistics:* The quantity of product in standing inventory in the consumer goods manufacturing industries is estimated to be in the hundred billions of dollars. More creative placement of inventory, better forecasts, and reduced shipping time can mean significant savings in inventory costs.

- *Customer satisfaction:* Many retailers deduct from manufacturers' invoices if the product is not delivered at the time when the bay in the warehouse dock is assigned. Shippers are really another supplier to the manufacturer, and management of their quality is critical. The actual deduction and the cost of handling are measurable items.

- *Product development:* Identification of coincidental product usage can identify the need for a brand-line extension. For example, examining detailed purchases of cake mixes established the need for a frosting product to accompany the existing cake mix.

- *Product refinement:* If failures on a disk drive or an airplane are higher based on take-off and landing plus environmental conditions such as heat or salt air, investigations and engineering evaluations can be conducted to reinforce or determine whether more inspections or other maintenance procedures are required to avoid complete failure.
- *Promotion events:* The most effective promotion events can be determined, considering shelf price, advertising, in-stock position, and competitive activity.

Transportation

In the transportation industry, a sector that spans the range of transportation services for travel agencies to trains, from the airline industry to trucking firms, the benefits of the application of technology to customer relationships are many.

For example, British Airways uses a data warehousing system for complete business analysis, resource allocation, and customer relationship management. The system provides a range of information — which customers are traveling, where, when, and how often; it estimates resources and inventory required, based on customer-centric data; and it builds a knowledge-base of customer actions and transactions to predict the future and manage its operation based on these activities.

Also, British Airways and six other major international airlines use data warehousing to provide a number of business solutions beneficial to their operations, including:

- On-line query of all resources and schedules
- Ability to manage planes/loads/usages
- A financial management system
- Resource planning and system scheduling
- Knowledge transfer to all levels of business users

Some of the general benefits for the transportation sector are described below.

- *Analysis of asset utilization:* In railroads, reduction of dwell time in the rail yard can eliminate the purchase of one locomotive, which can pay for a substantial data warehouse. In airlines, analysis of yield and resulting marketing activities can ensure that every seat is filled with the highest possible fares.
- *Analysis of agent activities:* This analysis can identify agent situations reflecting fraudulent practices, for example, where agents book tickets to receive compensation and then later cancel them.
- *Analysis of origin/destination patterns:* An analysis of passenger origin or destination points, plus competitive information, can identify the opportunity for new routes. This could result in a reduction in weeks or months of

effort to identify new routes, as well as providing more revenue by adding just one additional route with greater productivity.

- *Analysis of frequent flyer activity:* Identify profitable customers to provide incentives for retention and potential additional travel. In one travel campaign, an airline saved an estimated $100 million by marketing directly to 26 million customers, versus conducting a mass media campaign.
- *Analysis of agent performance:* This analysis assists in selecting agents who are placing more business than market average, or more profitable business based on type of fare.
- *Analysis of alternatives:* This analysis develops crisis plans for unusual business incidents such as the grounding of aircraft due to defects, investigations, etc., or the strike of a competitor.

The General Value of CRM

There are some general features of data warehousing and CRM implementations that apply to any organization, wherever there are customers, and no matter what business sector they are in. Some examples of these features are provided below:

- *Benchmarking* — compares sales organizations or departments against each other and against prior periods to identify good performers and those needing additional coaching
- *Customer one-to-one marketing* — identifies unique interests of potential customers based on purchase patterns
- *Direct marketing* — reduces the cost of mailings by tracking responses and householding,
- *Identifying opportunities* — cross-sells additional products across lines of business
- *Customer profitability* — identifies the total cost of doing business with individual customers based on the type of products, usage of discounts, selling time and effort, and logistics costs
- *Initiative management* — gathers information across functions on the execution as it happens, for new product or promotional initiatives, which allows mid-campaign adjustments or campaign termination that can save a significant portion of the campaign's value or cost

Determining the ROI for a CRM Solution

Ultimately, most organizations will want to have basic and well-understood ROI/business benefit measurements to evaluate the implementation of a data warehouse and a subsequent CRM solution, with all of its components. This can be accomplished most effectively by looking at the ledger before and after the technology is implemented and comparing the costs and revenue.

It is important to address the collection of ROI data before starting the data warehouse development and incorporation of the other technologies on the way to a CRM solution, because collecting data after the fact will be difficult. This is one of the items that needs to be monitored by the data warehouse and CRM solution project team. There are several ways to estimate savings:

- *Precise before/after savings:* The budget for the CRM project may need to be reduced to justify the use of the newly created budget excess.
- *Flat overhead:* One company increased its business by 30 percent without increasing the staff overhead needed to manage it.
- *Leverage large cost:* This assumes that a small change on a large cost item could pay for the data warehouse.
- *Productivity elimination:* This is often defined in terms of "saving one hour per month per person for 1000 people"; however, those fractional personnel savings are never realized. Instead, for an activity that is recognized as being important, such as building revenue forecasts, estimate how many people it would take to accomplish the equivalent analysis without the data warehouse.
- *Redundant systems elimination:* One company eliminated 22 reporting applications, and the reduction in operations and staff costs amounted to $2.5 million per year savings.
- *Hidden gems:* One customer identified $234 million in unbilled business with one of the first applications of its data warehouse.
- *Risk protection:* Estimate the cost of a business catastrophe such as a product recall. Identify the savings possible in narrowing the scope of the recall or speeding the identification of a suspect product.

Justifying Data Warehouse Growth

If the data warehouse and the CRM solution are successful, they will grow rapidly. New users will bring new information to the warehouse to support their information needs, and the combination with the existing data will enrich every user's information experience.

Most organizations spend months of staff resources attempting to justify the initial data warehouse and subsequent CRM solution expenditures, and then become complacent, immersed in the technology and its projects. When the usage grows and the system grinds to a halt, corporate management may challenge requests for more capacity. This issue can be addressed by paying close attention to the business objectives and by using periodic reviews to ensure that the CRM solution continues to meet them.

The Ultimate Benefits of CRM

The data warehouse and CRM solutions, as noted previously in this Handbook, must be operated and evaluated on their merits, in a businesslike manner, and when properly used and assessed for ROI, they will more than justify their implementation (see Exhibit 1).

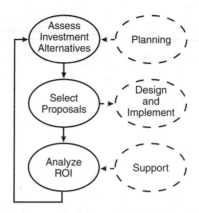

Exhibit 1. Analyzing Investment — Management Methodology

The successes described in the CRM case studies of Chapter 4 and the benefits of CRM detailed in this chapter, sector by sector for several major business areas, amply support this assessment of the overall benefits of data warehousing and CRM.

Measuring ROI: An Ongoing Process

As noted previously, the measurement of ROI must be an ongoing activity in the management of the data warehouse. Users must participate in gathering information about the business — cost savings, increased revenues, easier processes — any benefit that can be classified as a business benefit. What manager would invest $10 million in new manufacturing capacity and not be asking if it was helping to generate new business and retain existing business?

In the business of the 21st century, the time and effort required to perform many analysis and reporting functions are costly. A data warehouse can make all the relevant source data available in a single integrated platform and database, enabling more efficient use of the data and leading to lower operating costs.

With an understanding of the patterns provided from data in the data warehouse, costs can be reduced, productivity improved, and new business opportunities identified. Like the "tools of the trade" in traditional occupations, the data warehouse is merely a tool of the IT trade, with an enterprise reach, that extends the capability of humans and enhances productivity.

Tangible and Intangible

Building on the data warehouse and other technologies described in this Handbook, it is obvious that there are significant, intangible, job-oriented benefits to be derived from the application of technology to customer relationships, not to mention the tangible benefits noted in several chapters.

Inside the enterprise, employees achieve a sense of control over their job responsibilities and careers, problems can be recognized before they occur,

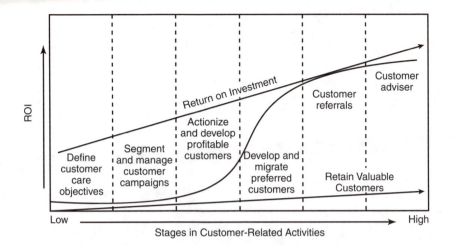

Exhibit 2. ROI Potential Based on Enhanced Customer Service

and energies can be focused on thinking and creating rather than on laborious and tedious information gathering and processing.

Outside, at customer touchpoints, better customer service results, with subsequent enhancement of three important customer parameters: (1) satisfaction, (2) loyalty, and (3) retention (see Exhibit 2).

While these intangible benefits are important, they are difficult to recognize in the "bottom line." The business world requires measurable benefits to justify spending on programs such as CRM, so the tangible, sometimes immediate benefits, as well as those that are less tangible and longer-term, need to be presented, described, and justified.

Ultimately, these measurable benefits, as well as the intangibles, will prove the positive impact of CRM for organizations just entering this important corporate process, as they have for those organizations that have achieved success in meeting their CRM objectives.

Appendix A

Glossary of CRM and Data Warehouse Terminology

Active Loyalty — Customers who repeatedly purchase products and services from the same company are described as being actively loyal. For example a customer could have a bank account for years but not actively use it. Time is not an indication of loyalty. The same customer, when needing to apply for a loan, may do so with a different bank. Customers who continually interact and transact with their bank are described as "actively loyal." (See *Passive Loyalty*).

Analytical CRM — Refers to the analysis of data created on the operational side of the CRM equation for the purpose of business performance management. Analytical CRM is directly related to data warehouse architecture.

Association — Refers to rules that enable correlations to be determined that establish the presence of one set of items with another set of items

Attrition — A term used in the banking industry to describe when customers leave to use the services of another bank. The more commoditized products become, the more frequently this process takes place. In the telecommunications industry, the same process is called "churn."

Business Drivers — External influences that affect a business and cause a shift in focus or change in course — e.g., increased competition may force an increased investment in R&D to maintain a competitive position.

Campaign Management — Management of single- and multichannel marketing campaigns based on customer intelligence gleaned from mining a data warehouse.

Channel Management — Monitoring the effectiveness of sales and distribution channels (e.g., Web, ATMs, face-to-face, call center, etc.) to ensure maximum return on investment and increased client satisfaction. Information on the way customers currently use different channels is analyzed to increased efficiency and improve overall customer service.

Chief Customer Officer (CCO) — Many organizations that implement a CRM strategy have a Chief Customer Officer (CCO). The role of the CCO is to oversee the continued implementation of the CRM strategy, ensuring that the cultural and customer interaction changes necessary for successful CRM are in place.

Churn — A term used by telecommunications companies to describe the loss of customers to competitors. (See *Attrition.*)

Clustering — A data mining approach that attempts to identify distinguishing characteristics between sets of records, and then place them into groups or segments.

CRM — A companywide, ongoing process whereby customer information is intelligently used to service customers more efficiently, thus optimizing customer satisfaction and company profits.

CRM Architecture — The infrastructure of CRM software, also described as the data warehouse architectural model that supports analysis of customer relationship management systems through the use of technology, tools, and applications for the purpose of business performance management.

Collaborative CRM — Refers to the application of collaborative services (e.g., e-mail, conferencing, real-time) to facilitate interactions between customers and organizations and between members of the organization around customer information (e.g., customers to sales, sales to marketing, community building), for the purpose of improving communication and coordination, raising customer switching costs, and increasing customer intimacy and retention.

Conditioning — Preparing data for input to the data warehouse or data mart.

Corporate Culture — Refers to the operating parameters of an organization, the way it conducts business and manages customer relationships, in general, the way it presents itself internally and externally.

Customer Interface/Point of Interaction (POI) — The point of interaction (or contact) between a customer and an organization. This can include Web, telesales operator, call center, and counter.

Customer Retention — The strategy of keeping existing customers and often the goal of marketing campaigns.

Data Cleansing — The process of removing inaccurate and historical data from operational systems to use in a data warehouse. Data must be accurate and consistent in order to increase the accuracy of the data mining process.

Data Mart — A departmental data warehouse or summary data store, usually storing only one specific element of a corporation's customer data, at a summary level.

Data Mining — Refers to the sorting and exploration of data with a view to discovering and analyzing meaningful patterns and rules found therein. A variety of tools and techniques is used, some of which have been developed explicitly for this purpose, others which have been borrowed from statistics, computer science and other disciplines. These include clustering, classification, time series analysis, and OLAP (Online Analytical Processing).

Data Models — To analyze data it is often necessary to build what is called a "data model." In its most simple description, a data model takes a given number of inputs and produces a given number of outputs. For example, a churn data model might take in information on customer transaction history, demographics, and product information and provide an indication on how likely a customer is to leave the company.

Data Warehouse — A database of information, explicitly designed for decision support purposes. Unlike a database, which is just a means of recording and storing transactional data, a data warehouse is designed to make the right information available at the right time. It may contain data from a number of different sources which have been brought together to provide information to the same decision-support application.

Delta Updating — A learning algorithm that uses a linear approximation to an error function to compute and apply a correction factor.

E-CRM — Electronic CRM is the use of Web channels as part of the overall CRM strategy, and may include other electronic business elements, such as E-sales, E-marketing, E-banking, E-retailing, and E-service.

Event-Driven Campaigns — Campaigns whose genesis comes from customer intelligence, e.g., banks conducting a marketing campaign for car loans based on the knowledge that a target group "X" will be graduating soon and are likely to start work, have a disposable income and therefore are prospective new car buyers.

Operational CRM — Refers to the automation of horizontally integrated business processes involving customer touchpoints — sales, marketing, customer service, call center, and field service — via multiple, interconnected delivery channels and integration between front office and back office.

Pareto's Law — Also known colloquially as the "80/20 Rule" — 80 percent of profits are derived from the top 20 percent of customers. Some analysts increase this to 140/20 when dealing with financial institutions, especially banks.

Passive Loyalty — Customers may appear to be loyal on examining the database; however, they may not have transacted business with an organization in years. This is passive loyalty. These are customers who have not left yet because there is no better option or offer from competitors. (See *Active Loyalty*).

Pilot Test — The small-scale implementation of a new CRM system within a small section of a company. This process provides feedback, helps solve any unforeseen problems prior to full implementation, and evaluates different approaches to achieving CRM objectives. A pilot test helps employees become familiar with CRM concepts.

Points of Interaction (POI) — (See *Customer Interface*) The point of interaction (or contact) between a customer and an organization. This can include Web, telesales operator, call center, and counter.

Recency and Frequency — Both recency and frequency are used to measure customer loyalty. Recency refers to the last time that a customer contacted an organization, and frequency refers to the regularity of the contact. Both definitions exclude contact initiated by the company to the customer, e.g., direct marketing campaigns, telemarketing, etc.

ROI — Return·on Investment — the return, in terms of increased revenue, that can be achieved from an investment in a CRM strategy.

Segmentation — Consumers are individuals. Different customers have different needs and privileges. Traditionally, marketers have divided their target market into segments with homogeneous characteristics such as lifestyle, demographics, or even consumer behavior. The ultimate goal of CRM is to treat every consumer as a "segment of one," i.e., know the customer so intimately that the company can provide a product/service specifically tailored to the customer's needs and preferences.

Terabyte — One million gigabytes.

Transaction History — The data recorded after every customer transaction, which is often used in data mining to gain valuable insights about customer segments and behavior. This includes information on any interaction involving money and would therefore exclude data on inquiries or complaints.

Visualization — This process takes large amounts of data and reduces them into more easily interpreted pictures.

Appendix B

References and Bibliography

References

1. Brown, Carol. V. Ed., *IS Management Handbook,* 7th ed., Auerbach Publications, Boca Raton, FL, 2000.
2. Burrows, Cathy. The Royal Bank of Canada (Canada), Client relationship management — a journey not a destination. In *Proceedings of "The Power of One" CRM Conference,* Nice, France, May 2000.
3. CGI Group Inc. White Paper, Building Competitive Advantages through Customer Relationship Management, January 2001.
4. Curry, Jay. *The Customer Marketing Method: How to Implement and Profit from Customer Relationship Management.* Free Press, New York, 2000
5. Hackney, Douglas. *Architecture and Approaches for Successful Data Warehouses.* Enterprise Group, 1998.
6. Inmon, William. Creating a healthy centralized data warehouse. *Teradata Review,* Spring 1999.
7. Meltzer, Michael. *Data Mining — Dispelling the Myths.* NCR Corporation, 1998.
8. Meltzer, Michael. *Using Data Mining Successfully.* NCR Corporation, 1998.
9. Inmon, W. *Building the Data Warehouse.* John Wiley, New York, NY, 1993.
10. Inmon, William. *Building the Data Warehouse.* John Wiley, New York, NY, 1996.
11. Mackenzie, Ray. *The Relationship-Based Enterprise.* McGraw-Hill Ryerson, Toronto, ON, 2001.
12. Meltzer, Michael. *Data Mining — Dispelling the Myths.* NCR Corporation, 1998.
13. Meltzer, Michael. *Using Data Mining Successfully.* NCR Corporation, 1998.
14. NCR Corporation. White Paper. Scalable Data Warehouse Solutions: Overview. 1997
15. Swift, Ronald S. *Accelerating Customer Relationships: Using CRM and Relationship Technologies.* Prentice Hall, Upper Saddle River, NJ, 2001.
16. Atobatele, Ade. The race to real-time: operationalizing the data warehouse, *Teradata Review,* Fall 1999.

Bibliography

1. Adelman, S. *Project Management for Data Warehousing*. In Proceedings of The DCI Data Warehouse Conferences and The Data Warehouse Institute's Implementation Conferences, 1995–1999.

2. Anahory, Sam and Dennis Murray. *Data Warehousing in the Real World*. Addison-Wesley, Reading, MA, 1997.

3. Anderson, Paul and Art Rosenberg. *The Executive's Guide to Customer Relationship Management*. Doyle Publishing Company, Houston, 2000.

4. Anton, John. *Customer Relationship Management*. Prentice Hall, Upper Saddle River, NJ, 1999.

5. Berry, Michael and Gordon Linoff. *Mastering Data Mining: The Art and Science of Customer Relationship Management*. John Wiley, New York, NY, 1999.

6. Berson, Alex and Stephen J. Smith. *Data Warehousing, Data Mining and OLAP*. McGraw-Hill, New York, NY, 1998.

7. Bischoff, Joyce and Ted Alexander. *Data Warehouse: Practical Advice from the Experts*. Prentice Hall, Upper Saddle River, NJ, 1997.

8. Brobst, Stephen and NCR Corporation. Integrating Your Data Warehouse into the World of E-Business. In *Proceedings of "The Power of One" CRM Conference*, Nice, France, May 2000.

9. Burrows, Cathy. The Royal Bank of Canada (Canada), Client relationship management — a journey not a destination. In *Proceedings of "The Power of One" CRM Conference*, Nice, France, May, 2000.

10. Charles, Cheryl. Security, privacy, and trust in financial services, BITS financial services roundtable. In *Proceedings of the NCR Partners Conference*, Orlando, FL, October, 1999.

11. Church, Nancy W. Customer relationship management: solutions for the insurance industry. In *Proceedings of the Insurance Industry Roundtable Seminars*, New York, Boston, Hartford, and San Diego, 1999.

12. Curry, Jay. *The Customer Marketing Method: How to Implement and Profit from Customer Relationship Management*. Free Press, New York, NY, 2000.

13. Deviney, David E. and Karen Massetti Miller, Eds. *Outstanding Customer Service: The Key to Customer Loyalty*. American Media, New York, NY, 1998.

14. Direct Marketing Association. *Customer Relationship Management: A Senior Management Guide to Technology for Creating a Customer-Centric Business*. DMA Publishers, New York, NY, 1999.

15. Eckerson, Wayne W. *How to Architect a Customer Relationship Management Solution*. Patricia Seybold and Company Publishers, Boston, MA, 1997.

16. Newell, Frederick. *Loyalty.com: Customer Relationship Management in the New Era of Internet Marketing*. McGraw-Hill, New York, NY, 2000.

17. Shapiro, Andrew L. *The Control Revolution, How the Internet is Putting Individuals in Charge and Changing the World We Know*. A Century Foundation Book, New York, NY, 1999.

Index

A

Access Integrated Networks, 143–144
Ad hoc processing, 72
Advertising media, 4
AeroXchange, 190–192
Airline industry, 190–192, 194–195
Alberta Treasury Branches (ATB), 152–153
Alert/response systems, 41–44, 56
Allegiance Intelligent CRM, 176–177
Analytical data mining, 54–55
Analyzing stage of CRM strategy, 9–10
Anthem Blue Cross Blue Shield, 162–164
Application integration services, 53
Application programming interface (API), 79
Architected data marts (ADMs), incremental, 105, 107–108
Asset utilization analysis, 223
Association, 116, 122
AT&T Wireless Services, 141–143
Automotive industry, 139–141
Avaya, 166

B

Benchmarking, 224
Blue Cross Blue Shield, 162–164
BMG Entertainment, 149–151
Bottom-up enterprise data warehouse, 107–108
British Airways, 223

Burlington Northern Santa Fe Railway, 192–193
Business case, 26–27, 30, 32
    discipline testing, 50
Business discovery, 87
Business information directory (BID), 79, 81

C

Call centers, *See* Customer contact centers
Canada Post, 144–145
Canadian federal privacy policy, 208–209
Canadian Pacific Railway (CPR), 193–194
Canon Canada, 184–185
Cavoukian, Ann, 203
CenterVu Internet Solutions, 166
CGI, 143
Change, 57
Checkout scanners, 177
Clearwater fine foods, 197–199
Client/server application development, 94
Clustering, 116
CommerceQuest Inc., 175
Communications sector, 141–146, 220–221
Consultants, 14, 87–88
Cross-functional teams, 16, 33, 171
Customer alert/response systems, 41–44, 56
Customer Care Consultant system, 140–141

Customer-centric model, 4, 8, 20, 23–24
 benefits of, *See* Customer relationship
   management, benefits of
 dialog testing, 49
Customer contact centers, 140–141,
   152–153, 155–156, 166–167,
   171–172, 175–176, 184–185
Customer demographics, 48
Customer-driven value proposition
   development process, 32–33
Customer feedback, 7–8
Customer information:
 exact transaction analysis, 28, 37–38
 personal information privacy, *See*
   Privacy issues
 sources of, 34–35
 transforming to customer value,
   24–25
 two-way communications flow, 34,
   40–41
Customer loyalty, evaluating, 46–47, *See
   also* Customer retention
Customer one-to-one marketing, 224
Customer profiling:
 case studies of CRM implementations,
   141–143
 data mining applications, 124
Customer referrals, 43–44, 45–46
Customer relationship management
   (CRM), 3, 17
 analytics in data mining, 54–55
 cultural readiness, 173
 implementation process, 15
 implementation review, 53
 market of millions to market of one,
   7, 19
 challenges, 5
 commitment to, 14–15
 core capabilities, 23
 customer input to, 40–41
 definition, 13
 functioning solution, 14
 lessons from successes, 22
 new marketing paradigm and, 19–20
 planning, *See* Planning
 priorities, 6
 privacy concerns, *See* Privacy issues
 program management, *See* Program
   management
 rationale for, 40
 seven factors for improving, 5

 support tools, 18
 technologies, *See* Technology
Customer relationship management,
   benefits of, 2, 28, 219–227
 business case, 26–27, 30, 32, 55–56
 communications sector, 220–221
 determining ROI, 224–225
 general value, 224
 insurance industry, 221–226
 intangible benefits, 226–227
 manufacturing sector, 222–223
 transportation industry, 223–224
 ultimate benefits, 225–226
Customer relationship management, case
   studies of successful
   implementations:
 automotive industry, 139–141
 communications sector, 141–146
 energy sector, 146–149
 entertainment industry, 149–152
 financial institutions, 152–160
 fund-raising, 160–162
 healthcare sector, 162–167
 insurance industry, 167–169
 investment, 169–170
 packaging industry, 170–172
 recruiting and training, 172–175
 retail sector, 175–183
 technology sector, 184–190
 transportation or travel industry,
   190–197
 wholesale sector, 197–201
Customer relationship management,
   testing and evaluating
   solutions, 44–51
 dialog testing, 48–49
 discipline testing, 49–51
 discovery testing, 47–48
 program management, 51–54
Customer relationship management
   strategy:
 alternative to mass marketing, 15–16
 applying, 35
 customer-driven development
   process, 32–33
 generating early wins, 33
 gradual approach, 13–14
 implementation issues, 29, 32, 36
 integrated business design, 32
 issues, tactics, and methodologies, 36
 matching with business strategy, 22

trans-organizational strategy, 13
workshops, 36–37
stages of, 9–11
twelve-stage model, 29–35
Customer retention, 5, 167
   case studies of CRM implementations,
      141–143, 145–146, 151–152
   CRM system priorities, 6
   identifying customers at risk, 220
Customer satisfaction, 222
   core competency, 6
   marketing challenges, 5
   primary issues, 1
Customer value, 24–25, 33–34
Customers, 1–2
   answering typical questions about,
      20–21, 35
   at risk, identifying, 220
   difficult and demanding, 44–46
   segmentation, 48, 168
   shifting relationships, 3–4
   types, 2, 8, 39

D

Data analysis, 33
   tools, 99
Data cleansing, 119–120
Data cleanup, 76
Data clustering, 99
Data granularity, 73, 132
Data marts, 61–63, 67
   advantages of, 68
   business applications, 69–70
   consolidation, case study, 195
   data requirements, 69
   data warehouses versus, 68–70
   incremental architected data mart
      (ADM), 105
   legacy ("legamarts"), 105
   limitations of, 59, 61–62, 65
   marketing campaigns and, 70
   summary data issues, 65–67
   supporting technologies, 69
   transition to data warehouse, 70
Data mining, 35, 77, 97–98, 114–115
   analyzing links, 121
   applications, 124–125
   case studies of CRM implementations,
      150–151, 185

creating models, 120–121
   CRM analytics in, 54–55
   CRM solutions and, 118–119
   data cleansing and transformation,
      119–120
   detecting deviations, 121
   difference from other tools, 117–118
   exploring corporate assets, 117
   integrating front- and back-end
      systems, 97–98
   modeling techniques, 121–122
   segmenting databases, 121
   selection and extraction, 119
   techniques, 115–117
   tools, 122–123
Data quality issues, 74–76, 125–127
   critical success factors, 127
   standards, 98–99
Data sharing requirements, 69
Data stage/data mart, 104
Data transformation, 63, 94, 119–120, 126
Data visualization, 123
Data warehousing, 9, 17, 35, 58–62,
      67–68,*See also* Data mining
   adding new data, 128
   architectural design, 88–89
   architecture options, 102–105
   audit, 102
   avoiding pitfalls, 71–72
   benchmarking, 82–83, 113
   benefits of, 219–227, *See also*
      Customer relationship
      management, benefits of
   business application, 69–70
   business contents, 74
   business discovery, 87
   business value, 84–86
   case studies of CRM implementations,
      141–143, 145–146, 150–151,
      152, 157, 159–160, 163–164,
      167–169, 178–180, 182–183,
      188–190, 192–193, 194–195,
      196–197
   computer platforms, 81–82
   consultants, 87–88
   costs of, 68
   CRM project management, 85–91
   customer relationships and, 61
   data conceptualization and
      categorization, 66
   data granularity, 73, 132

data mart approach, 61–65, *See also* Data marts

data marts versus, 68–70

data quality issues, 74–76, 125–126

data separation, 126–127

data warehouse characteristics, 60–61

database technology, 95–96

decision support systems and, 110–111

departmental versus enterprisewide solutions, 91

design and construction, 65–66

determining database requirements, 96–97

determining ROI, 224–225, 226

development methodology, 92–95

development process, 73–74

ensuring stability, 131–132

establishing data standards, 98–99

exploration warehouses, 130

implementing the enterprise data warehouse, 105–110

infrastructure components, 78–79

justifying growth, 225

logical modeling, 88

long-term approach, 59

management of, 95

marketing campaigns and, 70

measurable results, 91

mentor approach to building, 83

metadata infrastructure, 130–131

monitoring, 129

multidimensional OLAP, 111–112, 118

new job functions, 129–130

objectives, 59–60

operational data warehouse (ODW), 76–81

organizational growth, 131

planning, 72, 86–87

privacy concerns, *See* Privacy issues

proactive administration, 131–132

problematic issues, 64

processing environments, 72

processing methodology, 84

product quality assurance application, 188–190

project implementation, 89–91

project team challenges, 109–110

query tool methodology, 84

relational online analytical processing, 112

restrictions of summary data, 65–67

scalability, 90–91

scope and resources, 86–87

solution integration, 100

special function warehouses, 104–105

support and enhancement, 99–102

supporting technologies, 69

transition from data mart, 70

tuning, 101

user training, 132

virtual data warehouse, 110–111

Database management systems, 95–96, 112–114

case studies of CRM implementations, 145–146

data model complexity, 113

data volumes, 113

data warehousing development, 92, 93–94

multiple users, 113

processing environment complexity, 114

Database requirements, 96–97

Decision-making support tools, 99

Decision support systems, data warehousing and, 110–111

Decision trees, 123

DEFINITION checklist, 72

Delano Technology Corporation, 161

Delta Airlines, 194–195

Dialog testing, 48–49

Difficult and demanding customer, 44–46

Direct mail campaigns:

data mart/data warehouse applications, 70

data mining applications, 99

Direct marketing, 224

Direct marketing opt-out, 215–216

Discipline testing, 49–51

Discovery testing, 47–48

Distributed data warehouse/data mart (DDW/DDM), 104

Distribution logistics, 222

Distribution networks, dialog testing, 49

E

Eagle's Flight, 172–174

eBusiness Applications, 153, 199

E-business solutions, 143–145, 153, 154–155, 161–162, 165–166, 181–182, 194, 198, 199–201
E-commerce, 4, 48, *See also* E-business solutions
    exchange (AereoXchange), 190–192
    privacy issues, 212–213
    recruiting service, 174–175
Economic forces, 4
eConsumer goods, 200
EDS, 141
eFinance, 153
eFrontOffice, 154
Electronic-commerce, *See* E-commerce
E-mail marketing, 186–188
Enbridge Consumers Gas, 146–148
Energy sector, 146–149
ENMAX Energy, 148–149
Enterprise application integration services, 53
Enterprise data warehouse (EDW), 102–103, *See also* Data warehousing
    bottom-up implementation, 107–108
    top-down implementation, 106–107
Enterprise Marketing Automation (EMA), 150
Enterprise Resource Planning (ERP), 198
Entertainment industry, 149–152
Estimation, 117
European Directive on Personal Data Protection, 208
Exact transaction analysis, 28, 37–38
Exploration data warehouses, 130

F

Federated data warehouse/data mart (FDW/FDM), 104
Federation of Migros Cooperatives, 177–180
Finance Demand Chain Network, 169
Financial institutions, 152–160
Food industry, 197–199
Fraud detection, 115, 124, 222, 223
Fujifilm France, 199–201
Fund-raising, 160–162

G

Gartner Group, 75
General Motors (GM), 139–140
Global information sharing, 185–188
Global Interactive, 174–175
Goldmark, Peter C., 219
Great Plains Siebel Front Office (GPSFO), 173
Guaranty Bank, 154–155

H

Harrah's Casinos, 151–152
Healthcare sector, 162–167
Hewlett-Packard (HP), 185–188
Home Depot, 175–176
Hourihan, Anthony, 57

I

IBM Global Services, 198
Incremental architected data marts, 105, 107–108
Individualized or personalized services, 7–8
    case studies of CRM implementation, 154–155, 161–162
    maximizing customer experiences, 35–36
Information sharing, global, 185–188
Information technology (IT) department, 18
Information technology (IT) vendors, 133–135
Informational data warehouse (IDW), 96
Initiative management, 224
Inmon, Bill, 84
Insurance industry, 167–169, 221–226
Intelligent agents, 99
Interacting stage of CRM strategy, 9–10
Internet, 4, *See also* E-business solutions
    discovery testing, 48
    privacy concerns, 205
Inventory management, case studies, 182–183, 190–192
Investment services, 169–170
Iterative processing, 72–73

J

Just-in-time (JIT) systems, 77, 80

K

Knowledge management system,
　　197–198

L

Leadership, 31, 37
Learning, 9–10, 33
Legamarts, 105
LGS Group, 174
Logical data model, 88, 206, 217
Logical design review, 101

M

M&M Meat Shops, 176–177
Management support, 32, 37, 127
Manufacturing sector, 222–223
Market basket analysis, 116, 124
"Market of millions to market of one," 7,
　　19
Marketing, 3–4
　　CRM and new paradigm, 19–20
　　CRM strategy versus mass marketing,
　　　　15–16
　　customer-centric model, 4
　　customer retention/acquisition
　　　　challenges, 5
　　data marts and data warehouses and,
　　　　70
　　general value of CRM, 224
　　mass, CRM strategy versus, 15–16
　　reducing expenses, 220
　　use of point-of-sale data, 177–180
Marketplace analysis, 49
Massively parallel processing (MPP)
　　server, 192
Media outlets, 4
Metadata infrastructure, 79, 80, 81,
　　130–131
Migros Cooperatives, 177–180
Mission statement, 30
Modeling:

logical data, 88, 206, 217
physical data, 93–94
predictive, 121, 141–143, 157
techniques, 121–122
MQSeries, 175
Multidimensional online analytical
　　processing, 111–112, 118
Multimedia capability, 196

N

National Bank of Canada (NBC),
　　155–156
NCR Corporation, 157, 163, 180, 182, 188,
　　196
Neural networks, 122
Nortel Networks, 154

O

Online analytical processing (OLAP)
　　data, 78–79, 111–112
Online Privacy Alliance, 215–216
Onyx, 148
Operational data warehouse (ODW),
　　76–81
Opt-out rights, 212, 215–216
Oracle Corporation, 186
Oracle Exchange Marketplace, 190
Organization for Economic Cooperation
　　and Development (OECD),
　　207, 211
Organizational growth, 131
Outsourcing assessment, 53

P

Packaging industry, 170–172
Parallel processing, 76, 182, 192, 196
PeopleSoft, 184, 194
Personal data disclosure opt-out, 216
Personalized customer service, *See*
　　Individualized or personalized
　　services
Pharmaceutical industry, 165–166
Physical data modeling, 93–94
Physical database design review, 101

Pilot teams, 16, 171
Pivotal, 169
Planning, 9–10, 14, 25–28
 business case and, 26–27, 30, 32
 CRM plan of action, 26–27, 31
 data warehousing, 86–87
 modular approach, 26
 priorities of functionality, 26
 selecting technology solutions,
  27–28
Platform for Privacy Preferences (P3P),
 213–214
Point-of-sale data applications,
 177–180
Point-of-sale presentation, 200
Postal system, 144–145
Predictive model, 121, 141–143, 157
PricewaterhouseCoopers, 169
Pricing, 221
Privacy Diagnostic Tool, 209
Privacy issues, 39–40, 203–218
 access control, 207
 benefits, 217
 corporate policy, 205
 defining privacy, 206–207
 demand for privacy, 205
 E-commerce and, 212–214
 establishing infrastructure, 209, 211
 fair information practices, 210
 government initiatives, 207–209
 guidelines, 211–212
 industry support, 215
 *Platform for Privacy Preferences
  (P3P)*, 213–214
 logical data model, 206, 217
 opt-out rights, 212, 215–216
 protecting personal privacy, 216
 third-party information disclosure,
  216
Proactive customer alert/response
 systems, 41–44, 56
Procurement applications, 144–145,
 190–192
Product concepts, 46
Product development, 32, 222
Product forecasting, 222
Product pricing, 221
Product quality assurance, 188–190
Product recall, 222
Product refinement, 223
Program diagnosis, 52

Program management, 51
 guidelines, 51–54
 data warehousing and, 85–91
Promotion events, 223

Q

Quality assurance, 127, 188–190
Query and reporting tools, 118

R

RadioShack Canada, 180–182
Railway industry, 192–194
Rapid application development (RAD)
 tools, 78, 80
Raw material cost analysis, 222
RBC Financial Services, 156–158
Recruiting and training services, 172–175
Referrals, 43–44, 45–46
Relational database management
 systems, 96, 112–114
Relational online analytical processing,
 112
Repetitive processing, 72–73
Retail sector, case studies of CRM
 implementations, 175–183
Return on investment (ROI), 27, 30
 determining for CRM solutions,
  224–225, 226
Risk clustering, 222
Royal Bank of Canada (RBC Financial
 Services), 156–158
Rule induction, 123

S

Sales force automation (SFA), 186
SAP, 144, 165
SAS, 150
Saturn Corporation, 140–141
Scalable data warehouse, 90–91
Senior management support, 32, 37, 127
Sequence-based analysis, 116
Sequence discovery, 122
Siebel, 153, 171, 199–200
Siebel 2000, 174, 198
Snowflake schema, 97

Software solutions:
  benchmarking, 82–83
  case studies of CRM implementations,
        150–151, 166–167, 169–170,
        173, 175–176, 176–177,
        184–185, 190–192, 194, 198,
        199–201
Star schema, 97
Statistical analysis tools, 118
Strategy review, 52
Supervised induction, 122
Supplier quality analysis, 222
Surplus inventory, 191

T

Technology, 8–9, 18, 21, 38–39, 57–136,
        See also Data marts; Data
        mining; Data warehousing;
        Database management systems;
        Software solutions; *specific
        applications*
  customer feedback, 7
  outsourcing issues, 155
  selecting solutions, 27–28
  vendors, 133–135
Technology sales/service sector, 184–190
Teradata, 157, 163, 180, 182, 188, 196
Test and control-based measurement, 33
Testing and evaluation, 44–51
Third-party information disclosure, 216
Tipper tie, 170–172
TLC Laser Eye Centers, 166–167
Top-down enterprise data warehouse,
        106–107
Training, 132
Transportation industry, 190–196,
        223–224
Travel industry, 196–197
Travel Unie, 196–197
Triversity, 176
Two-way communications flow, 34,
        40–41

U

Union Bank of Norway, 158–160
United Way of Greater Toronto, 160–162
U.S. Federal Trade Commission, 207
Utilities industry, 146–148

V

Value Analyzer, 157
Value potential, 25
Vantive, 184, 194
Vendors, 133–135
Virtual data warehouse, 110–111

W

Wal-Mart, 182–183
Web site performance, dialog testing, 48
Web sites, case studies of CRM
        implementations, 139–140,
        181–182, 185–188, *See also* E-
        business solutions
Western digital, 188–190
Wholesale sector, 197–201
Word-of-mouth referrals, 43–44, 45–46
Workopolis, 174–175

X

XML and XML-based systems, 43, 81

Y

Yorkton Securities, 169–170

Z

Zurich Kemper Life Insurance, 167–169